D1569926

ILLEGITIMACY AND SOCIAL STRUCTURES

ILLEGITIMACY AND SOCIAL STRUCTURES

Cross-Cultural Perspectives on Nonmarital Birth

LEWELLYN HENDRIX

BERGIN & GARVEY
Westport, Connecticut • London

Library of Congress Cataloging-in-Publication Data

Hendrix, Lewellyn.
    Illegitimacy and social structures : cross-cultural perspectives
on nonmarital birth / Lewellyn Hendrix.
      p.   cm.
    Includes bibliographical references and index.
    ISBN 0–89789–467–7 (alk. paper)
    1. Illegitimacy—Cross-cultural studies. I. Title.
HQ998.H45 1996
306.874—dc20   95–39390

British Library Cataloguing in Publication Data is available.

Library of Congress Catalog Card Number: 95–39390
ISBN: 0–89789–467–7

First published in 1996

Bergin & Garvey, 88 Post Road West, Westport, CT 06881
An imprint of Greenwood Publishing Group, Inc.

Printed in the United States of America

The paper used in this book complies with the
Permanent Paper Standard issued by the National
Information Standards Organization (Z39.48–1984).

10 9 8 7 6 5 4 3 2 1

Copyright Acknowledgment

The author and the publisher gratefully acknowledge permission to use
the following:

Excerpts from Lewellyn Hendrix, "Illegitimacy and other Purported
Family Universals." *Journal of Cross-Cultural Research* 27: 212–231.
Copyright © 1993 by Sage Publications, Inc. Reprinted by permission
of Sage Publications, Inc.

Contents

Illustrations

TABLES

FIGURE

Preface

In my discipline of sociology, attention often shifts to new theories before older frameworks are fully tested. Scholarship on illegitimate birth is a prime example. As new approaches have appeared, we have cast aside older theories without carefully testing them. To conduct such a test, I have dug through numerous ethnographies to find 122 minimally useful descriptions of illegitimacy sanctions and matched these with other published data codes for these same societies. My cross-cultural research shows that these older theories are no less valid than newer ones: each set has its strengths and weaknesses. The findings suggest also that we need more complex, multifactor accounts of how societies deal with illegitmate birth.

The bibliography for the ethnographic descriptions used in the research is located in Appendix B. Works are organized according to their number in the Standard Cross-Cultural Sample and their use in coding. References to these works in the chapters give the author, date of publication, and the Standard Sample number. This may cause confusion for some, but many readers will want to see which ethnographic sources were consulted and which were used in the actual coding of information for the research.

I am grateful to many people who have contributed to this research or helped me prepare for it. My university has provided release time and graduate assistance. The people who have assisted, cajoled, critiqued, inspired, and prodded me include Shaheen Ahmed, John Alessio, Bridget Austiguy-Preschel, Joel Best, Neal Blackburn, Grant Bogue, Tom Burger, Mindy Diltz, William Douglass, Mel Ember, Jerry Gaston, Ben Gorman, Marleigh Herr, Zakir Hossain, Cathie Hutcheson, Mary Hutchinson, Suzanne Keller, David Johnson, Marion Levy, Jr., H. A. Nimmo, Charles Speck, Clarence Storla, Tracy Thibodeau, and Margaret Winter.

1

The Puzzles of Illegitimacy

Societal responses to illegitimate birth have puzzled sociologists and anthropologists for over a century. When we examine the ways societies regulate nonmarital birth, we are confronted by a dazzling array of practices and ideologies. At one extreme of the array are societies such as the Rwala Bedouins, who attach great shame to illegitimate birth for the woman and her family. If a woman gave birth to a child before her wedding, she was cast out of the group or killed by her own kin, but women and their families tried to avoid this great shame. If a woman conceived before her wedding, she first would try to get her lover to marry her. And, if this did not work, she might resort to secret abortion or even suicide (Musil 1928, no. 46). Needless to say, nonmarital fertility was virtually nil in this society. Near the other end of the spectrum, the northern Lapps were lackadaisical about illegitimacy (Pehrson 1957: 60, no. 52). Over one-fifth of Lappish women gave birth before marriage. The Lapps disapproved of illegitimacy, but it was not a grave moral matter and did not affect a woman's chances for marriage. If a woman became pregnant but did not regard the father as a good marriage partner, she could wait until she found a man she liked. The few illegitimate children not taken into a marriage were formally adopted by the mother's kin.

Why do the Lapps and Rwala Bedouins react so differently to the same behavior? Variety in reaction, a primary puzzle of illegitimacy, is the focus of this book. Several theories, to be examined in subsequent chapters, have attempted to deal with this puzzle. Other puzzles involve these theories and the way they have accumulated without being cumulative. Curiously, these theories are mostly lacking in empirical confirmation through research. Their authors sometimes cite cases in support of their theories, but virtually no cross-cultural testing has been done. In this book, my emphasis is on cross-cultural testing of hypotheses from various theories and not on adding to the social science literature of conjectures. My main research question is: Under what conditions do societies use more severe sanctions for nonmarital conception or birth? Most theories of illegitimacy include severity of sanctions as one important aspect of control, either explicitly or implicitly. Hypotheses about severity of sanctions can be derived from the theories and tested. In this way, this research may be useful in making a comparative assessment of the empirical adequacy of the theories. I hope to sort out those aspects of theories that are more empirically adequate from those that are less so. I will not offer a new theory of illegitimacy, although the findings reported here provide leads for new directions in constructing theory.

WORDS AND VALUES

Some may ask why I use the term *illegitimacy*. It sounds old-fashioned to some people and politically incorrect to others. It seems to disapprove of people's behavior in advance. It seems to be sexist in being based on the woman's unmarried state without regard to the man's marital status. The phrase *illegitimate child* seems to blame the victim by labeling the child for the sins of the parents. The criticisms are important insights on the cultural definition and control of illegitimacy in America and some other Western societies. They point toward the shifting meanings of nonmarital birth in America. The questioning of language and the attempt to change it is also an attempt to change norms and ideals. Criticism should be directed at America's cultural definitions, and not at research on these and other groups' definitions. I think it is useful to employ illegitimacy in a technically neutral sense, leaving a society's value judgements as a variable for study. The juxtaposition of the Lapps and Rwala Bedouin should make this clear.

There are several reasons for using illegitimacy. Some brief word or phrase is needed to refer to unmarried women's conceiving and giving birth. I am not sure we currently have a brief neutral phrase other than *nonmarital birth*. While this phrase does not convey the issues of norms and control that I examine here, I use it as a synonym for illegitimacy.

Next, history suggests that some neologism (such as *nameless children* (Zingo and Early 1994), or *generic children*) would be of little help. Over time, Western societies have moved from the language of spurious and bastard children to illegitimate and out-of-wedlock children. As older words took on connotations of immorality, concerned members of polite society engineered new words to refer less disparagingly to the same behavior, only to have these new words take on moral overtones as their novelty wore off. Also, important theories come from a time when the term illegitimacy was in vogue, and it is the term they use. It would be rather tortuous to analyze these theories without using their principal term. This would be analogous to explaining Marxism without the concept of *class struggle*! I intend my technical use of the word illegitimacy to be morally neutral. It is an ubiquitous but varied cultural trait, a puzzle that ought to stir our scientific curiosity instead of stirring urges to enforce political correctness. I ask readers to distinguish between the technical term and the folk usage.

ILLEGITIMACY AS THE BASIS OF KINSHIP INSTITUTIONS

Various normative aspects of family and kinship structure have been conjectured to be universal among the societies of the world. These include marriage itself, the incest taboo, nuclear family structure, men's authority over women, the division of labor by sex, the family's part in socializing children, and the prohibition of illegitimate birth. While research would be valuable on any of these conjectured universal features of family and kinship, illegitimacy has received less close inspection than any of the others. Here the need is greatest.

To be sure, there is an enormous body of research on illegitimacy rates and ratios in contemporary societies and in historical settings. Family historians have studied illegitimacy primarily as an indicator of the growth of personal freedom and romance in mate selection or of other aspects of relations between the sexes (Shorter 1971, 1975; Gill 1977; Laslett et al. 1980; Fairchilds 1984; see also Flinn 1981). There is a large and rapidly growing body of policy-oriented research on illegitimacy as a social and psychological problem. More specifically the topic of adolescent pregnancy and birth receives much research attention today as one of the items on the standard list of social problems in America (see Miller and Moore 1990 for a review). In neither the historical nor the contemporary work is the cultural definition of illegitimacy or the sanctions for it the main object of study.

While illegitimacy may be a social problem in some modern societies, it is an ancient and widespread concept. Many societies, like the Lapps, have not considered nonmarital birth to be much of a social problem, but rather see it as one option following premarital conception. The social problem approach is not concerned with explaining why there are cultural norms and sanctions for illegitimacy but instead asks about the reasons and consequences for nonconformity. The approach presupposes the existence of the norm, and does not solve the puzzle of why some societies consider illegitimacy to be a social problem while others do not.

ILLEGITIMACY AS THE LINCHPIN IN OTHER FAMILY UNIVERSALS

We can see the importance of studying illegitimacy by examining its place in the accounts of other purported family universals.[1] Various family norms and structures have been conjectured to be universal among the societies of the world. I will show here that the principle of legitimacy is logically prior to these other supposed universal family features.

The cultural concept of legitimacy/illegitimacy, as formulated by Malinowski (1930) is a linchpin concept in these purported family universals, underlying and intertwined with the others. Malinowski's universal principle of legitimacy is that all societies assign one man to be the social father—the guardian and protector—of each child. To put it differently, he argued that everywhere reproduction is regarded as legitimate only if a social father is linked to mother and child in the family unit. Malinowski recognized the enormous variation in ideologies of reproduction and in the kinds of positive and negative sanctions used in implementing the principle of legitimacy. Yet he believed that the principle of legitimacy promotes and regulates parenthood everywhere, and that this is the basis of all family and kinship structures. He saw that societies recognize fatherhood even if they do not recognize biological paternity, even if they are matrilineal, and even if they are technologically simple foraging groups. I will argue that Malinowski's concept of the social father is implicit, if not explicit, in the accounts of the universality of the incest taboo, marriage, the nuclear family, male dominance, and the division of labor by sex. Theories of these family features assume the prior existence of the social father: the father role is part of the "givens" within each account. I will structure my argument by looking at accounts of each universal feature and showing how social fatherhood is a part of the account.

I want only to show the place of illegitimacy in the logic of various accounts of family universals. My major concern is not whether these are truly universal features or with whether the theories are really true. Each of the features is recognized to be tremendously widespread among the world's societies. This ubiquity, along with the theoretical accounts of these features, certifies their importance to understanding the family. Showing that illegitimacy is an integral part of the explanation of other purported family universals makes a powerful argument for its theoretical significance.

Some Views of Illegitimacy and Fatherhood

A special stimulus for seeing illegitimacy as the linchpin among the family universals comes from Wilson (1983). He speaks of the father-child relation as the primordial feature of kinship, in contrast to other family ties. Wilson sees the mother-child tie as being defined primarily on the basis of biology. That children are born of mothers and that mothers nurse their infants are obvious empirical facts. He views culture as being important in assigning particular meanings and values to motherhood, which shapes mother-child interaction. But the culture is an overlay, stemming from experience of the biological link. Similarly, Wilson argues that the sibling relation is based on the experience of the biological link of two children born from the same mother.

Today we perceive a biological link between father and child. Wilson theorizes that this was not so for early humankind, that fatherhood was a great social invention in human prehistory. The father-child biological link is less obvious than other biological links in the family. Wilson points out that while mother-child and sibling ties are cultural extensions of biological links, the father-child tie is a more purely cultural innovation. He does not develop his argument further to show that this primordial cultural invention underlies particular features of family and kinship, as Malinowski does.

In contrast to Wilson's cultural-innovation interpretation of the father role, other scholars have argued that there are biological underpinnings to fathering behavior. Draper and Harpending (1982) give a biosocial interpretation to the findings of studies on the impact of single-parent families on adolescent offspring. Rather than seeing the single-parent home as producing dysfunctional offspring, Draper and Harpending feel that either of these reproductive strategies may be effective in the setting in which it is initiated. They cite findings that father-absent boys are more aggressive, scornful of women and femininity and that father-absent girls have more negative attitudes toward males, become sexually active earlier, and are less able to establish long-term heterosexual relationships. These findings suggest that reproductive strategies may be triggered by family experience during the first few years of life (but influenced by later experiences also). For both males and females who have grown up in single-parent families, the reproductive strategy is one in which there is less permanent bonding of mates and less paternal investment in offspring. Offspring of two-parent families are more likely to use reproductive strategies involving long-term bonding with mates and greater paternal provisioning for mate and offspring. Father-absence sets a learning environment for boys and girls to acquire reproductive strategies in which they minimize reliance on one partner of the opposite sex.

Mackey (1985), on the contrary, believes that the two-parent strategy is the only workable one on a large scale mainly because of the extended need for provisioning, monitoring, and nurturance of human offspring. Nurturant fathering is a biosocial necessity and universal feature of societies today according to Mackey. He argues that men have a strong biological capacity for nurturing but have a higher threshold for this behavior than women do. In public observations of thousands of public child-adult interactions in eighteen societies, he finds that over half involve men alone, or men and women. Men respond to children in much the same way women do in these interactions.

These biosocial accounts are less opposed to Wilson's view than they seem at first glance. Wilson's statement by no means precludes the idea that *fathering behaviors* existed before the invention of the *role of father*. Undoubtedly he could agree that particular fathering behaviors are reproductively rational under given circumstances. His point is that people experience women's part in biological reproduction as intimate and direct. Men have no experiential counterparts to women's gestation, birth, and lactation. People must invent the idea of fatherhood. The common theme in these treatments is that fatherhood appears early in human societies. If this is so, then the father role—or the principle of legitimacy—can be seen as a key element in other purported family universals, to which we now turn.

The Role of Illegitimacy in Accounts of Marriage

The marriage relationship is said always to involve an exchange, or a contract, in which rights are acquired and obligations are incurred (Radcliffe-Brown 1950; Stephens 1963).   These rights and obligations may variably include the right to one's spouse's labor, rights of sexual access, and the right to procreate—or the right of the husband to claim the wife's offspring. This procreation element in the marriage contract institutionalizes father-child ties, specifying the father's claims over the child and his obligations to it.

In fact, it is difficult to distinguish between marriage and similar relationships without invoking the idea of reproductive rights. Several Western nations have recently moved toward equalizing the rights of legitimate and illegitimate children, but the question has been raised as to whether this can be done without reducing marriage to simple cohabitation (Eekelaar and Katz 1980; Tapp 1980). Davis (1985) points out that the expectation of reproduction distinguishes marriage from mere cohabitation. They are alike in other respects, including residential and sexual arrangements. Esther Goody (1982) notes that some African societies may grant unmarried women the right to reproduce following their puberty rituals. Other evidence indicates that marriage is needed in many of these societies to give the child rights vis-à-vis the father. Among the Bemba the *chisungu* ritual for adolescent females makes unwed birth a less serious offense. However, the child is not fully legitimate unless the mother is married (Richards 1956, no. 7).

These observations lead to the conclusion that it is impossible to define marriage, to distinguish it from similar relationships, other than by presuming that the culturally defined father-child relation is a part of the basis of marriage itself. [2]

The Role of Illegitimacy in Family Universality

Accounts of the universality of the nuclear family and of the family as an agent of socialization also presume that societies legitimate reproduction for married couples. Murdock (1949) argues that the nuclear family is universal among the world's societies either as an isolated structure or as the basic building block of composite polygamous and extended family structures. Since the nuclear family consists of a married man and woman and their children, the father-child relation is presumed in the definition of the family.

Murdock makes a causal argument also. He attributes this universality to the four functions the nuclear family performs everywhere. These are the sexual function, the educational (or socialization) function, the economic function of cooperation, and the procreative function. All but the sexual function presume a father-child relation.

The economic function is defined as a division of labor between spouses and between the generations for the benefit of the nuclear unit. This cooperation involves sharing between both parents and children, so a father-child relation is presumed.

Added to this is the procreative function, which is that married couples have obligations to provide for survival and basic sustenance of their offspring. Murdock (1949) notes that abortion, infanticide, and child neglect are regulated in all societies. The education function consists in parents imparting basic cultural skills and knowledge. He notes that while various other agencies may be involved in educating children, the parents always have a role.

This argument about the four family functions says that nuclear families are institutionalized in all societies in part because of the societal survival need for biological and social reproduction, which is accomplished efficiently by combining legitimate reproduction and child socialization with other functions in the family. Father-child ties are presumed in three of the four nuclear family functions: the reproductive, the economic and the educational.

The most renowned "exception" raised in the debate on the universality of the nuclear family is the Nayar of India (Gough 1968). This case shows the importance of illegitimacy even though it is contrary to the purported universality of the nuclear family. Nayar husbands and wives did not live together per se, but rather lived with their families of orientation. Hence, residential families existed but were not nuclear and did not include a married couple. Instead, a woman had a symbolic marriage to a religious functionary, after which she could legitimately reproduce with men of her caste—her "visiting husbands." A small gift from any one of her visiting husbands was sufficient to legitimate her child and acknowledge it as his. This is a minimal recognition of the social father, but an institutionalized arrangement nonetheless.

To argue that the nuclear family is universal is tantamount to saying that fathers are ideally a part of the family unit everywhere and that they have binding obligations to their offspring. As the Nayar case shows, legitimacy may be important even when there is no residential nuclear family.

Illegitimacy as a Cornerstone of Sexual Inequality

Functionalist scholars have asserted that sexual inequality is universal (Davis 1949; Levy 1966), and Marxists (Engels 1972; O'Brien 1981) have argued that sexual inequality stems in part from men's concerns in late prehistory about the paternity of the children that women bear. The latter theories explicitly assert that the formation of illegitimacy norms is bound up, partly as a causal factor, with the evolution of sexual inequality. They also see the differential resources of men and women as an element in men's ability to make the rules and establish control of women's reproduction. Engels argues that after a division of labor by sex arose in prehistory, technology enabled people to create a surplus. This surplus was a basis for wealth and private property. Men overthrew mother-right because they wanted to pass their wealth on to their "legitimate" sons. Also, to ensure that their wives' offspring were their own, men made wives into chattel, domestic and reproductive laborers.

In this theory there is a clear presumption of a culturally recognized bond of father to child. All of the features that Engels saw in the civilized family are consequences of men's desire to ensure the legitimacy of their wives' offspring. Illegitimacy concerns are one immediate cause of sexual inequality.

O'Brien (1981) has a different Marxist account of patriarchy that identifies a motive for men and sees social fatherhood as a key factor in the origin of sexual inequality. She believes that men's experience of reproduction does not link them to the next generation, that men are alienated, in the Marxist sense, from reproduction. This alienation provides reason for men to assert claims over women's offspring and to control reproduction through the control of women. O'Brien's theory is like that of Engels in that it sees the nascent idea of social fatherhood as a key factor in sexual inequality. By extension, the principle of legitimacy is one mechanism underpinning men's control of women.

Illegitimacy and the Division of Labor by Sex

Functionalists sometimes attribute uniformities in the division of labor by sex to the roles of women and men in reproduction. To my knowledge, no one has tried to link this division to legitimacy (although Murdock comes close), but such an argument can be made. In a nutshell, the division of labor by sex is usually seen to be within the family primarily between husband and wife, for the sake of legitimate offspring of the married couple. In a cross-cultural perspective on the uniformities in the division of labor by sex, women tend to perform tasks such as grain grinding, cooking, fetching water and firewood, hoeing in gardens, and foraging for vegetal foods and small animals. Plowing, herding large animals, and hunting large animals tend to be performed by men (Murdock 1937; D'Andrade 1966; Murdock and Provost 1973), along with combat roles (Adams 1983). Some tasks, like potting and weaving, may be assigned to women in one society and to men in another. As Ember (1981) and Schlegel (1989) note, one common thread in this division is that women's work roles in most premodern societies seem to be those that can be combined with infant and child care, which tends to be predominantly women's work. Women's tasks tend to center in and near the home more than men's do and involve repetitive or routine work. Male strength also may be a factor for some task assignments, but this may play only a small part in task assignment (Schlegel 1989). With the exception of plowing, men's tasks do not necessarily involve greater physical strength. Carrying water, firewood, and offspring are hard physical tasks for women, as is grinding grain with hand tools. The tasks mostly assigned to men may involve greater danger or unscheduled sudden action, as in the case of chasing large game or defending against enemy attack. From a reproductive point of view, men are the more expendible sex (Parker and Parker 1979).

Nor can the division be characterized as a split between "productive" work and "reproductive" work.[3] It is estimated for ethnographically described societies that women produce an average of 40 percent of the food diet (Aronoff and Crano 1975). The social division of labor appears to be built upon the biological division in reproduction, with women doing tasks that combine readily with infant and child care, and men doing residual work, especially dangerous work.[4]

By and large, these features of the division of labor by sex have been considered in the abstract. Little attention has been paid to the question of who receives the fruits of whose labor. Is there a family-based division of labor everywhere, or is there sometimes a nonfamilial basis? I do not believe that I am going too far out on the argumentative limb to say that husbands and wives loom large in this division, although other sex roles are relevant. On occasion, the men and women of a community may pool their catch from a hunt. In some matrilineal groups, men contribute to their married sisters' larders. The division of labor in these cases, and in the case of warfare, is made on a community or a descent group basis. Most frequently, however, the division of labor by sex takes place within families, with mothers and daughters doing some work while fathers and sons perform other tasks, with all family members sharing the fruits of this labor. Once the marriage and family basis of the division of labor by sex is pointed out, the same ideas about illegitimacy underlying the universality of marriage and the nuclear family can be again applied: The division of labor by sex is grounded in the notion of husband and wife cooperating to sustain themselves and their legitimate offspring in the family. This relates to Murdock's (1949) point in his discussion of the economic function of the nuclear family, where he argues that the cooperative division of labor between husband and wife is one of the bases of the universality of the family.

The Role of Illegitimacy in Incest and Exogamy

The incest taboo, more often than anything else, has been taken as the primordial rule of human family and kinship systems. Levi-Strauss (1969) expresses this view in saying that incest avoidance in mating is both a biological and a cultural phenomenon. Indeed, all societies known to present-day social science appear to have forbidden sex and marriage in parent-child and sibling relations for most of their members most of the time.[5] Arguably, illegitimacy is equally or more primordial, but before showing this, let us see what the lines of argument on incest have been.

Incest and family endogamy are held to be forbidden everywhere because of either genetic or social difficulties that would arise from their practice (Westermarck 1894; Davis 1939a, 1949; Murdock 1949; Levi-Strauss 1969). Westermarck's biological reasoning, and that of some contemporary authors (Parker 1976), is that the inheritance of harmful traits tends to result from inbreeding. Because of this, our species evolved with a potential for sexual avoidance triggered by close interaction during infancy and early childhood. Cultural taboos are built upon this biological foundation, forbidding what most people do not want to do and feel uneasy about. Seemanova (1971) presents medical evidence of the severe impairment and deformation of children of incest as compared with nonincestuous half-siblings. Some evidence of avoidance exists for several nonhuman primate species (reviewed by Parker, 1976). Evidence for human populations comes from studies of the lack of sexual pairing among age mates in the Kibbutzim of Israel (Talmon 1964; see also Spiro 1965 and Shepher 1971) and studies of *sim-pua* marriages in rural Taiwan (Wolf 1966, 1968; Wolf and Huang 1980). Wolf has found that *sim-pua* marriages, in which the wife is raised from infancy or early childhood with the husband, have more symptoms of sexual incompatibility than marriages contracted in adulthood. Studies of father-daughter incest in western societies similarly suggest that early association limits incestuous attraction. Stepfathers coming into the home after the daughters are several years old, or who are uninvolved in infant care, are most likely to commit incest (Russell 1984; Parker and Parker 1986; Gordon and Creighton 1988).

Other accounts say that incest and family endogamy are forbidden for social reasons. The taboo encourages broader networks of cooperation and peaceful alliances between kin groups (Fox 1967; Levi-Strauss 1969) or prevents disruption and disorganization in the family in the form of sexual jealousy, status-confusion, and the disruption of authority and socialization within the family (Davis 1939a, 1939b, 1949). There is much anecdotal evidence supporting the revered argument on alliance, but the only cross-cultural studies examining the empirical association between exogamy and peaceful or hostile relations find no support for it (Ember 1975; Kang 1979). Case studies of father-daughter incest in modern societies suggest that family disorganization may precede, as much as result from incest. The often-involuntary withdrawal of the wife-mother from her role is sometimes an enabling factor (Kaufman et al. 1954; see also Elbow and Mayfield 1991). The anomie, or lack of institutionalization, of remarriage and stepfamily relationships (Cherlin 1978, 1981) also may be a contributing factor to higher rates of incest in stepfamilies.[6]

The social and biological accounts of the incest taboo, taken together, see incest as the link between culture and biology and as the primary principle underlying family and kinship structure everywhere. Is incest really the primary underlying principle, or does illegitimacy share that place?

While the universal aspect of the incest taboo may be grounded in biologically based avoidances, as a social rule it presumes a social role structure. The rule cannot be expressed without referring to status-roles. There can be no rule against father-daughter sex unless there is a cultural recognition of father and daughter status-roles and relationships. A recognition of the kinship statuses of father and daughter in norm formation suggests at least a minimal kind of legitimacy—a social definition of fatherhood. The logic of the situation demands that we see illegitimacy as developing before or concomitantly with incest taboos. This is perhaps one of the reasons that Malinowski (1930) saw parenthood, not incest and exogamy, as the basis of kinship and social structure.

Another argument for the logical priority of legitimacy is that several theories of incest are not so much about the sex in incest as about the procreation that might come from it. They raise questions about the biological fitness of offspring of incest or about placing incestuous offspring into the kinship structure. Incest taboos and family exogamy—sex and marriage[7]—are equated in these theories as rules specifying who may procreate with whom legitimately. These theories hold a triple presumption about legitimacy. In addition to the general presumption just described, these explanations of the incest taboo outlaw certain reproductive relationships. In circumscribing who may legitimately procreate with whom, even as the incest-endogamy taboo is being formed, it may create a category of illegitimate birth—that of incestuous illegitimacy (Davis 1939a; Goode 1964, 1982). In these theories on the social or biological fitness of incestuous offspring, it is the birth that is forbidden, much more than the sex. Thirdly, these theories based on consequences for offspring imply that people recognize a link between the incestuous genitor and his offspring. If a society forbids incest because women's offspring by their fathers or brothers turn out stillborn, deformed, or retarded, that society has at least moved toward the invention of legitimacy. The society may not know of a biological connection between genitor and offspring, or even between sex and reproduction, but could construe the prohibition in terms of magical or spirit-produced defects in offspring. A hypothetical early society might have believed that if a woman has sex on a regular basis with a man in her family rather than with an outsider, spirits will cause deformities in her offspring. A belief of this sort would establish a minimal link between an adult male and a child—between the one who, along with the mother, instigated malevolent spirit action and the child who was acted upon by the spirits. By the same token, this belief would exert pressure on the group to recognize a paternal link between the healthy child and the mother's regular outside partner. If this reasoning is correct, the principle of legitimacy and the incest taboo may be seen to grow out of the same processes, which entail the institutionalization of family status-roles, including the father-child role, and the regulation of reproduction.

We must conclude that there are convoluted logical interconnections between illegitimacy and the formation of incest taboos. On the one hand, all intrafamily incest cannot be tabooed without there being a status of father. On the other hand, the development of the taboo, as some major theories see it, implies the concurrent development of concepts of paternity and legitimate reproduction. We cannot fully understand incest without understanding illegitimacy.

THE STRATEGIC IMPORTANCE OF STUDYING ILLEGITIMACY

We can see from these considerations that illegitimacy is a linchpin concept underlying and intertwined with the other purported universal features of the family, although few social scientists have seen it in this light. Understanding illegitimacy has implications for understanding other purported universals, including marriage, family structure and function, incest and exogamy, and the sexual division of labor and inequality.

We need to study illegitimacy cross-culturally in the manner that incest, the division of labor by sex, sexual inequality, and the other purported universals have been studied—in terms of behavioral, normative, and biological components. Recent cross-cultural research (Mackey 1985; Hewlett 1992) has drawn attention to fathering behaviors. These works begin to inform us about the range of variation in some aspects of fathering behavior, of some of their sociocultural concomitants, and of possible biological grounding of some behaviors. Additional work is needed on the interplay of social and biological factors in fathering and its effects on offspring. While research in America documents the economic and reproductive behaviors of father-absent offspring, we do not know if the findings of this work are generalizable to other cultures, although some may be (Munroe and Munroe 1992).

We can see from these considerations that the cross-cultural study of illegitimacy is of strategic importance. The principle of legitimacy helps define the father role, which is logically prior to the other purported universal features of the family, although few social scientists have seen it in this light. There is a void in the empirical literature. My aim is to help fill this void by looking at variation in the handling of illegitimacy. As is the case with other purported family universals, our sociological conception of this one conceals much diversity. It is a diversity that cries out for more attention.

PLAN OF THE BOOK

My research aims to test theoretical ideas about possible factors involved in the severity of social regulation of illegitimacy. It is important to understand precisely how each theory accounts for the sanctions for illegitimacy. The next two chapters provide a chronological overview of theorizing on illegitimacy and analytically dissect the theories to find useable hypotheses. Today, many scholarly articles and leading textbooks misinterpret Malinowski's principle and do not mention competing interpretations of illegitimacy. This wholesale misreading is another of the puzzles of illegitimacy. A preliminary step is to clear up "what Malinowski really meant." Malinowski had far broader things to say about illegitimacy than the status placement hypothesis he is often credited with today. When I place Malinowski's principle of legitimacy in its historical context, we will see that the status placement argument would have been puny. I further show the gradual modification of Malinowski's principle of legitimacy until the current status placement version came into vogue.

This tracing out shows another of the puzzles of illegitimacy—that in some respects theorizing on illegitimacy has gone full circle. Around the turn of the century, there was a concern with variation in societal reaction to illegitimacy (Malinowski 1930), and a consideration of conflicts of interest stemming from social and sexual inequality in the production of cultural definitions and social

controls (Engels 1972). Before mid-century, theory began to treat the definition
and control of illegitimacy as a constant factor across societies and over time.
As the status-placement hypothesis developed, a link between the stratification
system and legitimacy of birth was initiated. In the 1980s, the radical or
"conflict" branch of sociology (Collins 1988), along with feminist theory
(O'Brien 1981), had again begun to consider cultural evolution and cross-
cultural variability in the social control of nonmarital procreation. Like Engels
at the close of the nineteenth century, several writers today emphasize that the
social control of illegitimacy stems from a matrix of social and sexual inequality
and operates in a way that constrains and represses those without power.[8]

In this circular history, there is less sign of progress in scientific
understanding than one would like to see. There is little evidence that newer
theories have built on the strengths of earlier conjectures while discarding their
excesses. Instead, the recent theories yield a potpourri of conjectures about
factors pertinent to the regulation of nonmarital birth—factors such as societal
need, moral consensus, sexual inequality and socioeconomic inequality, innate
bonds to offspring, and economic practicality of offspring. Indeed each theory
seems to attend to a limited set of social structural conditions and to one or two
motives giving rise to cultural norms and sanctions. To some extent the theories
center on early stages of the life cycle, when the notion of legitimacy is not only
about birth and childhood but also about adulthood rights and duties. Several
aspects of structure and several kinds of motives have been identified by
competing theories as pertinent in an understanding of illegitimacy, but
comparative empirical work has been uncommon. The paucity of empirical
research makes it difficult to even identify the strengths and weaknesses of any
of the theories set forth over the past century, except from the perspectives of
formal logic or of one's personal biases. Thus, there are pressing needs for
theory construction and integration and also for comparative empirical research.

Subsequent chapters describe variation in societies' systems of control of
illegitimacy and present statistical evidence from the cross-cultural study. I also
analyze case examples as a way of documenting and elaborating some of the
factors involved. To test hypotheses, it is important to get information on
societies throughout the ethnographic spectrum and not to limit ourselves to the
concepts and contexts of Western civilization; some of the theories themselves
have dealt with the entire gamut of human history (and even prehistory).

The findings I describe here take us beyond the confines of Western
civilization to examine societal reactions to nonmarital conception and birth
across the full ethnographic spectrum. The focus in Chapter 4 is on describing
and classifying variations in the systems of control of nonmarital birth among
the nonindustrial societies of the world. I classify the various modes of social
control of nonmarital birth into four main types. These four types are arrayed
along a dimension of increasing stigma or punishment.

Following Chapter 4 on variation, separate chapters look at particular factors
purported to play a major role in the development of severe sanctions on

illegitimacy. Some major factors include technological development and the growth of social hierarchy, rules of marital residence, sexual inequality, and parent-child ties.

Chapter 9 discusses how the findings do not show extensive support for any particular theory. The sample data suggest that the principle of legitimacy is universal, but variable in ways that are not precisely predicted by any one theory. I suggest a preliminary framework for an account of illegitimacy norms and sanctions. It holds that the structure of a society triggers, or allows expression to, certain constellations of interests, which then mold the society's principle of legitimacy.

America is placed in a cross-cultural perspective in Chapter 10. America's principle of legitimacy has been becoming less repressive. For centuries Western law has been moving away from a definition of legitimacy based strictly on marriage and toward one that takes away fewer rights of illegitimate offspring and assigns obligations to biological fathers, regardless of marital status. Reproductive technology is being used in ways that seem to challenge this legal trend, but thus far most cases have been decided within the framework of existing family and illegitimacy law. The social trend is consistent with the legal trend. In America this century, both middle-class white communities and lower-class black communities are reacting less severely to nonmarital pregnancy and birth.

I use some of the statistical findings to help account for these trends and apply the theoretical framework from Chapter 9. While we can be sure that men's interests have been important in shaping laws and community responses to illegitimacy in America, I discuss the importance of women's and offspring's intergenerational interests in shaping this trend in the American principle of legitimacy.

A cross-cultural study obviously does not apply directly to the current American issues on welfare and illegitimacy, and it cannot come up with ready-made solutions. Nonetheless, viewing these issues in a broader framework may help in identifying the underlying structural sources of our definitions of paternity and maternity, against which the new reproductive technology grates. As Glendon (1987) suggests in her comparative analysis of abortion and divorce law, a broader perspective can help in rephrasing the issues or in developing more thoughtful and caring ways out of these conundrums.

NOTES

1. Large portions of this section are reprinted with slight modifications from Lewellyn Hendrix, "Illegitimacy and Other Purported Family Universals," *Cross-Cultural Research* 27: 212-231, 1993.

2. I have phrased my argument in terms of Malinowski's principle of legitimacy, which holds that everywhere the social father is recognized and expected to be part of the domestic family unit. The argument applies to mother-child relations as well. Nobody has questioned the universality of mother-child relations, or whether the mother

is always expected to be a part of the family. This does not excuse us from seeing that there are cultural definitions of the link between mother and child and that the mother-child relation may vary from one society to another. Too often, we assume that the mother role is a cross-cultural constant. The socially defined mother-child relation also underlies marriage, but that issue is not addressed here.

3. Except in the Marxist sense of capitalist production for the market, the notions of productive work vs. other types of work, or production vs. consumption, make little analytic sense. As Marion Levy (1966: 390-93; 1989) points out, there is no production without consumption, for production requires the consumption of energy and raw materials. When we consume, we also produce something. When a "consumer" purchases raw food and cooks it, edible food is produced. When the new mother digests this food, mother's milk for the newborn is produced. Other "products" of her food preparation and consumption include body maintenance and health, energy, fat, excrement, and garbage. Excrement and food scraps may be consumed by sewage plants in the production of sludge. The sludge may be consumed by farmers who use it to enrich soil for the production of grass for livestock or vegetables, which are eventually purchased by consumers. If we see the full cycle of consumption-production, then we are drawn to the conclusion that the distinction between productive work and nonproductive work is usefully seen as a folk category within modern western culture, or as a misplaced abstraction.

4. In urban industrial states analogous patterns can be seen. Men are assigned combat roles more often than women. "Protective" legislation prevents women from entering some hazardous jobs. Over half of married women are in the labor force in the United States, and some 80 percent work for some part of their married lives outside the home, but the proportions are higher for married men. Studies of housework continue to find an extreme imbalance between husband and wife, even for two-paycheck couples. When a wife increases her share of paid work outside the home, there usually is not an equal decrease in her housework duties (Strong and DeVault 1986; Scanzoni and Scanzoni 1988).

5. Incest and family endogamy have been allowed for some nobility or on rare occasions in various societies. A few societies have allowed limited sex between parent and child on certain occasions. Hendrix (1975) reports cultures that allowed one episode of parent-child incest construed to be for sex education, and others that practiced father-daughter incest in nighttime rituals before hunts to give hunters more courage. The incorporation of ordinarily forbidden, criminal behavior in normative ritual may seem peculiar. However, Gluckman (1967) points out that one often finds some amount of license in ritual. This gives them a "safety-valve" latent function. Brother-sister marriage was practiced among royalty in some ancient civilizations, such as in Egypt, Hawaii, and among the Incas. For Roman Egypt there is evidence that brother-sister marriages were accepted among commoners as well. Middleton (1962) presents funerary evidence that some people in brother-sister relationships married in Roman Egypt, but the frequency and acceptability of these marriages are not inferable from the data he presents. Hopkins (1980), using census records, letters and other archival evidence, documents that marriages involved "actual" rather than "classificatory" brothers and sisters. Letters, horoscopes, and invitations from the period strongly suggest that these marriages were not only acceptable, but preferred, and that offspring were hoped for. Hopkins raises a serious question on the universality of the incest prohibition.

6. Leavitt (1990) suggests the findings on the biological basis of incest avoidance are not fully convincing on empirical grounds. He suggests primarily that biosocial writers have overlooked some research that does not support their claims, and that they have exaggerated the strength of support in the studies cited. He finds the evidence "far from conclusive" (Leavitt 1990: 983), and does not believe the theory empirically valid enough to displace "cultural/environmental theory." I agree with his assessment to a degree, but believe that cultural theories have even less empirical validity than the biosocial theory.

7. Robin Fox (1967) wryly notes that while most adolescents understand that sex and marriage are very different things, some otherwise brilliant anthropologists theorizing about incest and exogamy have been unable to see any difference.

8. Guttentag and Secord, in *Too Many Women* (1983), also hold this type of view. While they draw from mainstream social psychological theories of power rather than from feminist or Marxist theory, they are influenced by the feminist viewpoint.

2

The Development of Theory

My task in this chapter and the next is to examine explanations of the control of nonmarital birth as sources of useful, testable insights. Secondarily, I will document my assertions in the first chapter on the circular, non-cumulative history of theory. As I stated, theory testing is sorely needed since many conjectures have accumulated without culminating in an enhanced understanding of the empirical world. To facilitate this secondary task, explanations are lumped into three sets:

A. Early theories emphasizing variability.
B. The development of the status-placement explanation in mainstream sociology.
C. The potpourri of contemporary theories.

The theories of illegitimacy discussed in this chapter consider how, in the absence of a concept of illegitimacy, issues would arise during some epoch in human history, or recurrently in all societies, to spur its invention and its control. Each theory centers on a particular phase of the life cycle. As various people experience this phase, illegitimacy issues arise again and again until some set of people evolves or creates control mechanisms for illegitimacy, and then gets others to implement them. The life stages, the particular intergenerational interests, and the agents involved vary from one theory to the next. Because of these differing assumptions about agents, stages, and interests, the theories come to divergent conclusions about the origins and nature of illegitimacy as a cultural category. By making these covert assumptions explicit, the causal connections posited in each theory are clarified. Two benefits stem from this task: the divergent conclusions of theories become comprehensible, but equally important, this step is needed to tease out hypotheses for empirical testing.

For the first two sets of works, I will summarize the main points of each and follow up with my analysis. The analysis will include the theory's view of the variability of illegitimacy control mechanisms and of the agents, life stages, intergenerational interests underlying the development of illegitimacy norms, and the social structures that trigger or enable norm formation based on these motives. My list of independent variables will be derived from this analysis. For some theories, one must "read between the lines," making inferences about possible assumptions from clues in the texts. Some theories have such gaps that it is impossible to tell, for example, precisely what motives drive its actors.

THE EARLY THEORIES

Bronislaw Malinowski produced the most influential theory of illegitimacy, encapsulated in the phrase, "the principle of legitimacy" (1930). However, an earlier treatment of illegitimacy exists in the writings of the unilinear cultural evolutionists of the late nineteenth century. Frederick Engels (1972) used a cultural evolutionary model to construct a Marxist interpretation of the origin and development of the family, private property, and the state. A crucial factor in the development of the family for Engels's model is men's concern about legitimacy and offspring, which he believed to have appeared in later evolutionary stages. Malinowski reacted to this notion of Engels and other evolutionists, arguing for an earlier, universal base for the social institution of fatherhood.

Most of the subsequent theorizing on illegitimacy in sociology of the family has flowed out of one brief paper by Malinowski on the principle of legitimacy. While Malinowski's work continues to be cited, it is often misinterpreted, and Engels's emphasis on legitimacy is almost forgotten. Each theorist had insights that are ignored in sociology today.[1] Our faulty recollections of these theories need correction. They are superior in some respects to the status-placement theory and some of the ideas in the contemporary theoretical grab bag.

Engels's Evolutionary Theory

Engels emphasizes the inequality between women and men, more than class inequality, as the basic factor giving shape to the regulation of procreation and to the family more generally. Engels sees men's concerns about legitimacy of offspring rising with the development of civilization and following the vast time spans of progress through the stages of "savagery" and "barbarism." This type of unilinear evolutionary thinking has largely been discarded,[2] but Engels's insights on illegitimacy are sources of testable hypotheses, even if one questions unilinear evolution.

Description of Engels's Theory. Here briefly is Engels's three-stage treatment of the origin of bastardy norms. In the first stage of savagery, the food supply of early human society, procured through foraging, was barely sufficient for survival and was not adequate for the accumulation of a surplus.[3] The few material goods that existed were owned communally. Sex roles were undifferentiated, and there was little social regulation of people's lives, including their sexuality and procreation.   There was no concept of incest or of illegitimacy, since early promiscuity made it impossible to recognize paternity (if people had had that concept).   Over the centuries, promiscuity was narrowed somewhat by ruling out first parent-child, then brother-sister incest. With this narrowing, groups of men married groups of women as whole categories.

During barbarism, the next stage, clan ownership grew out of communism. Group marriage gave way to "pairing" marriage, in which the husband and wife each had a primary spouse but secondary ones as well. Paternity came to be recognized with pairing marriage, but social organization was still matrilineal. Engels believes that women wanted and helped bring about this form because they had suffered more from the excesses of earlier forms, and because they still had the power to effect change.

The domestication of plants and animals for food production introduced the third stage, civilization, as exemplified by classical Greece and Rome.   As animals began to be herded, a domestic division of labor arose between men and women, with men producing most of the food.   The level of food production subsequently increased, resulting in a surplus.   The surplus fell into the hands of men, who controlled the means of production, since they were the primary food producers.   The concept of private property grew from men's controlling the surplus.   Over the generations, as men owned surplus goods and could market them, they accumulated wealth and became concerned about passing this wealth to their offspring as opposed to the offspring of other men.

This situation gave rise to a concern about the paternity of children.   In the preceding stage, the uncertainty of paternity resulting from promiscuity and multiple spouses had led to matrilineal inheritance.   What few goods a man might have had were passed to his sisters' offspring.   Now men with wealth or power wanted to pass it on to their offspring, and not to their sisters' offspring as they had under the matrilineal pattern, and here we come to the crux of the matter.   Undisputed paternity was required in order that "these children may in due time inherit their father's wealth as his natural heirs" (Engels 1972: 68-72). Women, being dependent on men, became objects of lust and mere instruments of reproduction (Engels 1972: 68).   Men invented monogamous marriage as a way of controlling their wives' sexuality to guarantee the paternity of their wives' offspring.   Wives were secluded and guarded to make sure that only the husband had sexual access.   Men did not wish to constrict their own sexual activity to marriage.   Women now could be accused of sexual or procreative transgressions and punished by their libertarian fathers and husbands or by society at large.   This double standard could work only if there were separate classes of sexually available women—prostitutes, slaves, concubines—for men's use outside of monogamous marriage.

Hence for Engels, the concept of illegitimacy, the double standard of sexuality, prostitution, and monogamous marriage all emerged as parts of the same package of sexual oppression and from wealthy men's concern about the paternity of their wives' children.   The "traditional" Western family structure came about as the solution to the problem of legitimacy.

After the onset of civilization, various types of marriage were mixed together in Europe, resulting in some tempering of the portrait of monogamous marriage in the early civilizations of Greece and Rome. Under early capitalism, Engels believes that the features of marriage and family life were determined by class position. More specifically, the package of sexual oppression existed mainly in the bourgeois classes. The absence of property in the proletariat made for less domination of women, more affection between husband and wife, and less concern about paternity. Engels believes that prostitution and adultery played an almost negligible role here. However, earlier practices carried over somewhat, and bourgeois domination creates additional problems (Engels 1972, 79-80).

Analysis of Engels's Theory. Engels sees immense variation in the extent to which societies attempt to control illegitimacy. The main dimension of variation is from a complete lack of concern to severe, repressive sanctions. These sanctions apply to mothers and illegitimate children more than to men.

Who are the agents of creation, and what are their interests in this theory? In Engels's scheme on the creation of repressive illegitimacy controls, wealthy married men are the primary agents who struggle with women to create the notions of paternity and legitimacy. Men's control of property gives them power over women, who are excluded from ownership. Sexual inequality and economic inequality are important facilitating structural conditions. Without sexual inequality, women would have more input into the content of family norms and sanctions, which would then be patterned some other way. Without the accumulation of wealth by a few men, there would be little question of the inheritance of property, and these men would not have the power to implement their solution to the problem of uncertain paternity. The struggle is primarily between husband and wife, but also between father and daughter, and between men and women in nonmarital sexual liaisons. Hence, Engels's agents play their parts in the sexually active adult years in general, more than any highly specific life stage.

For Engels, men have two motives—an interest in erotic freedom and variety and an interest in their own biological offspring inheriting their estates. The self-interested sexuality of Engels's men is understandable, if he assumes that the drive for sexual variety is universally powerful. Engels did not assume that women shared this powerful drive, but in other aspects this desire for sexual freedom without family responsibility is in line with the rest of the theory. The other motive does not fit Marxist theory. Engels's men oppress their wives and daughters, but are altruistic toward sons by their wives. It is not clear why these self-interested men would want to single out certain sons, their offspring by their closely watched wives, as heirs to their property. This altruism is an incongruous element in the personality make-up of Engels's otherwise oppressive and self-interested men, and is made more mysterious by their unwillingness to form obligations to their offspring conceived by their mistresses.

Why would these oppressors care who inherits their wealth? This is the motor for Engels's theory of the family, but he gives no direct answer to this question. Let's consider some possibilities. He may have presumed implicitly that there are innate father-child bonds behind the concern. Other people of his day made such presumptions. He may have been assuming extrinsic interests of fathers in sons. A materialist argument could be made in which powerful men were interested in alliances. Sons would be chief allies, and the loyalty of legitimate sons could be kept by promise of an inheritance. Although this would be consistent with the general tone of Engels's writing, he does not make this argument or any other to back up his notion that men want legitimate heirs. He seems to have blindly followed Morgan's (1963) lead in interpreting Greek and Roman marriage as based on men's concern for certainty of paternity, without adding a materialist account of it, and consequently leaving a theoretical gap.

Discussion of Engels. Engels's account of repressive sanctions for nonmarital birth fails because of this lack of an intergenerational interest consistent with the theory. Since illegitimacy concerns are the foundation for monogamous marriage in Engels's evolutionary theory, this is a significant problem. O'Brien's century-later materialist account of reproduction, described in the next chapter, provides one solution.

Engels provides some vital leads for understanding illegitimacy, which stem from his view of the control of illegitimacy as a variable response to changing structural conditions. He alerts us to the importance of the cultural recognition of biological paternity, to the part of economic development in the accumulation of surplus wealth, and to the concept of property inheritance. Foremost, his theory hypothesizes that repressive controls of sex and reproduction occur with the development of social and sexual inequality in agrarian states. In an importance sense for Engels, the repressive control of illegitimacy unfolds at the intersection of social and sexual stratification. This conceptualization is helpful in understanding the one-sidedness of illegitimacy controls in cases such as in the historical West, where stigma and loss of rights have fallen more heavily on the mother and child than on the father. When men of the upper classes are allowed to have sex and procreate with prostitutes, slaves, and captured enemy women without sanction or legal obligation, but women of the upper classes face the threat of degradation and loss of position for analogous actions, we see the interaction of the two forms of inequality. While these assertions are plausible, their status as general explanatory principles lacks cross-cultural empirical validation. There may of course be other structural conditions under which repressive controls appear. Also, repressive controls may not always occur at the intersection of sexual and social inequality if there is not some important interest of adult men in claiming some offspring but avoiding ties to others.

In the statistical findings reported in later chapters, several hypotheses from Engels are tested. These link the treatment of illegitimacy to inheritance rules, descent, subsistence technology, social stratification and centralization, and sexual inequality.

Malinowski and the Prinicple of Legitimacy

Malinowski is, one might say, the father of the sociological problem of legitimacy. Mainstream sociology has ignored Engels's ideas and built upon Malinowski's (1930) thinking. In fact, the development of mainstream sociological thought on the topic can be seen as the gradual modification of Malinowski's original notion of the universality of the "principle of legitimacy."

The Modern Misinterpretation. The curious thing about this development is that many sociologists today mistakenly believe Malinowski to have emphasized the role of the father in status placement of offspring. Coser and Coser's (1974) examination of the principle of illegitimacy following social revolution and Blake's (1979) examination of recent changes in American family patterns both cite Malinowski as saying that the principle of legitimacy is universal because of the role of the father in status-placement. Some leading textbooks (Scanzoni and Scanzoni 1988; Skolnick and Skolnick 1989) on family sociology misinterpret the principle of legitimacy in the same way. Scanzoni and Scanzoni attempt to rework Malinowski's theory. They believe that the function of the social father for Malinowski is "to serve as a pipeline to the social and economic rewards of a particular society" (1988: 220). They critique this idea on the basis that it does not fit the facts for Europe and America today. Single mothers in higher occupations, they say, can place their offspring well within the status system. Poor single women receive government aid—not the father's aid—in rearing and placing their offspring. These are misguided critiques.

Background to Malinowski's Principle. This common misinterpretation necessitates a clarification of Malinowski's ideas on illegitimacy. While he does use the terms "full legal status" and "full sociological status" of the child, the status placement function is not the main thrust of his argument. To understand more clearly what Malinowski is saying, we need to look at two sources of his ideas: Edward Westermarck's view of the family and Malinowski's own fieldwork in the Trobriand Islands of the South Pacific.

Westermarck and Malinowski were personal acquaintances (Montagu 1956), and Malinowski (1930) acknowledges his influence. Westermarck (1894) had argued against the cultural evolutionary model of family and kinship as it was being set out by Bachofen (1861), Morgan (1963), and others. Whereas the evolutionary model held that the family appeared far after the origin of humankind and after some degree of technological development, Westermarck held the family, consisting at least of male and female parents and children, to be universal among human societies. Hence, there was no primitive promiscuity, as the evolutionists had hypothesized. Westermarck posited on the one hand that the human family is a reflection of our heritage from the higher primates. On the other hand he posited that the cooperation of man and woman in procreation and child care (that is, the family) is necessary for species survival. For an effective survival strategy, there needs to be a male to cooperate in subsistence activities and to act as protector of the mother and infant.

Malinowski preferred this view of the family consisting of at least two parents and children over the notion that some societies simply had not limited sex and procreation to individual relationships, with the consequence that fatherhood been unknown. In his 1931 debate with Robert Briffault on the BBC, Malinowski said:

A whole school of anthropologists, from Bachofen on, have maintained that the maternal clan was the primitive domestic institution, and that, connected with this, there was group marriage or collective marriage. In my opinion, as you know, this is entirely incorrect. (Malinowski 1956: 76)

Malinowski's fieldwork in the Trobriand Islands most certainly strengthened this view. His field observations show parallels with his later theory. Contrary to the evolutionary model, he found a strong two-parent family even though biological fatherhood was not recognized and descent was matrilineal. With matrilineal descent, one's mother is the more important parent in status placement. This greater importance stems from the fact that children become members of their mother's clan and inherit from their maternal uncles and aunts. However, Malinowski was particularly impressed by the vibrant father-child bonds flourishing in this setting.

The Trobrianders believed spirits cause women to become pregnant but a woman must have sexual intercourse with a man at least once to open the birth canal. They saw sex as necessary for procreation, but they saw no natural link between any one male sex partner and the woman's child. The Trobrianders allowed extensive sexual freedom for unmarried youth, and these youth were very active sexually. Malinowski, puzzled over why so few illegitimate children were conceived in this youthful promiscuity, conjectured that conception is less likely when a woman has diverse sexual partners.

Nonetheless, the woman who did bear a child before marriage in this matrilineal society was strongly stigmatized. The Trobriand people cherished children and believed that each child should have a father (that is, a mother's husband). Although there was no specific prescribed punishment, illegitimacy was frowned upon and pitied. The illegitimate child was considered "unfortunate," and the mother "reprehensible." She became less desirable as a marriage partner and perhaps unmarriageable.

Malinowski's several examples of illegitimacy mostly involve women who were considered undesirable as spouses (albino and ugly women) by Trobriand standards, opening Malinowski's interpretation to question. However, one case did involve an attractive woman. In this one case, the woman's constant and exclusive lover abandoned her when she gave birth (Malinowski 1929: 194). Illegitimate children were "concealed" because of this social reaction, and sometimes adopted by their mother's married sisters (Malinowski 1929: 20, 196, 201).[4]

The Trobriand father had enduring, close ties with his children, but had little part in their status placement. Since descent group membership, inheritance, and political succession were matrilineal, the mother and her kinsmen were important in status placement. Despite the father's limited authority in the family, his ties with his children were enduring and affectionate. The mother was primarily responsible for infant care, but the father had an active role beginning in the third month. Fathers cleaned and washed infants and fed them mashed vegetables. During the evenings the father held and amused the baby. During weaning, the child slept with its father or grandmother (Malinowski 1929: 18-20, 235).

Malinowski believed these close ties led to patterned deviance from basic social norms. At puberty sons went to live with their maternal uncles, and upon marriage were supposed to bring their wives into that village. Fathers sometimes subverted this accepted practice by setting up a marriage between his son and his sister's daughter (patrilateral cross-cousin marriage was culturally preferred), and an irregular matrilocal residence. This combination of cousin marriage and residence would place the son back in his natal community near his father. The father would then try to give his son the use of property to which his nephews were entitled, causing problems within the father's descent group.

In these shenanigans stemming from the affectionate father-child ties and in the stern treatment of illegitimacy, Malinowski saw, like Westermarck before him, the operation of a natural, necessary, two-parent family. He did not see a powerful status placement function of a socially defined father. Had he done so, it would have been quite incongruous with his observations.[5] The Trobriand father's role in status placement was limited and often a deviant one. His role as a guardian, caretaker, and companion to his children was richly developed.

Description of Malinowski's Principle of Legitimacy. What then is the principle of legitimacy? Malinowski formulates it this way: "The most important moral and legal rule concerning the physiological side of paternity is that no child should be brought into the world without a man—and one man at that—assuming the role of guardian and protector, the male link between the child and the rest of the community" (Malinowski 1930: 137). The emphasis here is on the father's responsibility in guarding and protecting the child, on being a buffer between it and the larger community.

Malinowski says this is a universal principle that varies in its implementation. Children may be linked with a father figure either through negative sanctions in some societies or through positive inducements in others. This depends upon the society's value or contempt for virginity, the permissiveness of premarital sex norms, its ideas about the mechanism of procreation, and above all whether the child is a burden or asset to its parents. Malinowski (1930: 144) indicates that sometimes there is a logical connection between the native theory of procreation and the shape of social fatherhood but sometimes there is "a complete disconnection." He also reverses or qualifies his hypothesis on premarital sex norms affecting the implementation of the principle of legitimacy, by suggesting that the allowance of some nonmarital sex is an "adjunct" to mate selection, or a pressure valve, encouraging stability of subsequent co-parental relationships (Malinowski 1930: 142). This language suggests that premarital sex norms are as much consequence as cause of the principle of legitimacy, or both are part of what we might call a "legitimacy complex." The strong factor then is the practical value of children. If children are practical assets to parents and virginity is not valued, "the unmarried mother is more attractive because of her offspring," otherwise she is "degraded and ostracized on that account" (Malinowski 1930: 138).

In this diversity, Malinowski (1930: 138) sees "the rule that the father is indispensable for the full sociological status of the child as well as of its mother, that the group consisting of a woman and her offspring is sociologically incomplete and illegitimate. The father, in other words, is necessary for the full legal status of the family." Malinowski's point here is that procreation without a recognized father is everywhere socially and legally unacceptable. The principle of legitimacy does not refer to status placement in a stratification system as many sociologists have come to believe, but rather refers to the social and legal acceptance of the family unit.[6]

Malinowski (1930: 140) translates the principle of legitimacy into the idea that marriage is not merely a license for sex but a contract legitimizing procreation.[7] His thinking about why this licensing of procreation is universal is scattered in various works. His observations of father-child ties in the Trobriand Islands led him to posit a biological basis for parent-child ties (Malinowski 1927: 214; 1930: 127), which is also important in his view of illegitimacy. He thinks there is an inherently strong mother-child bond that is triggered during pregnancy and childbirth, but he recognizes that culture shapes motherhood in numerous ways. The father-child biological bond is less powerful, being formed only indirectly as the father guards and cares for the mother during pregnancy. Unlike women's bonds to infants, men's bonds are not strong enough to uniformly motivate men to see to the welfare of their children. Cultural reinforcement of these biological predispositions is needed. Nevertheless, they are strong enough to produce cultural elaborations on the theme of legitimacy. Drawing on Westermarck, Malinowski argues that fatherly care for mother and child is necessary if reproduction (that is, child survival) and socialization are to take place. In short, society cannot continue into the next generation unless mothers have help with sustenance and child care. Partners who stick with women during pregnancy and birth are the most motivated men to provide these services. In these ideas on why the principle of legitimacy is universal is an account of why two-parent families are likely to be interactional realities and why societies institutionalize this unit and encourage procreation within it.[8] There is not a shred of a status-placement function in Malinowski's principle of legitimacy.

Analysis of Malinowski. Malinowski sees the regulation of illegitimacy as even more varied than Engels does. Whereas Engels sees controls ranging from repression to indifference, Malinowski conceives the regulation ranging from repressive controls to illegitimacy-as-inducement to marriage. Like Engels but with less elaboration, Malinowski suggests a set of cultural and structural factors producing this variability. These factors include the value placed on virginity, the native theory of procreation, but *especially important* is whether children are a burden or an asset to parents. Unlike Engels, Malinowski thinks that there is always regulation of illegitimacy, and he attributes this to societal necessity and biological bonds triggered during birth and pregnancy.

Malinowski's explanations of the universal and variable parts of the principle of legitimacy involve several human agents. Mostly these agents are in the life-cycle stage of parenthood or they are soon-to-be parents. In the universal part of the principle of legitimacy, the motives of these agents are explicitly biological: the mother, and to some extent, the father, are said to have innate affectional bonds with their own offspring.

Other people in society seem to be the audience to the individual parental couple and child. In societies in which children are not economic assets, some other people in society must care enough about children in general, or about society, to attempt to enforce the principle of legitimacy and give men the extra boost (or threat) they need to get them to shoulder the tasks of fatherhood. Malinowski has neither an account of who these other people are nor why they care. This is a common problem with functional analysis, and the standard functionalist response is to say that societies just die out or are swallowed up by other societies if they do not take care of societal requisites for survival.[9] Members of society just have to care, and that's that.

In addition to these universal intrinsic biological interests in children, Malinowski also hypothesizes that in some societies parents have extrinsic interests in children. This is his key to variation in the social treatment of illegitimacy. Ironically while Engels the Marxist does not see a political-economic interest in offspring, Malinowski the functionalist does.

Discussion of Malinowski's Theory. For the purposes of my research Malinowski offers some significant leads. He suggests that intrinsic and extrinsic adult interests in children work together to produce positive or negative mechanisms for the control of illegitimacy. It is plausible that extrinsic interests in offspring lead to positive controls on illegitimacy. These economic interests vary across societies and historical periods, although they are difficult to measure.

There are some additional problems with the notion of intrinsic interests. Malinowski thinks of the universal intrinsic interests as rooted in socially triggered biological bonds. Malinowski would surely admit, were he alive today, that the extent of bonding, at least between father and child, must vary from society to society because it is triggered in social relationships that vary between groups.[10] However, there is more trouble with this idea. While there has been research suggesting the potential for maternal and paternal bonding in humans during the minutes and hours following birth (Klaus and Kennell 1976), it has not been replicated by independent investigation (Lamb and Hwang 1982, cited in Rossi 1984).[11] Nonetheless, we can think of father-child, and parent-child closeness and intimacy, whether rooted in the mind or in the body, as a relevant factor. While it would be premature to dismiss some degree of biological grounding for some components of parent-child ties, we know that empirical parent-child relationships vary enormously in intimacy across societies (Mead 1935; Rohner 1975; 1980; Rohner and Rohner 1981) and historical eras (Aries 1962, Shorter 1975). It was this *empirical* social interaction among the Trobriand Islanders that had Malinowski puzzled, so it is the empirical interaction that will be of concern here.

In statistically testing Malinowski's theory of the social control of illegitimacy, the severity of sanctions is hypothesized to be linked to affectionate ties and to the economic value of offspring. I will argue in a later chapter that the economic value of offspring has less to do with children's labor than with family structure.

ILLEGITIMACY AND STATUS

Malinowski set the stage for subsequent functionalist theorizing on illegitimacy. While these theories brought some useful ideas on how the control of illegitimacy relates to social class and other systems of social statuses, the mainstream understanding centered on the one factor of status placement. Kingsley Davis began this emphasis on status, but it came to fruition in the debate on Caribbean family structure and the place of the "principle of legitimacy" in the Caribbean family.

Davis: Moral Consensus and Status Placement

In contrast to Malinowski, Kingsley Davis views the control of illegitimacy as universally repressive and punitive. While his work is a continuation of Malinowski's functionalism, it suggests new leads for analysis. Davis's two major papers on illegitimacy contain related essays on the necessity of negative sanctions for illegitimacy and on the inevitability of illegitimate birth. In one paper, Davis (1939a) argues that forbidding and penalizing illegitimacy helps maintain family patterns and certain status-role systems, thereby perpetuating society. In the other essay he reacts to the social welfare approach to illegitimacy, arguing that neither illegitimate birth, nor the stigmatizing of illegitimacy, nor the unequal rights of illegitimate offspring, can be ended (Davis 1939b).

Description of Davis's Theory. Any human society, according to Davis (1939a), can survive only if its members' activities are organized and integrated in such a way that necessary societal functions are performed. These organized, integrated activities are not self-maintaining, but people must be taught these patterns and motivated to value and maintain them. These norms will be impressed "so early and so deeply in the psychic constitution that the individual will take them as part of himself, condemning without thought and without respite those who depart from such behavior" (Davis 1939a: 77). This conditioning cannot preclude deviance altogether, for no social structure is perfectly integrated, and cultural norms never coincide exactly with "fleshly desire and capacity" (Davis 1939a: 77). Thus, both deviance and its condemnation are inevitable.

Since procreation is an indispensable functional activity, it must be organized and integrated with other functions in this way in all societies.

If this activity were not carried out according to given normative patterns, the function of reproduction could not be socially guaranteed, the necessary cooperative behavior in caring for children could not be organized, and reproduction could not be integrated with other functional activities. Procreation outside the familial channels will *inevitably* be condemned, for without such condemnation the structure itself could not exist and the society could not operate. (Davis 1939a: 77-78)

The attitudes against illegitimacy are so ingrained and diffused throughout society that people "attack the mother even before her confinement, because she and her family and friends all feel a moral horror at the idea of unwed pregnancy" (Davis 1939b: 227). When Davis points out that unwed mothers feel moral horror at their own pregnancies, he is clearly ruling out any cultural pluralism, or any "bastardy prone subsociety."[12]   Davis (1939b) argues that the disabilities placed on the illegitimate child are not punishment for its parents' sins, but protection of the rights of legitimate families and their members. The rights of legitimate and illegitimate children cannot be equalized so long as the institution of marriage exists.

Davis calls Malinowski's principle of legitimacy the central principle of family structure, but believes that the effects of specific forms of illegitimacy need to be analyzed. He examines premarital, adulterine, incestuous, and intercaste illegitimacy, along with procreation by those in normatively celibate groups. For each type of illegitimacy, Davis considers its social consequences and why it is handled in a particular way. For example, premarital illegitimacy is more strenuously disapproved of if the sexual liaison is transient. At the other extreme, illegitimacy during betrothal may arouse gossip, but it can be remedied through legitimation by subsequent marriage. The threat of condemnation is rarely implemented.

Adulterous illegitimacy is more socially difficult. There is no possibility of marriage of the partners without disrupting existing marriages.[13] If the father is married and the mother is not, the rights of his legitimate offspring are impacted if he is required to take in his illegitimate children. If the mother is married, the illegitimacy is more difficult to detect. Davis notes that if a society attributes no importance to physiological paternity, this type of illegitimacy does not exist. Instead, all children born to a married woman are the legitimate "offspring" of her husband. However, if paternity is a supreme value and an indispensable ingredient in fatherhood, an illegitimate child born to a married woman is regarded as one of the worst kinds of illegitimacy because of the ease of concealment. Since detection is problematic, the law tends to presume the husband's paternity. This makes it more urgent for husbands to monitor their wives' fidelity (Davis 1939a: 82-83).

Davis (1939b) deals more with the notion of paternity as an ingredient in social fatherhood. In arguing that the seeming disabilities of the illegitimate child are in effect protecting other legitimate children, he singles out patrilineal societies in a discussion of descent, inheritance, and succession. He points out that the bastard child cannot inherit, but will be assigned to the physical custody of the parent "that is not lineally significant" (Davis 1939b: 224). In a patrilineal system the child is theoretically taken by the mother, which protects other legitimate offspring of the father who stand to inherit or succeed.[14]

Davis explains that incestuous illegitimacy creates havoc with kinship relationships, and here is the beginning of the status-placement explanation. Consider the son of father-daughter incest. From his father's point of view, he is son and grandson (daughter's son) simultaneously. From his mother's point of view, he is son and brother (father's son). For other children in the family, he is brother and nephew at once. The child does not fit into any single status and has contradictory relationships with family members.

Similar confusion can happen with intercaste illegitimacy. Societies with castes (or slavery) tend to forbid intermarriage and hence forbid legitimate procreation between members of different castes. Davis reasons that marriage presumes social equality of the husband and wife and of their families.[15] Intercaste marriage contradicts this presumption, and the child becomes an outsider to the castes and the families of both parents—a misfit in the status system. Norms prescribing caste endogamy prevent these misfits.

These effects of intercaste illegitimacy are more pronounced in racial caste systems than in non-racial caste systems since the offspring's biological traits cannot be hidden, Davis (1941) explains in an essay on caste. In nonracial caste systems, special rituals or fines may make intermarriage permissible. With these special mechanisms, men may marry women of lower caste, and offspring may be socialized into the subculture of the father and take his status. Davis states that matrilineal caste societies may not fit this model, but they are rare.

Analysis of Davis. The universal social response to illegitimacy in general is one of moral condemnation and legal inequality in Davis's theory. The response is universal to all societies and to all members of any given society. However, people respond differently to different types—such as illegitimacy during betrothal as opposed to incestuous illegitimacy. The agents in Davis's theory are all of the socialized adult members of society, reacting, as they have been conditioned to do, to the births of children to women by men to whom they are not married. The general motive of the public in shaming bastards and their mothers seems to be moral indignation or outrage that their values and way of life are threatened. Davis indicates that this motive has special implications in "civilized" and "patrilineal" societies where physiological paternity is an important ingredient in fatherhood.

Discussion of Davis. Davis's analysis is at once an advance over previous theories and a regression. His brand of functionalism dealing with the requisites for society can be easily criticized on the basis of oversimplification and tautology. To presume a universal moral consensus, that everyone (even the mother!) condemns illegitimacy seems an absurdity. Yet with this view, Davis is saying that women and men have a complicated mix of biological urges and internalized moral values that are not consistent. Davis's people are complex, but his society is simple. This simplification leads to his emphasis on universal condemnation among societies as well. Both Malinowski and Engels treat the control of illegitimacy as a cross-cultural *variable*, but Davis chooses not to use this aspect of their treatments.[16] Engels's view of societal indifference and Malinowski's view of children as inducements to marriage in some societies are thereby alien to Davis's theory. Illegitimacy sanctions range from weak moral condemnation and removal of offspring's rights to strong moral condemnation and removal of rights.

Functionalism sometimes appears to say that the effects of social patterns are their causes (Stinchcombe 1968), or it seems to explain the parts of social structure by saying that the whole cannot work without its parts. This is less an explanation than an analysis of how the parts fit together, but in analyzing how the parts fit with each other, some causal relationships may be suggested. For instance, Davis suggests that patrilineal descent and the importance of paternity in fatherhood cause illegitimacy to be handled in different ways, but he does not follow up to contrast matrilineal societies with patrilineal ones. Had he done so, it might have shown his implication that the bastard child becomes the burden of the father in matrilineal groups to be patently false, as we saw in discussing the Trobriand Islanders.

On the positive side, Davis's idea of the importance of physiological paternity to social fatherhood is more straightforward than Malinowski's ideas about the value placed on virginity and the native theory of procreation as factors affecting the handling of illegitimacy. Davis's concept of siring offspring as an ingredient in social fatherhood helps integrate Malinowski's hesitant formulation. Women's virginity is important in some societies because paternity is a prime ingredient of social fatherhood, and the ideology of procreation may help rationalize the importance of paternity (or lack thereof) in social fatherhood. Malinowski sees these ideological factors as pertinent to the control of illegitimacy, yet a connection is not always present.

We should credit Davis for the status placement hypothesis on illegitimacy for it is he, and not Malinowski, who brings up the notion that the illegitimate child must be handled differently from others if the status system is to be maintained. In examining caste systems and kinship systems as systems of status positions, Davis initiates the status-placement hypothesis of illegitimacy. His point is that the child of incest or cross-caste couples fits no existing status position whatsoever.   In both instances of castes and incest, marriage is forbidden: thus there can be no legitimate offspring to create confusion in the status system.   It should be noted that Davis' status-placement function is not particularly about status ranking (prestige), but about statuses as a system of structural positions within which people interact.

Davis's theory contains, just beneath the surface, an intergenerational interest other than those posited by Malinowski. Davis implies that any societies not condemning illegitimacy cease to exist, but provides no examples. This lack of examples suggests that people everywhere quickly catch on that illegitimacy is a challenge to their family patterns, their kinship structure, and everything they value about their way of life.   In fact, this suggestion of a moral basis is virtually explicit. For Davis, a peoples' way of life, their culture, is universally a learned and internalized moral phenomenon. Socialized adults have a moral stake in the continuity and preservation of their sociocultural system through appropriate procreation. Whether social life is threatened by deviant procreation or by external attack, Davis's people react with moral outrage and condemnation. Through internalization of group norms, self-interest becomes synonymous with interest in the continuity of one's society and culture, and these propagate concern for children being procreated within, and inculcated into, the group's standards and values. The motor in Davis's theory seems to be an interest in preserving one's valued way of life—an interest in offspring grounded in ethnocentrism.

A final important lesson for my research concerns the types of illegitimacy. Intercaste illegitimacy, incestuous, illegitimacy, adulterine illegitimacy, and premarital illegitimacy need separate analyses. My analysis focuses the latter type—on societal reactions to unmarried women being impregnated by men of their own social level, or by men whose identities are not publicly known.

The hypotheses in Davis's work that are amenable to cross-cultural statistical test are a subset of those of Engels and Malinowski. Davis posits that illegitimacy sanctions are somewhat stronger in patrilineal societies than in matrilineal ones because biological fatherhood is a key ingredient in social fatherhood.   Also, a social father is important in placing the child into the system of descent groups. Similarly, in highly stratified patrilineal caste societies, the sanctions for illegitimacy are stronger.

Placement in the Hierarchy of Statuses

At mid-century, a debate on family patterns in the Caribbean emerged. Scholars agreed that consensual marriage and legal illegitimacy were widespread among the lower classes of numerous Caribbean societies. One issue was whether these lower-class behaviors were normative patterns or deviant.

Goode's Theory. Goode (1960) extends the work of Malinowski and Davis in his influential analysis of illegitimacy in the Caribbean. Goode seeks to defend and reformulate Malinowski's thesis in light of the challenges to it based on the high rates of illegitimacy and cohabitation.[17] He argues against other authors who view concubinage, consensual marriage, and illegitimate birth as culturally approved equivalents to legal marriage. Nonetheless, Goode's close examination of these authors' works shows that legal marriage is an ideal, that families are upset at their daughters' nonmarital pregnancies, that most people do marry by the time they reach their later years. Consistent with this, Blake's (1961) research in Jamaica found expressed ideals for parental veto power during courtship, and for limiting procreation to the marriage relationship. That these are powerful cultural ideals is evidenced by the observation of women's personal shame from premarital pregnancy.[18]

In spite of this shame some women are drawn into careers of nonmarital procreation. Goode points out that many Caribbean lower-class peasants go through a period of living in consensual union and bearing illegitimate offspring even though they feel this is less than ideal. Commitment to legally sanctioned marriage and procreation is of a lower degree here than in the middle and upper classes.

Goode sees that it is necessary to reformulate Malinowski's principle of legitimacy if it is to apply to Caribbean societies.

The principle in fact rests primarily upon the function of status placement, not that of locating a father as 'protector.' . . . Violation of the norm creates some ambiguity with respect to the child, the parents, and the two kin lines. [Hence] commitment will be greater among the strata or kin lines which enjoy a higher prestige or in which concern with kin relations is higher. (Goode 1960: 27)

Concerns about maintenance of prestige and kinship translate into concerns about legitimacy.

A second factor, which Goode (1960: 29) calls *individual role bargaining*, is also relevant. Individual role bargaining means that courtship is done on an individualized basis, somewhat isolated and anonymous from one's parents. In some societies families are the bargaining units in "courtship," but not in the Caribbean. In the individualized and anonymous courtship situation, without her family to back her up, a woman has little bargaining power. At the same time, a man is able to argue against marriage because of the expense of the celebration. Even though she may desire formal marriage, the woman may have to settle for consensual marriage as a potential step in that direction, realizing that if her relationship breaks up, any children she has borne will make her less marriageable in the eyes of other men. She and her partner may eventually marry, or she may go through other relationships, before she eventually marries.

Analysis and Discussion of Goode. Goode's analysis of placement in the prestige stratification system is the main understanding of the principle of legitimacy in sociology of the family today. It has been questioned by some authors and built upon by others. Hyman Rodman (1966) offers a critique. He uses the concept of the "value stretch" to argue that the lower class in Trinidad accept contradictory ideals of legal marriage and of common-law marriage, because legal marriage may be impractical or impossible. This criticism does not severely challenge Goode's argument. It agrees that there is still some norm commitment among the lower classes, ambivalent though it may be.

Other analyses have used Goode's status-placement principle as their point of departure. Coser and Coser (1974) observe that attacks on the law of legitimacy follow successful social revolutions. They account for this by arguing that the norms of society are generally geared to the needs of the upper strata. They see illegitimacy norms as helping to protect lofty positions in ascriptive stratification systems. People with little wealth or prestige to pass on to their young will be little concerned about conforming to the norm for it is not especially in their interest to do so. Thus, when social changes reduce the importance of ascription, illegitimacy increases. Similarly, the main point of the Cosers is that in major social revolutions (in which the status system is attacked and there is a push for changes in values) there is a wish to eradicate the distinction between legitimate and illegitimate offspring and to end the disabilities of the latter. According to Coser and Coser, this fits with egalitarian values and helps put an end to the old order.

This status placement theme is echoed by Blake (1979: 191-194). She attributes the rising illegitimacy in the United States not to a breakdown of control, but to a "quiet revolution" in the family, in which Americans are subscribing less and less to the assumption that the husband-father ought to be the only one from whom children's status and life-chances are inherited. Goode's status-placement function has become an accepted explanatory principle.

Since Goode's work is so widely accepted in the mainstream today it deserves careful and critical attention. Goode centers on the incidence of illegitimacy and consequently gives little useful information directly about variations in mechanisms of control. His focus on social-class variation further limits the direct applicability of his interpretation for cross-cultural research, which tends not to deal with internal variation. On the positive side, his analysis does alter Davis's and Malinowski's notions, suggesting that the principle may work differently in highly stratified societies. Goode emphasizes that illegitimacy is higher in those classes having little prestige to lose, as the concern about prestige loss is minimal there. This is not the society wide moral consensus of Davis but a more limited spread of commitment to procreative norms, thinning out as it seeps into the lower levels. It is the interest in maintaining one's own rank, or one's family's rank, in the hierarchy of status that drives Goode's explanation, and not a concern for the system as a whole as it is for Davis. Those whose rank is higher and more valued show more commitment to reproductive norms. From this logic, highly stratified societies may have a different or an additional basis for regulating illegitimacy than more egalitarian societies do.

There are also theoretical loose ends. First, the explanation would not seem to work for matrilineal societies, for reasons I have given in talking about Malinowski and the Trobriand Islanders: the father is not primary in status placement.

Second, the account of intergenerational interest in Goode's theory is weak. Goode does not indicate why an illegitimate child would be a threat to one's rank. Once the norms are in place, having an illegitimate child may indeed be a threat to one's rank, but we cannot presume the norms and sanctions already exist if they are what we want to explain. Goode's assumptions about the motives underlying illegitimacy norms are not those of Malinowski (whose theory he claims to reformulate). Goode is not considering parent-child bonding or the practical utility of children in different classes. He may be using some assumption similar to that of Davis in which children represent cultural continuity, but not explicitly so.

The interpretation of social revolution built upon Goode's analysis shares this problem of not accounting well for human agency. For example, if revolutionaries were to repeal the law of legitimacy it would appear as a half-hearted and misdirected attack on the stratification system. It would be more effective to outlaw property inheritance altogether.

Third, Goode mentions sex differences in commitment to legitimacy norms without accounting for their presence. Goode's analysis of courtship bargaining power is done with much attention to the woman's point of view. Women are described as wanting to legitimate their offspring, but men seem less motivated in this direction. Goode theorizes men who want to avoid caring for other men's offspring, but who seem to have little positive motivation to care for their own. Does the greater concern of women stem from a greater concern with kin relations, or is it a more practical interest in securing the long-term commitment of a man in co-parenting? This is another of the loose ends.

Fourth, Goode mentions that cross-class concubinage is a common form of deviance in the Caribbean, without incorporating it into his analysis. He deals only with consensual unions in which both partners are lower-class peasants. According to Goode, middle-class and upper-class men marry within their class but also may take lower-class women as mistresses, whom they do not marry. These are the same men who are purportedly concerned about status placement and who therefore are committed to the rules. The key to this contradiction seems to be that these men are using the rules to their erotic or reproductive advantage, and that they are only selectively committed to the rules. The situation smacks of the kind of double standard that Engels investigated. From the high-status man's point of view there may be two classes of women: those of one's own class who are sexually inaccessible save through marriage, and lower-class women with whom the sanctions and consequences for nonmarital sex and procreation are almost nil. It may be this aspect of illegitimacy law that rebels attack following social revolutions. As Engels (and also maybe Coser and Coser's rebels) sees clearly, men with power can use the law to their erotic or reproductive advantage in liaisons with poor women. Status placement of offspring is no real problem from the upper-status man's point of view: the illegitimate children assume their mother's class position even though their biological father may be upper class. Obviously a more complete theoretical account of cross-class illegitimacy in the Caribbean is needed.

Perhaps the strongest critique of Goode one can make is that his analysis may confuse cause and effect. He does not analyze the way people create norms and sanctions when certain structures and motives crop up, as Engels, Malinowski, and Davis do. Goode has more of a theory of norm commitment than of norm creation. Goode may have not reformulated Malinowski's principle, but rather discovered that if status loss is the punishment then those with less status have less potential for being punished. On the positive side, Goode's influential work has brought to functionalist thought a greater awareness of the importance of social and sexual inequality in the social control of illegitimacy. Goode's theory suggests a hypothesis for cross-cultural testing similar to that of Engels: societal reactions to illegitimacy may be related to the levels of social stratification and sexual inequality in a society.

CONCLUSION

Within functionalist sociology, work this century has come to center more and more on social inequality as the basis for the norm of legitimacy, and in this way is showing some convergence with Engels's Marxist treatment. At the same time, the study of the social control of illegitimacy lost its earlier richness, shifting from a treatment of cross-cultural variety and multiple causes to a fixation on its ubiquity and its status-placement function. This fixation is so strong that Malinowski's principle has been rewritten in the minds of sociologists of the family to become the role of the father in status placement. Along with this fixation, the treatment of human interests and motives in creating this norm of legitimacy became weaker. A major puzzle is located in this theoretical shift: why has the status-placement interpretation been taken to heart by the mainstream to the neglect of the real content of the earlier theories without substantial empirical testing? The fact of this happening on so basic an issue raises a doubt about the scientific and scholarly status of other areas within family sociology.

NOTES

1. I emphasize *in sociology*. Some feminists scholars in other fields today are building on these early theories. O'Brien's (1981) application of Marx is discussed in Chapter 3. Sacks (1979) builds on Engels in an evolutionary account of sexual inequality in Africa.

2. Radcliffe-Brown (1965) criticized the evolutionary approach for speculating about an invisible, hypothetical past and suggested that a functionalist analysis of the interdependencies of contemporaneous parts of the sociocultural system would be more fruitful in understanding societies. Keesing (1975) points out that matrilineal societies are

better understood, and are generally understood today, not as an earlier stage of development but as an adaptation to particular ecological circumstances. Nonetheless, modifications of unilinear evolutionary theory are still around. Marxist-feminists, including Firestone (1970), Sacks (1979), and Coontz and Henderson (1986) find uses for unilinear evolution. Evolutionary thinking has re-emerged in recent conflict theories and biosocial theories on the family and illegitimacy.

3. See Harris (1977), Blumberg (1978), and Lancaster and Lancaster (1987) for examples of the growing view that this is opposite to the facts of human prehistory.

4. It is possible that there were more illegitimate children than Malinowski noticed. They could have been concealed through adoption into other families. He reports that abortion and infanticide were not practiced and is pressed to account for the paucity of illegitimate offspring. He indicates that adoption was so common that it was difficult to tell whether the children living with a family were actually that family's offspring or whether they were adopted. It is possible that many bastard infants were quietly taken in by their maternal aunts because of the shame attached to bastardy.

5. Some privileges and rights were conferred on the child because of its father. Although primary status placement was through the mother's descent group, kin ties on the father's side were recognized. The father link was important in the preferred marriage form of the son with his patrilateral cross-cousin (a daughter of his father's clan) in the Trobriands, but also in many other matrilineal groups as shown by Homans and Schneider (1955), although their explanation for this on the basis of sentiment has been disproven (Needham 1962).

6. This language of sociological and legal status does give one a misleading first impression of a status placement interpretation. However, it is apparent from the context that Malinowski means something akin to *citizenship* by these terms. Also Malinowski entitled his paper, "Parenthood: The Basis of Social Structure," which may have added to the confusion. Malinowski presented a peculiar construct called the "initial situation of kinship" in this paper. The initial situation corresponds to the experienced relationships into which people are born, which Malinowski took to be mother-child and father-child relationships. Thus, an implication of the title is that parent-child ties "on the ground" are the initial stimulus for the flowering of kinship structure and nomenclature in human society.

7. Ira Reiss and Gary Lee (1988) follow up on this insight by pointing out that courtship, or mate selection, is always regulated and restricted because it involves the selection of partners in parenthood.

8. The similarity of Malinowski's and Westermarck's explanations of family universality is apparent. Many recent formulations seem indebted to these, either in their reasoning about biology or in seeing the need for cooperation in child-rearing. These include Murdock's (1949) four universal functions of the nuclear family, Levy and Fallers's (1959) definition of the family as a small kinship-based group involved in socialization. Levy's (1965; see also Coale 1965) explanation of the two-parent family being necessary on grounds of biology and social efficiency reflects Malinowski's and Westermarck's lines of thought. It puzzles me that we have used so much of Malinowski's thinking and have contorted his meaning of the principle of legitimacy.

9. I will suggest what I think the hidden motive in functionalism is after I discuss more functionalist theories. Homans (1987) suggests that societies rarely if ever disappear because they lack suitable families, differential rewards, or are not taking care of some other functional requisite. They disappear because more powerful groups

invade, conquer, and impose their way of life on them.

10. Of course, he would not *want* to acknowledge this variability in bonding in response to the variability of the social trigger, for this would undercut his argument for the necessity and universality of the principle of legitimacy. His logic is that it takes a universal to explain a universal.

11. The suggestion in Klaus and Kennell's work is that those in contact with the infant as it is born, holding it, stroking it, nursing it, staring into its eyes, tend to become bonded to it. Even if this were empirically true, it would not help Malinowski's notion of father-child bonding much, as in most of the societies where birth practices have been described, birth is typically attended by women only. The ethnographic record indicates that fathers are more often not watching over the mother during birth and not immediately thereafter caring for the infant. In only a few societies where men are involved in birth could this involvement produce a father-child bond.

12. The phrase is Laslett's (1980). Davis in this quote seems to be restricting his analysis to societies in which paternity is held to be important in social fatherhood.

13. This is correct if the society allows monogamy only. Davis neglects societies allowing polygyny or polyandry, where a married man or a married woman respectively could marry an unmarried person with whom they had a child. This slip shows the difficulty in overcoming one's Western bias to think about how illegitimacy might be controlled in different settings.

14. There is an empirical problem here. First, this mother's taking custody of the illegitimate child in a patrilineal setting does not protect the rights and well-being of legitimate offspring in the mother's patrilineal descent group. Second, by implication, the illegitimate child in a matrilineal society would live with its lineally insignificant father. Davis does not develop this implication, but it is almost certainly empirically false.

15. In a later essay on intercaste marriage Davis (1941) points out that he does not believe that there is sexual equality in marriage, as his statement from his 1939 essay seems to indicate. Rather, husbands and wives ideally are from equal strata in the social class system, and the system of sexual inequality cross cuts the class system. Jack Goody (1976) qualifies this idea. He points out that many African societies do not assume spouses to be social equals but instead practice class heterogamy. Lifestyles do not differ radically among classes in these societies however. He argues that class endogamy is structurally important only when lifestyles become divergent among classes or castes.

16. Davis was aware of Malinowski's work and cited it. He alludes to what can only be the evolutionary theories of Engels and Morgan. He notes that husbands in our culture are very jealous and suspicious of possible adultery by their wives, so much so that "we have built theories of the family's origin on the assumption that primitive man invented exclusive monogamous wedlock in order to be sure his children were really his own" (Davis 1939a: 83). His emphasis on the cross-cultural constancy seems to be the outcome of a conscious choice to downplay variability.

17. Goode is one of the rare sociologists who accurately interpret Malinowski's principle as being the assignment of a guardian to the child.

18. Blake's survey research shows that first-time pregnant unwed mothers may indeed condemn their own deviance from procreative norms, just as Davis claimed.

3

The Recent Potpourri of Tangential Theories

As functionalism has ebbed, other theories, from sociobiology to neo-evolution and Marxism, have begun to reverse some of its troublesome trends. There is a renewed emphasis on variation and a move away from the status-placement account of the principle of legitimacy. These theories often do not deal with illegitimacy per se, but with tangential issues. While a few theories have explicit conjectures on illegitimacy norms, hypotheses have to be inferred from others. In this chapter, I will discuss the ideas from these theories that relate to illegitimacy.

THE STRUCTURE OF POWER

Several writers have made useful contributions to an understanding of illegitimacy as part of their works on the organization of power in society.[1] These contributions include a view of the family as based in property rights, an analysis of power and ritual in reproductive rights, and a treatment of courtship power imbalances stemming from variation in the sex ratio. A second set of contributions concerns the cultural invention and definition of paternity. These scholars are recasting evolutionary theory's speculation on the first recognition of biological paternity. Third, sociobiologists have formulated theories on family evolution and on conditions affecting paternal investment. None of these works have dealt with the social control of illegitimacy as a central issue, but each suggests hypotheses for this research. These recent works especially help to specify more precisely some of the independent variables to be included in the cross-cultural tests.

Property Theory

Collins (1988: 55-85) presents a "property theory" of the family, which is a quasi-evolutionary conflict theory. *Property* here refers to the rights that family members have in each other and to their rights in objects vis-à-vis each other. In other words, Collins views the family as a set of relationships defined in terms of rights in objects and rights in each other family members. The family is based on three forms of property. These include sexual property as the primary type, with economic and intergenerational property seen as consequences of sexual possession. Collins deals with illegitimacy norms through the concept of intergenerational property rights, which include children's right to inherit from parents and parents' power over children. In Collins's view, sexual property rights automatically carry reproductive property rights, or rights of legitimacy for children born from the union.

This theory extends Collins's (1971; 1975) work on sexual stratification, in which the sex drive is the motor, while sexual and reproductive property rights are shaped by the organization of force and the market positions of women and men. Sexual property can be either unilateral or bilateral (mutual egalitarian possession). The degree of inequality in sexual and reproductive property rights depends on the organization of force in society, for men's greater size and strength allow them to control both economic surplus and weaponry. For Collins, there are four combinations of the organization of force and the market positions of the sexes. These remotely resemble Engels's stages of evolution. They range from low technology tribal societies to affluent market economies with centralized states. The peak of unilateral sexual property, and (I infer) the most severe illegitimacy sanctions comes in the intermediate type, "fortified households in stratified society" (Collins 1975: 240-241). These societies are agrarian states in which the government does not have a monopoly on force, but large households or local kin groups control fighting and policing forces. With the advent in affluent modern societies of central bureaucracies monopolizing force, and with women gaining a better market position, inequality in family property rights declines. Hence, Collins sees the control of reproduction as being unilateral and repressive when men in local kin groups or households are armed and have a monopoly on force.

The agents in Collins's theory are men and women, both struggling to gain sexual possession of the other. The use of coercion and market position determine the outcome of the struggle. When men dominate, women have a limited role in norm formation. Collins's theory suggests a set of independent variables to be explored in relation to illegitimacy sanctions. These include centralization, stratification, presence of standing police forces, and sexual inequality.

Fraternal Interest Groups

Paige and Paige (1981) develop and test a novel, unifying framework for understanding reproductive rituals in stateless societies. Reproductive rituals consist of such things as male and female puberty rites, couvade, and menstrual restrictions. The Paiges theorize two ways in which men establish control over women's reproduction and establish paternity in stateless societies: through explicit contracts and through ritual.

They show that the type and focus of ritual depends on the strength of fraternal interest groups (FIGs). FIGs are local congregations of kinsmen, especially the patrilocal, patrilineal ones that often control weaponry in the way envisioned by Collins. Patrilocal and avunculocal marital residence tend to aggregate the male members of the kin group and disperse female kin, making for a strong fraternal interest group. Matrilocal residence on the other hand tends to aggregate female members and disperse males (Schneider 1961). FIGs are important in giving men greater capacity to mobilize for action. In societies with strong FIGs, men negotiate paternity rights with the men of other fraternal interest groups through explicit contracts involving arranged marriage or bride wealth. A man's own group can back up paternity claims through "ritual" surveillance or military action. Male circumcision rituals theoretically keep men with grown sons from breaking away from the group. Breaking away might be possible for men who have enough sons and nephews reaching adulthood to start a new FIG. In the absence of FIGs and of state power to regulate claims over offspring, men may have to resort to rituals as bargaining tactics to establish claims over their wives' and daughters' reproduction. Thus, female puberty rituals, the couvade and other forms of men's participation in childbirth tend to be greater where FIGs are weak. Men establish paternity claims not simply by the fact of marriage but by participating in birth ritual for the child.

Sanctions for illegitimacy are not an explicit concern for the Paiges. However, an implication of their theory is that sanctions for illegitimate birth are more repressive where fraternal interest groups are strong. They come close to saying this in noting a glitch in their findings. They indicate that if FIGs are weak, female puberty rituals sponsored by the father mark his right to control her reproduction and select her spouse. Here they find only a modicum of concern about sexual restrictions. With strong FIGs, however, there is great concern with premarital virginity for women, except (and here's the glitch) for societies in which any children are assigned to the husband in an "explicit contract" (Paige and Paige 1981: 93-96). The Paiges' discussion suggests they found little or no correlation of controls on premarital sex and birth with FIG strength. The "explicit contract" used to explain the glitch in the findings is a mere label for these divergent practices rather than an explanation of them.

Paige and Paige (1981: 44) assume explicitly that men are eager to claim offspring as economic and political allies. Offspring's value during adulthood is the motor of the theory. The Paiges treat this value as an unmeasured constant (among stateless societies), but one that triggers variable responses depending on the extent of men's local organization. This constant adds a motivating factor that both Engels and Collins lacked. It is similar to Malinowski's notion of the economic value of offspring but adds a political dimension. The Paiges' theory is centered somewhat on the stage of childbirth, but also on the stage in which offspring are coming of age.

The Paiges contribute a novel, parsimonious, unifying account of reproductive ritual. However, other factors that are plausibly correlated with both FIG strength and reproductive ritual may be confounding their analysis. Three unmeasured, possibly confounding, factors are sexual inequality, internal warfare, and descent rules.

It is widely recognized and documented by cross-cultural data (Whyte 1978b; Sanday 1981a) that women's status and authority are less in patrilineal, patrilocal societies (those with stronger FIGs) than in matrilineal or matrilocal ones. Collins and Engels emphasize that sexual inequality is a key variable in the control of reproduction. Hence, the effects of women's powerlessness may be confounded with the effects of men's organization in the Paiges' analysis. We need to ask how FIG organization and other sources of sexual inequality fit together in affecting the control of reproduction. One might even ask whether in some societies there are "sororal interest groups"[2] in which women are readily mobilized for action, and what input female groups have on the control of nonmarital birth.

Second, FIG organization has been found to be correlated with internal warfare, which may enhance the need for children as political-economic allies. Some, including Jeffery Paige (1974) have argued that FIGs directly stimulate internal warfare, feuding, or factional politics (Otterbein and Otterbein 1965; Otterbein 1968, 1970). The counterargument is that internal struggle and fighting produce patrilocal or patrilineal groupings while purely external warfare produces matrilocal or matrilineal groupings (Swanson 1968, 1969, 1974; Ember and Ember 1971). As Lee (1982) indicates, neither side is arguing about there being a correlation; they are arguing instead about the direction of causation. Regardless of which causes which, it is only when local FIGs are fighting among themselves that men need to have grown offspring as allies and warriors. If warfare is purely with other societies and there is little internal political struggle, there may be a need for offspring to be loyal to the society as much as to the father and his descent group. This stronger political need for offspring with internal fighting would contribute to the observed impact of FIGs on reproductive rituals.

Descent is a third confounding factor. Paige and Paige treat patrilineal descent as one factor in their measure of the strength of FIGs. However, descent theory points out that there is a key reproductive difference between matrilineal and patrilineal groups. Patrilineages reproduce biologically through wives while matrilineages reproduce through their female members. Matrilineal women bear offspring for their own descent group rather than for their husband's group. Matrilineal men have no part in the biological reproduction of their descent group's membership (Schneider 1961). FIG theory grates against descent theory when it speaks of matrilineal men claiming rights over their offspring. A comparative test of the two theories is needed.

The Paiges' novel and unifying work on reproductive ritual makes the FIG concept essential to my research on factors affecting the seriousness of sanctions for illegitimacy. My critique suggests also that the extent of internal warfare, the degree of sexual inequality, and descent rules also merit inclusion as independent variables.

Sex Ratio Theory

While FIG organization may promote repressive sanctions for illegitimacy, another structural factor hypothesized by Guttentag and Secord (1983) is the sex ratio. They argue that variation in the sex ratio creates imbalances in "dyadic power" (or courtship role bargaining power) of men and women. They assume that men always hold "structural power," which consists of economic, political, and positional resources enabling one to influence custom. In individual courtship dyads, there are market influences on power as well. With an imbalanced sex ratio, women's market position and dyadic bargaining power are altered. If the sex ratio is high, women are scarce and dear; if low, they are abundant and cheap. If women are scarce and dear, men will invest more in relationships and seek to control their partners, because of the lack of alternative partners. Men's and women's premarital sex is restrained, divorce is frowned upon, and illegitimacy stigmatized and uncommon. With a low sex ratio, women are easy to come by. Women have more sexual and reproductive freedom because men have less commitment and have less urge to constrain women.

Guttentag and Secord's theory is counterintuitive. Whereas other theories conceptually link severe illegitimacy sanctions to low female power, they link severe sanctions to *high* dyadic power of women. Unfortunately, I will be unable to test this theory directly because of the scarcity of cross-cultural data on the sex ratio.

There are problems with the theory itself however that seem to restrict its generalizability. It probably does not apply across the ethnographic spectrum. First, women's structural power need not be conceived as a constant. The balance of structural power between the sexes varies considerably from society to society (Whyte 1978b; Sacks 1979; Sanday 1981a; Chafetz 1984). Studies have found women's structural power to promote higher divorce (Ross and Sawhill 1975; Hannon et al. 1977; Pearson and Hendrix 1981, Booth et al. 1984; Hendrix and Pearson 1995). This confounds the theory's hypothesized effects of women's low dyadic power.

Secondly, Divale and Harris (1976) argue that frequent warfare causes men to be highly valued as fighters and women to be devalued, but also imbalances the sex ratio through male casualties during fighting. The devaluation of women may lead to female infanticide or neglect.[3] This interpretation sees the relationship between the sex ratio and female infanticide to be a spurious consequence of warfare. Also, common sense tells us that neglect and killing of female infants can imbalance the sex ratio, which according to the theory would lead to a stronger courtship market position and greater dyadic power for women.

Finally, the theory presumes monogamous marriage and ignores polygynous marriage. Polygyny is allowed in three-fourths or more of the societies in the ethnographic spectrum (Murdock 1949). In these societies, there must be theoretically a continual undersupply of women, since men are not removed from the courtship market when they marry. Women in polygynous societies would theoretically have high dyadic power. This is probably not an accurate analysis, however, for cross-cultural evidence indicates that polygyny itself may result from a shortage of men stemming from warfare mortality (Ember 1974; 1985).

SOCIOBIOLOGY AND THE BEHAVIOR OF FATHERS

One would expect, from its use of reproduction as its motor, that sociobiology would be applied fruitfully to the problem of legitimacy. Human sociobiology stops short of dealing with the question of why societies enforce certain parent-offspring relationships, although it deals with many of the concerns of the legitimacy theories. Sociobiology's concepts of inclusive fitness, certainty of paternity, kin selection, and reproductive strategies seem especially pertinent to legitimacy. Humans, as a species, invest intensively in a few offspring, rearing them to reproductive age or beyond, and through arranged marriages in some societies, even see that these offspring mate with suitable partners.

The issue of male investment in offspring—what others call fathering—has loomed large in sociobiology. Sociobiologists recognize that human males are on the whole quite high in parental investment among mammals (Lamb et al. 1987; Lancaster and Lancaster 1987), although female investment is greater. From the standpoint of biological evolution, female investment in offspring is favored because of the evolutionarily early differentiation of sperm and eggs in reproduction. Differences in mobility and size of reproductive cells, along with women's investment during pregnancy, make for greater female investment to continue behaviorally investing in offspring. Hence, men have greater "sexual plasticity" than women do (Trivers 1972), and may adopt varied reproductive strategies, especially mixed ones.[4]

Male promiscuity is limited for various reasons. One is the pregnant and lactating mother's need for protection and "provisioning,"[5] an investment that the male may be likely to continue. Males may reduce paternity uncertainty by guarding "their" females during fertile periods. This takes both the guards and those guarded against out of the mating market (Lamb et al. 1987). Courtship interaction and ritual can be interpreted not merely as a stimulant to sexual arousal but also as a guard against reproductive maltreatment for both women and men. Through courtship ritual, men reduce the chances that they will be cuckolded, and females can get some assurance that males will "co-parent" (Trivers 1972).

Contrary to criticisms of the approach, sociobiology conceives of reproductive behavior as being flexible and adaptable to varied environments. It can be used to explain variation among societies. This is because behavior is seen as a phenotype—a function of the interaction and developmental sequence of genotype and environment, including the sociocultural environment (Hughes 1988). Hence, there need not be a special gene for heavy investment in a few offspring or a gene for limited investment in a large number of offspring. Behavior responds not only to genetics, but also to individual definitions (whether conscious or unconscious) of what the best reproductive strategies are. Trivers (1972) suggests that this flexible behavioral adaptation applies not only cross-culturally but to microniches within society. For instance, Lancaster and Lancaster (1987) suggest that some lower-class men may be lacking in resources needed for high paternal investment.[6] Their remaining option is to move toward the opposite reproductive strategy, having many offspring by different women with minimal parental investment. This line of thought seems to dance around the notion of legitimacy without facing it head-on.

Sociobiological concepts have been used in accounts of several related topics such as family evolution (Lancaster and Lancaster 1987), matrilineal descent and inheritance (van den Berghe 1979; Gaulin and Schlegel 1980; Hartung 1985; see also Greene 1978), and father-absence (Draper and Harpending 1982). Each of these topics has some relevance to illegitimacy, although explicit hypotheses must be derived.

Family Evolution

Lancaster and Lancaster's (1987) basic argument is that scarcity of resources relative to population leads to a watershed shift in family formation and reproductive strategies. Their key variable is the family's control of needed resources for survival and reproduction. They contrast these strategies in low-density foraging and gardening societies and in high-density, sedentary, agricultural and urban societies. In the low-density setting, resources are seen as free goods that are there for the taking. Inheritable property in the sense of houses, land, and tools, is not important, although succession to position may be. Premarital norms are lax, and women may have several lovers before settling into parenthood with one of them. To maximize inclusive fitness, parents need to teach their offspring only basic survival skills. Family wealth is measured by the number of members. Among foragers, families tend to be small; a late age at weaning means that women give birth only once every four or five years on average. Sedentary low-density societies have smaller birth intervals and depend on older siblings caring for younger ones.

In high-density societies, resources are seen as scarce, leading each family to guard access to its estate. For reproductive success, at least some offspring must be provided with access to family-held property continuing into their adult lives. Relations within the family are regulated on the basis of differential access to goods and property controlled by the family.   Parents use a reproductive calculus to evaluate the cost of rearing each child and the gain from that child's contribution to the household purse.   Errant offspring can be disinherited or bastardized.   The child's chances in the marriage market are a part of the reproductive calculus as well for economic exchanges, such as dowry or bride wealth, come to mark marriages.   Female sexuality is severely restricted as a way of increasing women's marriage chances and as a way of enhancing the certainty of paternity of husbands.   Female virginity becomes a valued trait.

Lancaster and Lancaster's theory contains several of the concepts that Engels used to explain the evolution of family rules, including the rising importance of property and sexual inequality in access to property.   The stages of development, although different, are reminiscent of Engels's stages and Collins's as well.   The Lancasters's novel twist is to interpret many of the variables in Engels's theory from the standpoint of maximization of inclusive fitness.   The reproductive strategy changes because the environment changes.   In particular, family property is more important in high-density societies.   The theory has implications for illegitimacy sanctions also.   The selective reproductive calculus of the high-density society, and the value on virginity, implies that unwed mothers would be unmarriageable and subject to shame.   On the other hand, the lower cost of rearing children to reproductive age in the low-density society and the less stringent sexual restrictions on unmarried women suggests a more relaxed approach to nonmarital birth with less shame attached to illegitimacy.

Lancaster and Lancaster's implication of more repressive sanctions as society develops technologically converges with some hypotheses of Engels and Collins. The new variable useful for testing here is the form of the family.   The suggestion is that sedentary societies with larger multigeneration families will tend to have more severe sanctions for illegitimacy.

Matriliny and Uncertainty of Paternity

Sociobiologists use the concept of *uncertainty of paternity* to explain matrilineal descent in a way related to Engels's and the earlier cultural evolutionists account of "mother right."   From a biosocial viewpoint, women's promiscuity, or extramarital sex, makes paternity uncertain.   Maternity is always more certain, so under conditions of high promiscuity a man maximizes his fitness by investing in his sister's children.   This investment is said to be institutionalized as matrilineal descent or matrilineal inheritance in societies that have widespread adultery (van den Berghe 1979; Gaulin and Schlegel 1980; Hartung 1985).   While van den Berghe finds limited cross-cultural support for this hypothesis, Gaulin and Schlegel and Hartung produce more compelling correlations.

There is criticism of this hypothesis on the cause of matriliny.   Hartung (1985) has shown in a simple mathematical model that the probability of paternity would have to be not just less than 1.00 but less than 0.46 before men would rationally invest in their sisters' offspring, which he feels is too low to fit reality. Hartung concludes that women's inclusive fitness rather than men's is maximized in the high adultery-matrilineal situation. Broude (1980) notes, however, that much of the adultery in preliterate societies consists of forms such as kin adultery and wife exchange which lessen the effect on men's inclusive fitness, but which also may give women some fitness advantage over strict monogamy. Also, remember that matrilineal men do invest in their infants and children, as Malinowski demonstrated in the Trobriand case. A more exact measure of the extent of a man's investment in his own offspring and his sister's offspring is needed for a rigorous test of the hypothesis.

A testable corollary of the biosocial account of matriliny is easily derived. The corollary is that the sanctions for illegitimacy may be less severe in matrilineal societies or in societies with more adultery. Another biosocial concept, *male sexual jealousy* (Daly, Wilson, and Weghorst 1982), provides the link from certainty of paternity to illegitimacy sanctions. Paternal investment presumes some certainty of paternity and helps to maintain certainty of paternity. Male sexual jealousy is an evolved alert state with a potential for aggression that helps men be watchful for threats to their certainty of paternity. Daly, Wilson, and Weghorst (1982) present evidence that male sexual jealousy occurs even in sexually permissive societies, and that norms and laws allow its violent expression. However, they do not deal with cultural variation in the degree to which male sexual jealousy is allowed violent expression. Hupka and Ryan (1990) find that expressions of male sexual jealousy are related to cultural factors such as norms restricting marital choice, sex outside of marriage, and property arrangements. These data suggest that male sexual jealousy is less strong where there is less certainty of paternity and fewer material resources for investment.[7] With this logic, we can return to the certainty of paternity-matriliny hypothesis. Once adultery or "avuncular investment" has become a fixed pattern, male sexual jealousy consequently would be less strong. Consequently, social norms would less strongly opposed nonmarital sex and illegitmacy illegitimacy, and sanctions would be less punitive. In patrilineal groups (where the theory presumes that men invest more heavily in offspring), or for societies with less adultery, higher levels of male sexual jealousy will find expression as stronger sanctions for illegitimacy and nonmarital sex.

Father-Absence

An alternative biosocial treatment of paternal investment concerns father-absent families, which are seen to perpetuate low paternal investment. In this treatment, investment in offspring is everyday care-giving and providing rather than investment through inheritance. While in some societies, father-absence is a deviant pattern, it is quite normative in other societies, such as those having central men's houses in each community. Draper and her associates (Draper and Harpending 1982; Draper and Belsky 1990) have argued that father-absence, regardless of whether it is normative, tends to trigger certain reproductive strategies in offspring. The son from the father-absent family tends to mate with multiple partners and invest less in offspring, sometimes abandoning partners and offspring. The daughter from a father-absent family tends to begin mating earlier, to count less on her mate's investment in her offspring, and also to have more partners over a lifetime. Theoretically speaking, these are not pathological reproductive strategies, but may enhance offsprings' inclusive fitness in the right environment.   Father-present child rearing tends to produce reproductive strategies in offspring that emphasize more permanent pair-bonding and more paternal investment.

The father-absence theory makes no assertions about illegitimacy sanctions that can be tested in the statistical part of this research. However, the concept of sexual jealousy again provides a theoretical link. Father-absent child rearing results in lowered paternal investment and lowered male sexual jealousy. Thus, illegitimacy sanctions will not be severely punitive in cultures where father-absence is widespread. In societies where fathers are physically proximate to their infants and children and more involved in their care, male sexual jealousy will be expressed in severe sanctions for illegitimacy.

Being based in biological evolutionary theory, sociobiology develops more solid accounts of behavior than of cultural norms and values. It tends to view culture as an epiphenomenon, an outgrowth of widespread behavior patterns. Cultural norms reflect the evolved emotions and behaviors of the many toward the few who are different.   Yet hypotheses on illegitimacy sanctions are derivable from the biosocial approach. Severe illegitimacy sanctions are more likely to occur in societies that have extended families and sedentary residence, patrilineal descent, low levels of adultery, and fathers who are present and involved in child care.

PATERNITY AS A SOCIAL CONSTRUCTION

Perhaps part of the reason sociobiologists have ignored the legitimacy issue is that it is so saliently a cultural creation regardless of what biological foundations it may have.   On the face of it, paternity—that is, genetic fatherhood—seems "less cultural" than the notion of legitimacy and social fatherhood.   However, several authors have recently declared that both biological paternity and social fatherhood are cultural constructions.

The Invention of Fatherhood

Wilson (1983), as mentioned in Chapter 1, argues against a strictly socio-biological account of kinship and culture. He believes that while there is a biological basis for heterosexual pairing and for the mother-child relationship, fatherhood is a purely social creation. Fatherhood was invented during prehistory simply by making manifest the relationship implied by the maternal-child and heterosexual mating dyads. Hence, it became ubiquitous among the world's cultures. This goes one step beyond Malinowski's reasoning about biology and fatherhood.

Paternity as Ideology

Delaney (1986) goes further to say that paternity is not simply the empirical discovery that men also have a part in procreation, nor is it an analogy with maternity. The social definition of paternity links to religion, cosmology, and other parts of culture. Early Western and Middle Eastern civilization's concept of paternity gave the male a role in reproduction far surpassing that of the female. It was in no way in accord with today's scientific concept where each parent contributes genetic material. In Judeo-Christian culture, paternity has meant begetting, the primary and creative role, whereas women are not defined as active agents in reproduction. Judeo-Christian reproductive metaphors hold that the man plants the seed, and the woman is the field, the soil, the container, that nourishes and gives birth. The ideology encapsulated in these metaphors exaggerates men's role and devalues women's part in reproduction.

Delaney's analysis suggests that a culture's ideology of paternity is not an acknowledgement of certain facts, but instead a part of a system of meanings in the culture that is linked with religion, gender, and other spheres. Men do not claim offspring because they recognize the biology of reproduction. A culture's construction of reproduction may reflect and help maintain sex roles and men's rights to claim offspring.

Paternity Claims as Alienation

O'Brien (1983) gives a Marxist argument concerning men's assertions of paternity. She holds that ideologies giving men priority in reproduction result from men's natural alienation from the reproductive process. She tries to look at reproduction in the way that Marx looked at production—as lived experience shaping consciousness, and as a material basis on which social relationships (especially gender and generational relations) are built. O'Brien holds that men's experience of reproduction is different from women's. Women necessarily experience the process as a continuous whole, starting with sexual intercourse and the cessation of menstruation, to the growth of the fetus, and finally in labor, birth, and nurturing. This continuity gives women a sense of unity with offspring. In contrast men's reproductive experience is discontinuous. Following coitus, men are not necessarily involved in the remainder of the reproductive process. Men's early separation from the process yields a discontinuous consciousness and a natural *alienation*, in the Marxist sense of the word, from their seed, from reproduction, and from the human race (O'Brien 1983: 36). In O'Brien's view, men have a primordial need to overcome this reproductive alienation. They need to invent and objectify paternity and to appropriate particular children, actions they began during "dark prehistory" (O'Brien 1983: 54).

In O'Brien's view, paternity is not a natural relationship, not just an empirical understanding, but a *right* to a child. Paternity as a right presupposes a *political community* of men who compete and cooperate in establishing rights of access to women and in laying claim to their offspring. This support system and arrangement of rights, responsibilities and claims is labeled "patriarchy" (O'Brien 1983: 54).

O'Brien notes various ways in which paternity can be made certain or defined. If paternity is defined biologically, men can just trust each other, or they can limit physical access to women if they do not trust each other. Alternately, paternity can be defined in a nonbiological way, such as being married to the mother.[8]

Regarding hypothesis testing, these theories on the social construction of paternity do not bear much fruit. There is a general suggestion in Delaney's and O'Brien's works that implies that more severe controls of illegitimacy are associated with higher levels of sexual inequality, and with the way that paternity is defined. Unfortunately, ethnographic descriptions of the definition of paternity are rare, making statistical hypothesis testing difficult. The theories nonetheless underscore the importance of examining gender and sexual inequality as factors in illegitimacy.

RELEVANCE OF RECENT TANGENTIAL THEORIES

These ideas on the invention of paternity tie in both with recent writings interpreting legitimacy as an outcome of political conflict and struggle and with the earlier theories. Engels theorized that the recognition of a link between sex and procreation is a necessary condition for any principle or claim of legitimacy of birth. Malinowski saw that this was not true in the Trobriands, but developed an unpersuasive general argument that the native theory of procreation was among the factors making for positive or repressive control of illegitimacy. Davis likewise saw the definition of biological paternity as important to social fatherhood as a relevant factor. Delaney, and especially O'Brien, reverse the causal sequence and turn these hypotheses inside out. For them, patriarchal organization (a political community of men) is immediately responsible for the paternalistic ideology of procreation and for coercive control of women's reproduction.

Both Collins and the Paiges assume that societies vary in the extent to which there are active local political communities of men engaged in struggle with other similar communities. The Paiges provide some evidence that the control of reproduction is a function of explicit bargains and contracts when there is FIG organization and is a function of ritual when there is not. This seems to be a special case of O'Brien's notion of a political community of men being a necessary condition for the notion of paternity as a right.

One conclusion from these recent writings is that we should look toward the organization of power—among men, and between the sexes—in society as a causal factor shaping both the definition and the control mechanisms for legitimacy and illegitimacy. Questions in need of cross-cultural testing concern FIG and family organization, the concentration of power in the state with its police and armed forces, descent rules, father-child involvement, and the interplay of these structures with women's power.

Within these accounts emphasizing men's political organization are two notions about motive: the Paiges presume that men want offspring as allies in battle, and O'Brien holds that men want to battle their alienation from reproduction. O'Brien may have found the motive that Engels' theory is missing, but it brings problems for empirical research. In the newer biosocial approach, theorists presume a different intergenerational interest: people are motivated to reproduce their genes either through direct descendants or through investing in the offspring of close kin. Each of these imputed interests presents unique problems for measurement. The issues raised by these theories cannot be satisfactorily resolved without some measurement of the interests on which they are based. An important long-run research need is to develop explicit measures of these intergenerational interests and corresponding organizational forms to find out which do relate in fact to the social control of illegitimacy and to the other norms and behaviors specified in the theories.

FULL CIRCLE

Theorizing on legitimacy over the past century has gone full circle. Early evolutionary theories emphasized variety in definitions and control mechanisms, and Engels saw social and sexual inequality as causes. Functionalist theory moved away from this emphasis on variety, but later began to see inequality as an important factor. Unlike the functionalists, the most recent theories concern themselves with paternity claims and paternal investments rather than with legitimacy as a moral concept. They see inequality and power-struggle as important, and some are evolutionary or quasi-evolutionary theories. These recent tangential theories thus have completed the circle: their questions and concerns are more like those of Engels than of the functionalists of this century.

There has been some improvement in legitimacy theory during this century, but it is compartmentalized in small niches, and earlier theoretical strengths have been mislaid as limited gains were made. For example, an improvement in functionalist theory is the recognition that inequality is a factor and that moral consensus is not uniform and universal—that the lower classes may have less commitment to mores. The corresponding losses, as status placement became the focus, included an account of human agency and intergenerational interest, and a grasp of the extent of variation in definitions and control of illegitimacy. O'Brien's theory is an improvement over Engels in that it provides a male motive that drives the theory, although women's interests are arguably important in the formation of illegitimacy norms and sanctions. The notion that paternity is an invention is an improvement over Engels's notion of recognition. Yet O'Brien gives us no firm sense of any lines of variation in men's political communities, although this is provided by Collins and the Paiges.

Overall there has been limited progress in our theoretical understanding of legitimacy. After a century of scholarship, one would hope for some dialectical process in which the most recent theory would respond to both Engels and the functionalists, incorporating the strengths of each theory. We may ask why this has not occurred. One reason is that recent theories often push single causal factors to the exclusion of others. This is happening in an era when the standard presumption in mainstream methodology is one of multiple causation. Arguing for a single factor precludes a vision of what the effects of different combinations of factors might be, and thus hinders the development of theory. Monocausal theories obfuscate by creating typologies of societies, treating variables as constants, examining only one portion of the life cycle as crucial, and examining only certain intergenerational interests to the exclusion of others.

Theories with evolutionary typologies, such as those of Collins and the Lancasters, overly simplify combinations of factors. For example, to contrast high density, agrarian, stratified states on the one hand, with low density, foraging, egalitarian societies on the other is (if we are dichotomizing) to conceal eight possible kinds of societies in only two categories.

Related to this kind of oversimplification is the treatment of causal factors as constants. Most theories presume universal invariant factors (men's alienation from reproduction, the wish for offspring as allies, men's structural power) as pertinent factors in the regulation of reproduction. Most of these constants can readily be conceived as variables. This treatment also ignores possible combinations of the "constant" with other variables, which in conjunction may impact differently on illegitimacy.

Each theory of illegitimacy has dealt with a particular intergenerational interest as its motor and a limited part of the life cycle as problematic. Some intergenerational interests include men's concerns about inheritance by legitimate offspring (Engels), concerns about the continuity of society and culture (Davis), retaining cooperation of adult offspring (Paige and Paige), and maintaining status in the stratification system (Goode). Problematic life-cycle transitions include pregnancy and birth for many theories, infancy and childhood (Malinowski, Davis) and the maturing of offspring (Paige and Paige). Legitimacy is about the assignment of social parenthood, however, and parenthood is multifaceted. It encompasses all of these aspects and more. Esther Goody (1982: 6-34) points out that parenthood is about social reproduction generally and contains five separate tasks or dimensions. These dimensions are:

1. Bearing and begetting—these are biological aspects that may or may not coincide with other dimensions, depending on cultural definitions.

2. Giving birth-status identity—these are all of the entitlements and relationships acquired by the child by virtue of legitimacy of birth, including civil status.
3. Nurturance reciprocities—these are rights and obligations arising from child care and support, such as caring for elderly parents in the United States.
4. Training reciprocities—these include training in moral education, economic roles, etc., which entails some degree of authority and discipline. Some training may be delegated to others.
5. Sponsorship reciprocities—these involve providing the resources and certification for the offspring to assume an adult role in society. Sponsorship is highly variable.

These dimensions indicate that there are different kinds of parenthood—physiological, jural, and educational—which are of differential importance in different societies (Goody 1982: 17).

The theories of legitimacy have focused narrowly on how physiological fatherhood is linked with particular social dimensions, most typically on endowing offspring with birth-status identity. While the earlier functionalists emphasized tasks of rearing and nurturance, Engels and some recent theorists ignore or downplay these. In part, progress may be lacking in the study of legitimacy because different theories may be addressing somewhat different components of the parenthood role. If theorists have looked at different components, it is not surprising that they have isolated different causes of illegitimacy norms and sanctions.

Parenthood is not just an isolated social role or bundle of tasks. It is a social relationship, and relationships by definition always involve two people, just as roles entail counter-roles. Theories of legitimacy of parenthood have generally taken on the perspective of just one of these people in the relationship—the parent. More often than not they have focused the initial phases of parenthood. They have seen parents, or adults, or adult men, as the active agents creating illegitimacy norms and sanctions. Let us consider the further truism that adults are also someone's children. No theory has examined legitimacy from the standpoint of the adult who is interested in "offspring claims" against parents, rather than paternity claims. Seen from this particular angle, legitimacy is not so much about birth and responsibility for children's upbringing as it is about inheritance, succession, and parental death. It should be treated, at least in part, in the context of inheritance and succession. In general we see that the focus on the interests of parents is too narrow. Not only do adults struggle to claim (or avoid claims to) offspring, but offspring may struggle to claim parental possessions or offices, and the generations may struggle against each other. For theoretical advance in the longer run, the incorporation of multiple inter-generational interests and consideration of varied aspects of social parenthood is needed.

Finally, theoretical progress has been slight because of the paucity of empirical testing of theories. Goode and Guttentag and Secord give empirically based arguments on selected case societies, while Paige and Paige present extensive cross-cultural quantitative findings in support of their explanation.[9] Much more testing needs to be done to establish the empirical validity of the causes of illegitimacy sanctions imputed by the various theories. My cross-cultural findings on sanctions and mechanisms of control for nonmarital birth are one step toward this goal.

NOTES

1.   One would expect to find Marxist scholars dealing with inheritance and illegitimacy as part of the machinery through which social classes are "reproduced," but Engels's promising lead has only recently begun to be followed up. More central family issues for Marxism are the development of the distinction between public and private spheres of life (Zaretsky 1976), how housewives' domestic labor fits into capitalism (Seccombe 1973, 1975; Coulson et al. 1975; Gardiner 1975) and kinship-based modes of production (Siskind 1978; Sacks 1979; Coontz and Henderson 1986).

2.   I know of no one suggesting this as a theoretical concept, although feminist activists recognize that "Sisterhood is powerful." Yet Sanday's (1981a) cross-cultural female power scale combines items on women's economic and political power with women's organization and social interaction. In his search for cross-cultural dimensions of women's status, Whyte (1979b) found a cluster of items that seem to me to indicate the degree to which women are interacting frequently together and thus have the capacity for organized action. The fact that women can organize for political action can be seen in an event that happened in the Igbo, where women regularly congregate in marketplaces. Green (1947, no. 17) relates how Igbo women went on strike. Believing that the men had done something to bring hard times, the women from several villages left their homes and went to one central village to camp. They refused to serve or cook for their husbands until rituals were performed to end the difficulties. The men eventually performed the ceremonies and the women returned home.

3.   Divale and Harris's evidence in support of this has been roundly criticized on methodological and empirical grounds by Fjellman (1979) and Kang, Horan, and Reis (1979), and is currently "on hold" within the cross-cultural research community.

4. Sociobiologists place more emphasis on men's sexual flexibility than on women's. Women's flexibility in reproduction is in some respects different from men's and includes not only choosing single or multiple sexual partners but also "parenting" alone (or with one's family of orientation) or with the genitor, but also choices in the number and spacing of births. Note that an expansive array of ethnographically described societies practice abortion or infanticide as a means of family limitation (Devereaux 1955; Hendrix 1975). Hence, there is theoretical room for women's reproductive choice, although in some societies men's dominance of reproductive institutions may reduce women's flexibility.

5.   *Provision* is used by some sociobiologists (e.g., Lamb et al. 1987) as a verb instead of a noun, as in the sentence, "The father may provision his offspring for their first twelve years," when the more appropriate word is *provide*. The important point is to make salient, as some work on "parenting" in contemporary society does not, that producing food, or earning and sharing income with one's mate and offspring is part and parcel of parenthood.

6. This biosocial interpretation competes with Goode's hypothesis that less commitment to reproductive norms makes for less permanent relationships and more illegitimacy in the lower classes of societies.

7. This is my interpretation, not that of Hupka and Ryan. They are arguing against the biosocial concept of sexual jealousy as a universal constant and in favor of theories like that of Collins which view jealousy as a response to threats to socially defined sexual property.

8. O'Brien (1981: 54) does not think that trust between the sexes is likely as a basis for paternity claims, for unlike Engels she does not presume an innate monogamous urge in human beings, and because she sees the relations between men and women in reproduction as relations between the free and the unfree, between nonlaborer and laborer.

9. However the Paiges, as noted, do not deal explicitly with sanctions for illegitimacy as a variable, but rather with reproductive ritual.

4

Empirical Variations in the Control of Illegitimacy

Social control is usually defined as the application of positive sanctions for conformity to norms or negative sanctions for deviance from norms. Sanctions come in many empirical varieties and can be administered by various agencies or individuals. A system of control of illegitimacy consists of more than a set of sanctions—more than threats or inducements to marry. It is also connected to normative controls on sexuality and on mate selection. Additionally, an illegitimacy control system rests not only upon a definition of illegitimacy, but also upon an ideology of procreation and an ideology of legitimation, an ideology concerning how men's obligations and rights to offspring are established. Sanctions, the aspect of the illegitimacy control system to be examined here, are central to theory and are the aspect most frequently described in ethnographic accounts.

In this chapter, I present the typology of illegitimacy sanctions developed for this study. As a lead-in to that presentation, I discuss the research strategy, and the ethnographic descriptions of the dimensions underlying variation in illegitimacy control systems. By examining the kinds and quality of the available descriptions, I show the need for a simplifying typology reflecting theoretical concerns and the limitations of ethnographic descriptions.

A CROSS-CULTURAL SAMPLE

The research strategy is to combine original codes on illegitimacy sanctions with existing published data from the Standard Cross-Cultural Sample (SCCS) (Murdock and White 1969). The SCCS is a set of 186 ethnographically described nonindustrial societies from all major world regions, with the time and place of fieldwork pinpointed. Murdock and White encouraged other cross-cultural researchers to use the SCCS in their research, and to code variables for this sample, using the same ethnographic sources on particular communities and time periods. Over time, numerical codes for hundreds of variables have accumulated for this sample of societies, but only recently have codes on illegitimacy been published.[1]

Murdock and White selected societies for the SCCS on several bases. First, each society represents a cultural area within a continent or region. Within cultural areas, no societies closer than three degrees latitude or longitude are included and none showing linguistic evidence of common origin within the previous thousand years before the pinpointed time are included. The reason for this is that the use of statistical correlation and inference requires that each case be selected independently. Societies may share traits because of recent common origins, or because traits have diffused between neighboring groups. Diffusion and recent common origins can produce statistical correlations between traits, even though one does not cause the other. In addition to this guard against these autocorrelation effects, extensiveness of description is used as a selection principle for the SCCS.

Measures for all variables in this study, except severity of sanctions for illegitimacy, come from published data codes for the SCCS. If ethnographic discussions of illegitimacy were available for the SCCS pinpointed author and time, I used these to code sanctions. If not, I substituted, coding from descriptions of illegitimacy from a different author or for a different time period. This substitution may create random errors in the illegitimacy codes, which theoretically can lower their observed correlations with other variables from "true" levels.

I am willing to pay this cost because the benefit of substitution is that more cases become available for statistical analysis. The critique of theories in Chapters 2 and 3 indicates that I should expect to find interaction effects—effects where one factor alters the impact of another on illegitimacy sanctions. The statistical analysis employs gamma, a measure of ordinal association, and Goodman's (1966) test for difference between two gammas, which can show an interaction effect. Variables are dichotomized for the interaction tests.

DIMENSIONS OF ILLEGITIMACY CONTROL SYSTEMS

One can derive numerous dimensions from the ethnographic descriptions of systems of control of illegitimacy in the SCCS. These dimensions highlight the limited scope of theories in that only a few of these coincide with the dimensions of concern to theories. I will give examples of a number of dimensions and describe the availability of ethnographic description for each to show the basis and usefulness of the particular typology developed for this study.

For any given dimension, there may be excellent, poor, or no information for particular societies in the SCCS. Useable descriptions range from one sentence to several pages, with a few sentences being typical. This is to be expected since ethnographies ordinarily deal with culturally normative behavior more than deviance. Since illegitimacy is not one of the standard topics for ethnographic works, there are no regular reporting categories or conventional modes of presentation. This situation results at worst in idiosyncratic descriptions containing some distortion, and at best, in errors of omission. I will comment on the quality of ethnographic descriptions for each of the empirical dimensions of variation.

Norms Opposed to Nonmarital Sex

Western societies have been among those that seem to have tried to outlaw premarital sex as a way of ensuring legitimacy of offspring, although there has been considerable variation in the stringency and efficacy of these sex norms.[2] The rural Irish earlier in this century[3] forbade nonmarital sex, nonmarital conception, and strongly condemned nonmarital birth. Illegitimacy was a matter of great stigma that hurt a woman's marriage chances and could cause her to fall into disrepute. It brought ill feeling and shame to the father as well. For a man to "destroy a woman's character" was called "murder" (Arensberg and Kimball 1940, no. 51: 209). Some women, or couples, who conceived outside of marriage were forced to emigrate. A hastened, or even a forced, wedding was considered more respectable than nonmarital birth. The strong shame and the resulting banishment or hasty marriage all but eliminated illegitimate birth in rural Ireland in spite of a late age at marriage. Fifty percent of men and 42 percent of women in the 35-40 age bracket were still single. Ireland's effective control of illegitimacy is more restrictive and harsh than that of many societies, but some cultures have even more severe sanctions.

In both the Western and the non-Western world, restrictive sex norms are fairly uniformly associated with stigmatizing reactions to nonmarital birth. However, this is an imperfect correlation. While premarital sex norms are a part of the system of control of illegitimacy, and while data are more plentiful on nonmarital sex norms than on illegitimacy, it is an empirical mistake to infer illegitimacy norms from premarital sex norms. I have tried to avoid inferring illegitimacy sanctions from premarital sex sanctions throughout this research.

Norms Opposed to Nonmarital Conception

Some societies allow premarital sex but not premarital conception or birth. We recognize this combination as plausible for modern nations with their batteries of contraceptive techniques, but how do such norms fit into a nonmodern context. Ideology, along with abortion and infanticide, provides the answer. As Malinowski noted, the Trobriand Islanders' ideology of spirit impregnation allowed premarital sex, but forbade both premarital conception and birth. The woman who conceived before marriage was condemned. She was likely to lose her lover and any chance of marrying. The Konso of Ethiopia employed abortion to make allowance for premarital sex. They were an age-graded society in which women and men of certain corresponding age grades were allowed to marry at a certain point in life, and to procreate after marriage. While some premarital sex was practiced with little apparent shame attached, premarital birth was not allowed because the woman was not of the proper generation grade until she reached the age of marriage. Forced abortion was the normative response to premarital pregnancy (Hallpike 1972, no. 35; Jensen 1936, no. 35).

The Degree of Moral Opposition to Nonmarital Birth

The Irish morally condemned birth outside of marriage, while other societies, such as the Lapps, were less troubled by it. The northern Lapps disapproved of illegitimacy in a moderate way, not so strongly as the rural Irish. While the Lappish age at marriage was not quite so late as that of Ireland, over one-fifth of women conceived or gave birth premaritally, sometimes marrying a different husband than the genitor of the child. If a single woman became pregnant but didn't like the genitor, she could wait until she found a man she liked, for illegitimacy was not so strongly disapproved that it hurt a woman's position in the marriage market. Those few illegitimate children who were not taken into marriage by the mother were formally adopted by the mother's kin (Pehrson 1957, no. 52: 60).

The Lapps and rural Irish show differences in an important factor: the degree of moral condemnation of illegitimacy. Unfortunately, there is an insufficient number of descriptions of morality, shame, and stigma to base a typology solely on moral condemnation. Several ethnographies vaguely report only the moral attitude or emotional reaction to nonmarital conception or birth without any information on other sanctions or arrangements for illegitimate children. Others report extensively on rights and penalties for the people involved without mentioning the morality or immorality of illegitimacy.

Types of Sanctions

Many kinds of sanctions are available to societies for enforcing whatever norms of illegitimacy they may have. A basic distinction underlying the cases mentioned heretofore is Durkheim's (1964) notion of repressive versus restitutive sanctions. The shame, degradation, and loss of marriageability shown by the Irish and the Trobrianders are examples of repressive sanctions. Among the Mao, a woman who conceived outside of marriage could be made a slave of the king. These reactions express moral outrage and are meant to punish deviant procreation.

Durkheim (1964) thought that repressive sanctions, found today in criminal law, reflected the strong collective conscience—the shared morality—and mechanical solidarity of simpler societies. In more differentiated societies, he saw that organic solidarity based on contractual relationships overshadowed the collective conscience and the predominating kind of sanctions changed. With organic solidarity restitutive sanctions, meant to restore rights or redress imbalances in interdependence, became more common.   Without using Durkheim's entire argument, we can fruitfully employ his distinction between repressive sanctions and restitutive sanctions.   These types can be readily inferred from concrete descriptions of particular control systems.

Ethnographies for other societies report an array of arrangements for handling illegitimacy without mentioning moral values and reactions, as though the matter of arranging a father were solely a practical, contractual matter of little emotional or moral concern.   This is particularly true for some of the groups having the practice of bride wealth.   Among the Massa of Africa, payment of the bride wealth legitimated children and gave a man rights over them.   If a woman became pregnant, her parents would try to negotiate a quick marriage for her.   If the man could not raise the bride wealth, the woman's family would raise the child.   Were the child a girl, she remained with her maternal grandparents until marriage.   Her maternal grandfather negotiated her marriage and received the bride price except for one cow that was given to the natural father of the bride.   Were the child a boy he usually joined his natural father's group as an adolescent, and the natural father at that transition gave the mother's father some cattle for their efforts in rearing the boy (Garine 1964, no. 27: 159-160).   For the Massa, illegitimacy is not described as especially shameful.   We may infer that it is handled through the mechanism of compensatory payments between the physiological father and the family of the mother without any special sense of immorality.[4]

The Konso, whose abortion practices were mentioned already, provide an example of a preventive mode of dealing with illegitimate birth. The normative abortion of the Konso arguably is not a repressive sanction.   The lack of ethnographic discussion of moral outrage, or even embarrassment, suggests that abortion is meant to restore the damaged order of the generation grades of the society.   This is not to deny that women are not "repressed" in a different sense when they are compelled to have abortions, but it implies that abortion is not an expression of shame or moral outrage.   While no theories of illegitimacy explicitly use Durkheim's repressive versus restitutive distinction, it is an empirically useful one.   Descriptions of many substantively different types of sanctions can be classified readily according to this dichotomy.   Additionally, as suggested by Durkheim's theory, repressive sanctions appear to be accompanied by moral condemnation.   Descriptions of sanctions classified as repressive or restitutive may stand in place of descriptions of moral attitudes and reactions.

Severity, or Harshness, of Sanctions

Societies vary extensively in the severity of sanctions applied to illegitimacy. The arrangements of the Massa seem to have an almost voluntary quality about them and may involve only the payment of one, or a few, head of cattle.   Not only is this sanction different in kind from the Irish repressive sanctions, but it is less severe. The nomadic Lapps have especially mild sanctions. They seem to value children, perhaps as workers among other reasons, so that illegitimate children are seen neither as a burden nor an impediment to marriage. Other societies use corporal punishment, or even capital punishment for people who procreate outside of marriage.

The severity of sanctions, especially for women, is a major emphasis of Engels. It is not always easy to rate societies in terms of the relative severity of their sanctions. Gross judgments can be made however, and the dimension seems to coincide frequently with the extent of moral condemnation and with the distinction on the type of sanction. Restitutive sanctions are typically milder, and repressive sanctions are typically harsher, as Durkheim (1964) noted.

Who Is Sanctioned

To the modern Western mind, two people, the genitor and the genitrix, are responsible for a nonmarital birth. Cross-culturally we find that sanctions are not often imposed equally on both members of this pair and no one else. The child is the person outside the couple who is most likely to be sanctioned. The child is sometimes stigmatized and may lose important rights. In the native viewpoint this is rarely if ever explicitly considered a sanction for the child. It is instead a side effect of family norms and repressive controls. The parents' behavior reflects on the child in these societies.

Other people besides the genitor and genitrix may be affected by illegitimacy sanctions also. In some societies, a deviant procreation reflects on the person's family or kin group, because shame and honor are allocated to kin groups as much as individuals in many societies. Among the Kazaks, illegitimacy was a great shame for the mother's entire clan. While a hasty marriage might follow premarital conception, abortion was also used to conceal the offense and avoid stigma, and sometimes the infant was killed after birth (Grodekov 1899, no.65). A similar situation prevailed among the Rwala Bedouins where great shame was attached to illegitimacy. If a woman bore a child before her wedding, she was cast out of the tribe or killed by her own kin. Women and their families tried to avoid the great shame of this situation. If a woman conceived before her wedding, she first would try to get her lover to marry her. If this did not work, she might resort to secret abortion or even suicide (Musil 1928, no. 46).

In some societies, both members of the reproducing pair do not receive the same sanctions. Many descriptions mention punishments for the genitrix, but not for the genitor. The ethnographies for the Kazaks and Rwala Bedouins provide examples. While these may be errors of omission on the part of ethnographers, it may also be that there are no comparable sanctions on the genitor. There are many societies described as having sanctions or stigma only for the genitrix, or that are stronger for the genitrix than for the genitor. Given the amount of detail for the Kazaks and Rwala Bedouins, we may presume that the strongest sanction for the genitor was coerced marriage—a restitutive sanction—although we do not know what the means of coercion were. This pattern of more repressive sanctions for the genitrix is widespread.

Some societies find the genitor more culpable than the genitrix. The Lovedu valued female virginity, and illegitimacy was rare. In these rare cases, "great blame" fell upon the guilty man, who was fined twice as much as in the case of adultery. The bastard infant was said to be "a thing of joy to everyone," and the mother was congratulated by her kin and friends (Kriege and Kriege 1943).

Ethnographic information on who receives sanctions for illegitimacy is sparse. The descriptions are often obviously incomplete and generally uneven. Some sources discuss the implications for the child only, others the implications for the mother only, when there is obviously more to be said about other sanctioned persons. In creating a useable typology, some other basis for categorizing aspects of illegitimacy control systems is needed.

Who Imposes Sanctions

Agents of control of illegitimacy vary cross-culturally. Various agents, such as parents and other kin, age-grade peers, community elders, and "public opinion," sanction and stigmatize illegitimacy. These agents shame those who procreate outside of marriage, express outrage, administer corporal punishment, force marriage or abortion upon unwed mothers, or see that unwed fathers marry or pay fines. One agency is notable by its absence: nowhere is there a description of organized courts and police forces administering justice for cases of deviant procreation. The ethnographic record is spotty on the matter of the agents imposing sanctions, frequently with no mention of sanctioning agents, making this dimension fruitless in a quantitative study.

Identity of Genitor and Social Father

Societies vary in the extent to which they employ their ideologies of procreation to buttress their ideologies of legitimation, and their mechanisms of controls for illegitimacy. Among societies recognizing biological fathers, some insist that the unwed father step forth to marry the unwed mother, or receive punishment.

Several groups mentioned—the Irish, but also the Kazaks, Rwala Bedouins, Lapps, and Massa—put pressure on the biological father as a first step in controlling illegitimacy. Within this set, the two groups without repressive sanctions—the Lapps and Massa—are less concerned that the biological father be singled out for treatment. While they both recognize the role of the genitor in procreation, their systems of control are not built primarily upon the identity of genitor and social father, but allow options.

Many other societies allow options also. Among those societies in which bride wealth, or bride price, is defined as a gift-payment for the claim to offspring, there are some in which there is no attempt to pin the blame on the genitor. Anyone who pays the bride price, or sometimes a fraction of it without marriage, claims and legitimates the child. Paige and Paige (1981) view this situation as a matter of explicit contracts on reproductive rights between fraternal interest groups. A woman's natal descent group is able to claim her offspring as members with full rights until some other descent group pays her bride price. Her group has claim to her offspring regardless of who their genitors may be.

The Otoro Nuba differ from many other societies in the way they treated illegitimacy. They identified the genitor as the social father, even without marriage. Children were considered to belong to their biological father, and there was no discrimination against them. Nadel (1947, no. 30) claims that out-of-wedlock children were not seen as "illegitimate," but does not say what was done to find the genitor, or what rights and obligations were incurred.

The emphasis on the genitor and social father being one and the same man is an important cultural feature underlying norms concerning sex, marriage, and legitimacy. However, it is not often described explicitly, and it presents problems for quantitative research.

Age at Betrothal and Marriage for Women

Other societies deal with illegitimacy in a preventive way by having early betrothal and marriage for women, sometimes considering all of a woman's children to belong to her husband, regardless of whom the genitor may be. This is an effective strategy for reducing nonmarital birth without the use of negative sanctions. Mbuti pygmy women married soon after a ritual celebrating puberty (Turnbull 1962, no. 13). Among the Tiwi of Australia, female infants were betrothed to adult men and widows were immediately remarried, eliminating any possibility of nonmarital birth. Although extramarital sex was extensive, husbands were considered to be the social fathers of all their wives' offspring (Hart and Pilling 1960, no. 90). The Tiwi's tenacious belief in spirit reproduction enabled them to minimize the importance of biological paternity and to assign all of a wife's offspring to her husband, even when westerners told them their version of the facts of procreation (Goodale 1971, no. 90).

Age at marriage is almost never mentioned in ethnographies. Often the peoples studied do not have extensive numbering systems with which to keep track of their ages. Marriage age is a discernable factor in the ethnographic literature primarily when women uniformly marry before, or shortly after puberty. The few examples of the regulatory effect of early marriage are compelling, but there are too few data for extensive statistical testing of hypotheses about age at marriage.

Abortion and Infanticide

While some groups, such as the Konso, Kazak, and Rwala Bedouin, use abortion to limit illegitimate birth, others do not. In an emic view, the Irish moral aversion to abortion was rooted historically in Christian ideology, but a general sociological and etic explanation would look for the grounding of reproductive and religious ideology in other societal conditions. As various theorists have pointed out children may be valued as workers and political allies, and they may be seen as ends in themselves. Abortion might be regulated for these reasons or others.

The Morality of Abortion or Infanticide

Several ethnographic examples document the use of abortion or infanticide as a deviant means of escaping the repressive sanctions for illegitimacy. A handful of ethnographies examined for this study mention both abortion and illegitimacy only in noting that women may resort to secret abortions as a way of concealing their nonmarital conceptions or to prevent nonmarital births. These tantalizing fragments leave much unknown, but they suggest that the penalty for, or public opinion on, illegitimacy must be quite harsh. The methods used to induce abortion are typically painful and appear to carry considerable health risks for pregnant women. The extent of women's suffering is indirect evidence of a severe and repressive mode of control of illegitimacy. If mentioned in the context of a longer discussion of illegitimacy controls, such descriptions confirm the reliability of the ethnographer's understanding of the control system.

In other societies, abortion and infanticide are part of the normative apparatus used to control illegitimacy. They are employed for religious and moral reasons. The Manchus of Aigun village were very strict in killing illegitimate children for religious reasons. They felt that clan spirits could recognize only those offspring from proper exogamous marriages. The Manchus said that one could not be happy after death without legitimate offspring to look after one's tomb (Shirokogoroff 1924, no. 115). Thus, the spiritual well-being of both the parent and the child depended upon the legitimacy of births. The afterlife reflected the patterns in the material world that were kept orderly through infanticide for irregular births. Hence, Manchu religion, in contrast to the Catholicism of the rural Irish, justified infanticide.

Abortion and infanticide are considered to be acceptable and practical means of family limitation in some societies. Married and single women among the Tikopia used coitus interruptus, abortion, and (formerly) infanticide for this purpose. According to Firth (1936, no. 100), there was no shame attached to abortion or infanticide before (or after) marriage. Abortion and infanticide were used by married couples on firstborn offspring suspected of being another man's child, or for later conceptions after several children were already in the family. The match of the number of children to the family's available farm fields was

considered important.   Sex was an accepted part of courtship among the
Tikopia. Firth points out that it was not sex and not conception, but birth before
marriage that drew stigma.   The Tikopia had a caring but practical attitude
toward children, thinking they should only be born in a home where they have
two parents to provide for them. Couples who wanted to marry usually tried to
conceive. Premarital pregnancy was one of the two most common routes to
marriage in Tikopia. Unmarried pregnant women, if they could not, or did not
want to marry, often induced abortion or their mothers saw to it that the
newborn died.

Only a small minority of ethnographic descriptions mention abortion or
infanticide. Some descriptions do not relate these to illegitimacy, and some do
not clearly state whether the abortion or infanticide is normative or deviant.
There are not sufficient descriptions available for statistical analysis of the
normative-deviant dimension of abortion and infanticide.

Voluntary versus Forced Marriage

When premarital conception or birth is considered shameful, participants may
be pressured to marry. Several examples of this have been noted. In a few
societies, unwed parents need not be pressured to marry. Some societies have
been described as practicing fecundity testing. In these groups, couples usually
marry only after they conceive or give birth. Obviously a strong desire for
children is the motive for marriage in these societies. Some rural areas of
Europe were noted to have this "peasant bundling" pattern of bastardy before
modern times (Shorter 1971, 1975), which has been attributed to the economic
benefit parents received from offspring. This set of practices existed alongside
formal religious and legal doctrines opposing premarital sex and procreation.

Legitimation after Birth

The ease with which children can be legitimized after birth varies across
cultures. Greater ease appears associated with weaker moral opposition to
illegitimacy. The Manchus killed illegitimate infants in part because they
perceived no way to legitimize offspring after birth.   In ancient Rome,
nonmarital children could be legitimized only through adoption, even by their
genitor. Children can be legitimized after birth in some African societies
through bride price payment. When the peasant bundling pattern of bastardy
existed in England, the term "mantle child" referred to a child whose parents
married after it was born. A mantle, or cloak, covered the child during
religious ceremonies in which the religious functionaries "bent the rules" to fit
local practice. The mantle child was given most if not all rights of a legitimate
offspring. Questions of legitimacy of birth were more important among the
nobility than among the peasants, but quite a few nobles and royalty had bastard
offspring (Given-Wilson and Curteis 1984).

Very few ethnographies are explicit on the matter of postpartum legitimation, although it can be an important part of control systems in which premarital sex and conception are allowed. Many sample societies allow some premarital sex, and one might suspect that some ethnographers have not mentioned the possibility and frequency of postpartum legitimation through marriage or adoption.

Alternate Modes of Legitimation

Western societies have not considered offspring to be legitimized in ways other than by marriage or adoption. Some societies provide for illegitimate offspring in their maternal grandparents' homes, and these offspring may have inheritance rights there. Partial bride wealth payment in some African societies can legitimize offspring without establishing the full rights and obligations usually associated with marriage. An unusual case is the Fon, or Dahomeans, of Africa. In Dahomey, there were more than ten kinds of "marriage" that were diverse in the material transactions that accompanied them, and in the mixes of rights that were exchanged between spouses. These rights included some or all of the following: rights of sexual access, rights to offspring, rights to the spouse's labor, and rights to cohabit. A "marriage," depending on its type, may or may not have carried reproductive rights. The Dahomeans thus split what we think of as marriage into several kinds of legal relationships. Children were "legitimate" and had rights in some kin group regardless of the types of marriage their mothers had contracted (Herskovits 1938, no. 18; Bohannon 1949, no. 18). A child whose mother was not in any type of marriage probably was seen differently. There may be a loose association between a society's having alternate modes of legitimation and its having restitutive sanctions, little loss of rights to the offspring, and little moral opposition to nonmarital birth.

The main empirical difficulty with this dimension is that the ethnographic record on alternate modes of legitimation may be woefully incomplete. Very few thorough descriptions are available.

Intrasocietal Variation by Social Status

In discussing Goode's theory, I expressed my suspicion that it might be a mistake to study illegitimacy without distinguishing between intra-class illegitimacy and cross-class illegitimacy. The ethnographic record bears this out. Cross-class and cross-group illegitimacy are widespread practices accompanying legitimate marriage and procreation. The practice of concubinage sometimes is allowed for male members of a group or class with women from other groups that are considered morally or socially lower. While a child of a concubine usually does not inherit from its father or take its father social status, concubinage is not illegal or highly immoral in these societies. Although cross-class illegitimacy would seem to be a fruitful area for study, full ethnographic descriptions for both types of illegitimacy are not common. Hence, the quantitative part of this study necessarily will concern the illegitimacy norms and sanctions for partners who are of the same society and the same social status.

Frontline and Back-Up Mechanisms of Control

A few ethnographic descriptions of illegitimacy control systems are so thorough that they make it difficult to classify a society as having a particular type of control on illegitimacy. Some of the societies mentioned above try to get the couple married as the first step. If this fails they may try to find another man to marry the woman. If this fails, she may attempt to induce an abortion, or she may become an outcast. The difficulty presented is that the frontline mechanisms are often restitutive, while the backup mechanisms may be repressive, and more severe. I coded these more extensive descriptions according to the most typical outcome of premarital conception, if the frontline and backup mechanisms fell into different coding categories.

The "Missing Data" Problem

In looking at these diverse cases, we see that illegitimacy control systems comprise many dimensions that are interrelated in complex ways. Ethnographic descriptions tend to include one or a few of these dimensions, but the selection of dimensions differs from one ethnography to the next. This implies that creating typologies and coding for each of these specific dimensions separately would yield much "missing data," which would limit the number of cases available for analysis, thus making the search for complex interactive relationships methodologically impossible. What is needed is a typology for which various kinds of ethnographic observations on illegitimacy can be used to classify any given society—one which can minimize coding error while maximizing useable cases and theoretical relevance.

SOME CURRENT TYPOLOGIES

The few existing typologies of illegitimacy do not take advantage of these empirical variations among regulatory systems. An overview of two typologies will show this to be the case.

The Concatenated Theory

In her concatenated theory of illegitimacy rates, Hartley (1975) points out that beliefs, social structure, and other factors affecting the amount of illegitimacy in a group must do so by affecting one or more of a sequence of variables that are by definition linked to marital or nonmarital birth. This sequence of variables is:

1. Proportion of females in childbearing ages who are unmarried.
2. Proportion of unmarried females in childbearing ages who are sexually active.
3. Proportion of unmarried females in the childbearing ages who conceive.
4. Proportion of pregnant unmarried females who do not marry before childbirth.
5. Proportion of pregnant unmarried females who do not abort.

Hartley's typology is useful for examining *rates* of illegitimacy. Some of the empirical variations in illegitimacy controls coincide with the elements in the concatenated theory and thus may impact on illegitimacy rates. The Tiwi minimized the proportion of unmarried females in the population by betrothing them shortly after birth. The Irish did not press women to marry early but attempted to keep singles sexually inactive. The Kazaks, Tikopia, Iban, Rwala Bedouins, and Konso all reduced illegitimacy rates to some degree through induced premarital abortions. In many groups, including the Irish, Lapps, Kazaks, Tikopia, Iban, Massa, and Bedouins, some couples marry between the time of conception and birth.

This typology, emphasizing rates rather than norms and control, does not capture cultural dimensions that are important to my research. It omits the level of moral opposition, the possibility of postpartum legitimation, the general seriousness of sanctions, or the importance of the identity of pater and genitor.

Types Based on Social Disruption and Social Disapproval

Goode (1964, 1982) presents another typology of illegitimacy. He extends Davis's (1939a) typology by presenting fourteen forms of illegitimacy in the rank order of their increasing disapproval. The increasing level of social disapproval, as one moves down the list, is said to stem from their increasingly disruptive consequences to society:

1. Consensual unions
2. Concubinage
3. Illegitimacy within the lower class
4. Liaison of nobleman with mistress in preindustrial western society
5. Childbirth during betrothal
6. Casual sexual relationship, followed by marriage
7. Adulterous illegitimacy, only the man being married
8. Union of a person in a celibate status with another celibate or a noncelibate
9. Adulterous illegitimacy, only the woman being married
10. Adulterous illegitimacy, both parties being married
11. Illegitimacy from the union of upper-caste woman with lower-caste man
12. Incestuous illegitimacy, brother-sister
13. Incestuous illegitimacy, father-daughter
14. Incestuous illegitimacy, mother-son

A given form of illegitimacy might be more typical of one society than another. Hence, Goode's typology has some cross-cultural applicability. For example, in a society with early betrothal, childbirth during betrothal might be the modal form of illegitimacy. Since this is one of the less disruptive and disapproved forms, less moral opposition and less severe sanctions might be expected. There are restrictions to this applicability, however. Goode's typology is designed to deal with different kinds of illegitimacy *within* a society. The focus seems to be on more complex societies that assign importance to the social and biological father being the same person. It also does not take into account abortion and infanticide as controls. Furthermore, it does not strongly coincide with the empirical lines of cross-cultural variation in illegitimacy control systems.

DEVELOPING A TYPOLOGY OF ILLEGITIMACY SANCTIONS

In view of the problems in these existing typologies, a new typology of illegitimacy control systems was needed for this study. I began by using a sixty-item coding form whose topics resembled the lines of variation in illegitimacy control systems discussed above, with additional items for adulterous illegitimacy. I wanted to investigate the interrelations of the various dimensions and the correlates of each dimension. This turned out to be impossible within the general strategy of the research. The complex coding form did not yield rich data. It was difficult to apply and resulted mostly in blank categories, that is, missing data, on the specific variables, rather than useable data, because of the brevity and incomparability of most descriptions of control systems. Because of this problem, the coding scheme was abandoned.

Desiderata for the Typology

A simpler typology was needed. There are three particular desiderata for this typology, in addition to the standard requirements for typologies of categories being logically exhaustive and mutually exclusive. First, it must reflect several of the empirical lines of variation in illegitimacy control systems. The most commonly mentioned dimensions are the emotional-moral reactions and the specific sanctions applied.

Next it must maximize the number of ethnographic descriptions of control systems that can be classified and used in the study. The numerous causal factors emphasized by competing theories make this desideratum important. Multivariate analysis, which requires a large sample size for hypothesis testing, is needed. A simple typology with general, abstract categories is needed. Abstract categories allow for coding a society's control system from one or more of several ethnographically described specific features.

Finally, the typology must coincide with important dimensions of control emphasized in theories. The relative harshness or repressiveness of negative sanctions is the key factor.

The Severity of Sanctions for Illegitimacy

The typology employed here classifies the typical way of handling nonmarital conception or birth for intra-class unions. I interpret the typology as an ordinal scale of *the severity of sanctions for illegitimacy*. The social class coded is the one for which the data are most adequate.[5] The distinction between reaction to nonmarital conception and reaction to nonmarital birth is ignored, unless ethnographic sources mention a difference. Ethnographic descriptions of premarital conceptions or births are classified according to whether the handling is relaxed, restitutive, or repressive, with a fourth category added dealing with the range of people punished. This typology builds upon the interconnections among the dimensions of severity of sanctions, restitutive versus repressive sanctions, and the persons sanctioned.

1. *Relaxed Handling.* With this mode, illegitimate birth (or conception) is treated without coercion, penalty, or stigma by any of several means. Women may uniformly marry before, or shortly after menarche, thereby avoiding the possibility of nonmarital conception and birth. Cases of early betrothal are classified here, if nonmarital children are assigned to the betrothed. Alternately, men may voluntarily marry women who become pregnant. Illegitimate children may be raised by their mothers and incorporated into her family or orientation of procreation with full rights, or eagerly adopted by others.

2. *Restitutive Sanctions.* With restitutive sanctions there usually is little penalty or stigma attached to illegitimacy, although a threat of mild shame or coercion may be present as a backup mechanism to the frontline sanctions. Sanctions are in the form of corrective actions or compensatory payments. Couples who conceive may be pressured to marry, or a man may pay a portion of the bride wealth in order to claim the child. In other societies in this category, the father may be made to pay support costs or a fine to the mother's family or kin group, or he may be compelled to take custody of the child as recompense.

3. *Repressive Sanctions, I.* The mother, the child, or both, are stigmatized or punished, but the father is not punished (or there is no explicit mention of penalties for the father). Alternately, unmarried pregnant women furtively practice abortion or infanticide to avoid undescribed negative sanctions or stigma. Several ethographies describe secretive practices without mentioning specific norms or sanctions.

4. *Repressive Sanctions, II.* The mother and/or the child are stigmatized or punished, and the father also is subject to restitutive or repressive sanctions. Societies are placed in this category only if there is explicit mention of sanctions of some type for the man, in addition to the repressive sanctions for the woman and/or child.

Using this typology, a total of 122 societies of the 186 in the Standard Cross-Cultural Sample (SCCS) could be classified. With forty-four missing cases, the study sample cannot be claimed to be completely representative of the SCCS.

Yet, there are cases from each and every major world region, with each type of subsistence economy, and with each type of descent and marital residence. This is an adequate number of cases for using multivariate analysis to examine the suspected interaction effects on illegitimacy sanctions.

WORLDWIDE DISTRIBUTION OF THE TYPES OF SANCTIONS

It should be clear from the discussion of empirical lines of variation in illegitimacy control systems that the moral condemnation of illegitimacy is not universal (Davis 1939a, 1939b), nor even "nearly universal." Table 4.1 elaborates this impression by showing the frequencies of occurrence of these four types of control for the societies in the sample.

About one-third of the societies typically handle illegitimacy in a relaxed way. While a few of these may be "relaxed in their condemnation" of illegitimacy, most do not seem to view illegitimacy as a specifically *moral* problem. One instructive case in which the more moral evaluation is ambiguous is the Tiwi. Hart and Pilling (1960, no. 90) describe the Tiwi as having practiced early marriage because it rules out illegitimacy, possibly suggesting a moral opposition. However, it is not clear whether this is the native understanding or the ethnographers' interpretation of the situation for they do not substantiate it with description. Much of their work suggests that men desired daughters as objects of exchange and sons as laborers and allies. Wives were acquired through exchange of daughters or sisters and men often acquired

Table 4.1. Frequencies of Illegitimacy Sanctions by World Region

| Type of Sanction | World Region | | | | | |
	Africa	Eur-asia	Oceania	North Amer.	South Amer.	World-wide
Relaxed Handling	42%	34%	38%	26%	50%	38%
Restitutive Sanctions	27%	24%	24%	30%	12%	25%
Repressive for Mother or Child	21%	34%	38%	39%	31%	32%
Repressive for Mother or Child: Father is Sanctioned	9%	7%	0%	4%	6%	6%
Total Percent	99%	99%	100%	99%	99%	101%
Total (N)	33	29	21	23	16	122

several wives by their later years. These wives and unmarried offspring foraged and hunted, providing sustenance for the family. Since sons did not marry until their mid-thirties, they had put in many years of labor for their natal households. Daughters were not only productive workers but could be exchanged for additional wives. These practical benefits of offspring to parents appears to be a driving force behind the mechanism of early marriage, as much as a moral outrage over fatherless children.

Restitutive sanctions for illegitimacy are typical in another fourth of the sample societies. There is strong moral opposition in several of these groups, and this leads to forced marriages or other preventive controls. In others, such as the Massa with their cattle payments, illegitimacy seems to be a purely contractual matter regarding whether or not a particular man has acquired rights to a particular child.

About two-fifths of the societies, those using repressive sanctions, clearly condemn illegitimacy. Within this group there is considerable variation in the extent of moral opposition, and in the effectiveness of controls. The Kazaks, Irish, and other groups described above provide examples of extreme moral stigma and harsh sanctions. The functionalist theories (Davis 1939a, 1939b; Goode 1960; Coser and Coser 1974), building upon the notion of moral opposition to illegitimacy, apply to this category and to many other societies, but perhaps in as many as one-third of the sample societies illegitimacy is not a moral matter. Among the functionalist theories, Malinowski's conceptualization of diversity in attitude and mechanism of control is better able to handle this variation than the theories following his.

Engels argues that the double standard for illegitimacy developed only with monogamous, patriarchal marriage in the transition to civilization. Among the societies having repressive controls, only about one-sixth are explicitly described as having any sanctions for the father (although more certainly have some sanctions that are not mentioned). Rarely are the sanctions for the man equally harsh as those for the mother or child. Men in most of these societies are not subjected to the same level of shame and punishment. Engels's view of repressive controls being one sided seem to be on the mark. However, some societies having double standards with severe sanctions for illegitimacy are not in Engels's stage of civilization with patriarchal families. For the unwed mother in the matrilineal Trobriand Islands, there is extreme shame. Since biological paternity is not recognized, the father is not sanctioned at all. There is a double standard, but the society would be placed in an earlier stage of cultural evolution than Engels's theory predicts.

While some societies sanction the female more strongly than the male for illegitimacy, others sanction the male more. There is a connection between direction of imbalance of sanctions and type of sanctions primarily used. With repressive controls, the female often is more harshly sanctioned, but for other societies with restitutive controls, the male may be the one receiving the brunt of the penalty. Sometimes the male is made to pay a fine, provide support, or pay a portion of the bride wealth to the woman's family.[6] With other forms of restitutive control, such as forced marriage, both mother and father are equally ensconced in rectifying the situation. There are no sample societies with typically restitutive controls that put the burden more on the woman than the man. Although the resistant male partner may receive more pressure to marry in some of these societies, the female is equally involved in the marriage to the reluctant male, and both are made responsible for the child's upbringing. The societies having little moral opposition to illegitimacy, but which require restitution from men, appear to be fundamentally different from the familiar Western pattern in which women are held more morally culpable. This association of sex differentiated sanctions with type of sanctions has not been noted in any theory.

Table 4.1 also shows that the distribution of types of control of illegitimacy varies little by world region. Each of the three major types of control is found in each world region. This geographic distribution suggests that the principle of legitimacy is not a recent innovation with different types of control diffusing within different world regions. Rather, the relatively uniform distribution suggests that the principle of legitimacy is ancient, even primordial, in origin.

NOTES

1. These codes were published after I had completed the coding for my research project. They are for adolescent pregnancy rather than illegitimacy per se.

2. Numerous qualifications must be made to this statement of course for there has been much variation across countries, classes, and ethnic groups, along with historical shifts in the sanctions for premarital sex and birth. Trends will be discussed in the final chapter.

3. I do not necessarily imply a change in describing these attitudes in the past tense here. I simply refer to patterns existing at the time of the ethnographic observations. I will use past tense uniformly, rather than the "ethnographic present" for all case examples, since the ethnographies all refer to arrangements existing in the past. They may or may not be the same today.

4. I am inferring the absence of immorality from the absence of description. While this is not a good practice in general, it makes sense to do it when there is a thorough description, as is true for the Massa. There may be the problem that a few ethnographers ignore any sense of shame surrounding deviant procreation because they are concerned with describing patterns of exchange and legal arrangements.

5. In leaving social class free to vary, some measurement error is introduced, but it is thought to be small. While some sources pertain mostly to the upper strata—for example, the Romans—others pertain to the masses of poorer people—for example, the Haitians—or are descriptions of more homogeneous societies. To maximize the number of cases, I chose to use whatever description is available. The alternative would have been to specify a particular class location for coding and to ignore descriptions of other classes and of societies not having that specified class. Sample size would have decreased drastically with this procedure.

6. One could argue that the woman's having to raise the child alone is a penalty that balances out the situation or is harsher than the male's fines. In fact, she rarely raises the child alone, but it is often incorporated into her parents' family, and her family receives any benefits the child may bring in terms of labor, bride wealth, and so forth.

5

Illegitimacy, Sociocultural Complexity, and Family Structure

We have seen that recent theorists, such as Collins and the Lancasters, have revived some of the ideas of the unilineal evolutionists of a century ago. The general line of reasoning in most of these theories is that as technology for subsistence production develops and population increases (as either cause or effect of technology), societies become less nomadic with large extended families more likely. Societies lose their egalitarianism and hierarchies develop. They become more rigidly stratified and politically centralized with greater sexual inequality[1] and with parental authority in extended families reaching far into the adult lives of offspring. The outcome of all of this for illegitimacy is that the social control of sex and reproduction becomes more repressive. Additionally, mid-century functionalism came to see hierarchy as important (Goode 1960), but it was concerned solely with social and sexual stratification.

Although the theories vary in important ways (on motivation for example), they share many aspects of this general causal sequence in their explanations of reproductive controls. This shared sequence views the hierarchical structures—the extended family, the social class system, and the state—as *intervening* variables in the relationship between population and subsistence technology on the one hand, and repressive sanctions for illegitimacy on the other. Is this view of causality true, or do interactive relationships occur among some of these variables? The findings show some evidence in support of this idea of social structure as an intervening factor but indicate that modification is needed, especially in the case of the role of the family.

I discuss family factors in a later section in this chapter, after considering the part played by the state and stratification in cultural evolutionary theory. The associations of illegitimacy sanctions with subsistence technology and population are described first, followed by the associations with social structure—political centralization and stratification. Political centralization is measured both by the number of levels in the hierarchy and by the presence of police forces. Community size and population density are the selected population measures, with primary mode of subsistence economy and fixity of residence being the measures of technology. This contingency table analysis will be followed by a discussion of partial and conditional associations testing the hypothesis that family, government and stratification are intervening variables.

BIVARIATE RELATIONSHIPS

Technology and Population Factors

Theories relate illegitimacy controls to population and technology variables only through the intervening links of social hierarchy factors. Hence, modest but significant correlations are expected between the factors at each end of the chain.

Sanctions for illegitimacy have a slight, but significant, relationship to subsistence technology (gamma = +.17, pr. < .05). At the low end of technological complexity, 30 percent of the foraging societies (those relying mainly on hunting, gathering, or fishing) have repressive sanctions. Oddly, none of the hunting societies in the sample have repressive sanctions. At the upper end, 46 percent of societies practicing plow or irrigation agriculture have repressive sanctions. Societies that have repressive sanctions and also penalize men tend to be at the upper levels of subsistence technology.

Population density also has a modest but significant association with illegitimacy sanctions (gamma = +.19, pr. <.05). The relationship is most clear when extremes in population density are contrasted. The lowest density societies are twice as likely to have relaxed mechanisms (46 percent) as the highest density groups (23 percent), but the trend toward more severe sanctions is not altogether monotonic with increasing population density. The other measure of population, size of communities, is not found to be significantly associated with illegitimacy sanctions (gamma = +.06).

Fixity of residence—the degree to which a people is nomadic or sedentary—has also been thought to be one of the remote causes of harsh controls of sex and reproduction in the evolutionary theories. The findings show a connection in the predicted direction (gamma = +.27, pr. < .05). Just over one-fourth of the fully nomadic groups has repressive sanctions, but nearly half of the fully sedentary societies do.

These findings on food quest technology, population density, and sedentism are in the direction predicted by evolutionary theories conceiving of societies progressing through a series of stages. However, the association of the population/technology variables is scarcely high enough to justify the view that there are immutable stages that are qualitatively different from each other. Even if we grant that the evolutionary theories have a correct view of the original, prehistoric, pristine occurrences of technological development, we would expect to find only moderate correlations in a cross-cultural study because less developed societies borrow traits from more developed groups, or have traits imposed on them. Also, diffusion might go in the opposite direction in some instances. Regardless of whether these theories are right about the course of cultural evolution, the power of their cross-cultural predictions from technological and population variables appears even more modest than expected.

Illegitimacy Sanctions and Social Hierarchy

The associations of illegitimacy sanctions with political structure and stratification are expected to be considerably stronger than those with subsistence technology and population factors. This is because they are conceived of as more immediate determinants in the causal chain. Theoretically, they are the intervening links between technology and illegitimacy. This expectation is confirmed in the findings. The gammas between sanctions and the three hierarchy variables range from $+.24$ to $+.35$, as opposed to a range from $+.06$ to $+.27$ for the previous factors.

Societies with centralized states are more likely than stateless societies to have severe sanctions (gamma $= +.24$, pr. $< .05$). Considering the extremes of political complexity, three-tenths of the stateless societies have repressive sanctions, whereas half of the states with three or more political levels beyond the local community do so.

A second measure of the degree of centralization of political power is whether there is a specialized body of police for enforcing civil order in society. Most societies in the sample have no group performing a police function, but a few have multipurpose groups that do policing, and about a fifth have specialized police organizations. There is a relationship between police organization and illegitimacy sanctions (gamma $= +.35$, pr. $< .05$). Nearly half of the societies with only individual people enforcing norms have relaxed mechanisms of control of illegitimacy, but at the other extreme only one-sixth of those with specialized police forces take this approach.

The evolutionary theories also use differential wealth and the appearance of social classes to account for harsh social controls on reproduction. The finding of a positive association (gamma $= +.35$, pr. $< .05$) suggests that there is some merit to this idea. While over half of the classless societies handle illegitimacy in a relaxed way, only one-sixth of those with complex stratification do so.

Taken together, these findings on class and politics indicate that hierarchical societies do tend to have less relaxed and more repressive controls on reproduction, as one would predict from some of the evolutionary theories. However, my earlier remark on the weak effects of the population and technology variables holds for hierarchy variables also. The hierarchy variables are associated with illegitimacy in the direction expected from the theory, but the magnitudes of the associations are not sufficiently impressive to argue that distinct evolutionary stages exist. In fact, cross-cultural predictive power remains low.

DOES HIERARCHY INTERVENE?

Are political centralization and social stratification more immediate causes of reproductive controls than population and subsistence technology, as conjectured by the evolutionary theories? Are these social structures intervening links in a causal chain connecting technology and population to repressive sanctions as the previous findings suggest, or do they interact with population and technology? We can find out by examining the associations of illegitimacy with population and technology, while holding constant the purported intervening variables. If the evolutionary hypothesis is correct on this matter, there will be no interaction among the variables, and partial gammas will drop substantially below the levels of the zero-order gammas.

Holding Hierarchy Constant

Table 5.1 shows the effects of the population and technology variables with levels of political centralization controlled. The partial gammas are much smaller in magnitude than the zero-order gammas for subsistence technology and population density. This indicates that political centralization does link these variables to illegitimacy sanctions as predicted. However, the partial gammas for the other variables, sedentism and community size, do not drop so substantially, and these variables interact significantly with political centralization. Sedentism impacts on sanctions in centralized states, but not in stateless societies. Nearly half of stateless societies, and just over half of nomadic states, have relaxed controls, but only one-fifth of sedentary states have relaxed mechanisms for dealing with illegitimacy. Community size affects sanctions only in the absence of political centralization, or put differently, centralization makes a difference only in societies with larger communities. Among societies with smaller communities, only about two-fifths use repressive sanctions to control illegitimacy regardless of political centralization. Among societies with larger communities, fully half of the politically centralized groups use repressive controls, but under one-fifth of the stateless societies do so. The evolutionary hypothesis on centralization holds in societies with larger communities and in fully sedentary societies. It does not hold in nomadic groups, nor in societies with small settlements.

Does the presence of a standing police force link to illegitimacy sanctions in the same way as political centralization? Table 5.2, where presence of police is controlled, suggests that to some extent it does. The partial gammas for subsistence economy and density in Table 5.2 are near zero. While one partial gamma indicates a non-zero relationship of sanctions to density in societies with police, Goodman's (1966) test indicates no significant interaction effect on sanctions. For the relation of sanctions to sedentism, the partial gamma is substantially lower than the zero-order gamma, neither conditional gamma is significant, and there is no significant interaction. We are pushed to the

Table 5.1. Gammas for Severity of Sanctions by Population and Technology Factors Controlling for Political Centralization

Independent Variable	Zero-Order Gamma	Partial Gamma	Conditional Gammas	
			Stateless Societies	Centralized Societies
Subsistence Economy	+.19	+.09	+.09	+.09
Fixity of Residence	+.37	+.29	+.05	+.65*i
Population Density	+.19	+.06	−.14	+.29
Community Size	−.09	−.14	−.36*	+.16 i

* An asterisk denotes that the conditional gamma is significantly different from zero at the .05 level. No significance test is shown for the zero-order and partial gammas.

i The i denotes significant interaction effects. The gammas for stateless and centralized societies are −.05 and +.72 respectively when illegitimacy sanctions are collapsed into relaxed vs. more serious sanctions. These gammas differ significantly using Goodman's (1966) test: $W^2 = 7.43$, pr. $< .05$. When the relation of sanctions to centralization is examined with community size held constant and sanctions recoded as less severe vs. repressive, Q for societies with communities under 200 is −.05, and for societies with larger communities Q is +.81. $W^2 = 9.74$, pr. $< .05$.

conclusion that the presence of police is an intervening link between sanctions on the one hand and subsistence, density, and sedentism on the other.[2] However, there is significant interaction between community size and police force on illegitimacy sanctions. None of the other statistical indicators suggest that the presence of police is an intervening variable here. Indeed, the partial gamma is more than double the zero-order gamma, and one conditional gamma is significant and in the opposite direction from the other gamma. The interaction, and the direction of the partial gamma, is not that predicted by evolutionary theory. Societies with larger communities and no police are the least likely to have repressive sanctions (17%). In contrast, 42 percent of unpoliced societies with smaller settlements have repressive sanctions. Among societies with police, two-fifths of those with small communities, and just over half of those with larger communities have repressive sanctions for illegitimacy.

Both measures of the concentration of power, centralization and police, have somewhat similar effects on severity of sanctions for illegitimacy. Each significantly interacts with community size, producing effects on sanctions contrary to evolutionary theory. Each shows some tendency to interact with sedentism, but only the interaction involving centralization is significant. Subsistence economy and density of population do not seem to affect illegitimacy

Table 5.2. Gammas for Severity of Sanctions by Population and Technology Factors Controlling for Presence of Police Forces

			Conditional Gammas	
Independent Variable	Zero-Order Gamma	Partial Gamma	Police Absent	Police Present
Subsistence Economy	+.14	+.01	+.02	−.15
Fixity of Residence	+.33	+.18	+.14	+.56
Population Density	+.21	+.01	−.08	+.53*
Community Size	−.14	−.36	−.45[i]	+.18 [i]

* An asterisk denotes that the conditional gamma is significantly different from zero at the .05 level. No significance test is shown for the zero-order and partial gammas.

i With sanctions dichotomized as less severe vs. repressive, the conditional gammas for sanctions by community size are −.56 when police are absent and +.27 when police are present in society. Using Goodman's (1966) test, $W^2 = 4.63$, pr. < .05.

sanctions apart from their indirect effects on the concentration of power or other potential intervening variables not yet examined.

Table 5.3 shows the effects of the technology and population variables with the presence of social stratification held constant. While one of the eight conditional gammas (for sedentism) in the table is significant and opposite in direction to its mate, Goodman's test shows no interaction for this or any of the other technology-population variables with social stratification. While controlling for stratification reduces the effects of subsistence economy and population density, sedentism and community size have substantial partial gammas. The partial gamma for community size is over twice the magnitude of the zero-level gamma. Sedentism and community size appear to have effects on illegitimacy sanctions that are not mediated by stratification.

Qualifications on Hierarchy as an Intervening Link

Let's pause to summarize what has been uncovered up to this point. The data thus far give some support to the idea that repressive controls on reproduction are a product of sociocultural development, but this is not enthusiastic support. Two sorts of qualifications are needed. One is a reminder of the low magnitude zero-order relationships found. The other is the presence of interaction effects. While measures of sociocultural development, or complexity, relate in the expected direction to the severity of illegitimacy sanctions, they account for little

Table 5.3. Gammas for Severity of Sanctions by Population and Technology Factors Controlling for Social Stratification

Independent Variable	Zero-Order Gamma	Partial Gamma	Conditional Gammas	
			Egalitarian Societies	Stratified Societies
Subsistence Economy	+.19	−.05	+.15	−.10
Fixity of Residence	+.37	+.31	−.03	+.39*
Population Density	+.19	+.10	−.31	+.17
Community Size	−.09	−.19	−.20	−.19

* Conditional gamma is significant at the .05 level.

of its variability. None of the measures of population, technology, or hierarchy are so closely related to reproductive control as to rule out the possibility that other explanations may be of equal validity.

Writings from Marxist (Engels 1972) functionalist (Goode 1960), and conflict (Collins 1978) perspectives agree that social hierarchy makes for more severe illegitimacy sanctions. Most theories presume that hierarchy in turn is grounded in technological development and population growth. The findings confirm the idea that hierarchical forces—political centralization, specialization of police forces, and stratification—are intervening links between the levels of subsistence technology and population density on the one hand and illegitimacy sanctions on the other. However, the generalization that hierarchy intervenes between population-technology and reproductive controls appears less valid when we consider community size and sedentism. Some interactive effects of these variables with political centralization and police organization were discovered, and stratification did not appear to link them, as an intervening variable, to illegitimacy sanctions. No theory suggests that these interaction effects should occur. In fact, the significant partial gammas for the interactions involving community size were in opposite direction from what loosely might be supposed from the theories. The interaction effect involving sedentism and centralization involves a partial association that fits the direction of the theory. While this latter interaction effect could be taken into account with slight modification of theory, the two involving community size could not. Thus, we find that the theoretical chains are made up of weak links, and that some links are broken. While the role of the family is yet to be examined, it is clear already that evolutionary theory tells only a part, albeit an important part, of the story on how sanctions for illegitimacy come to be what they are.

THE ROLE OF THE FAMILY

A Theoretical Note

In evolutionary theories, illegitimacy sanctions are more intimately connected to the family than to the factors considered up to this point in this chapter. The extended family in agrarian societies is seen as the arena within which power arrangements between the generations and sexes are worked out, producing repressive controls of illegitimacy (Lancaster and Lancaster 1987; Collins 1988). Research has documented that extended families are most likely to exist in sedentary agricultural societies in the middle reaches of sociocultural complexity (Winch and Chase 1968). For two reasons, the extended family may promote more severe sanctions on reproductive deviance than the nuclear family does. First, the spouses of mature offspring must be assimilated into the extended family. By definition extended families have two or more generations of adults living together and cooperating economically to some degree. Second, the elder generation has more power over the junior generation within the extended family. Powerful elders often have greater ability to enforce reproductive norms. In contrast, in societies with nuclear families, the elder's power is diminished, and sometimes relinquished, upon the maturity and marriage of offspring.

Concerns about inheritance of wealth and scarce resources are seen to be most immediately linked to repressive reproductive controls (Engels 1972; Lancaster and Lancaster 1987). Engels thought that once men figured out biological paternity, they would want their legitimate sons to inherit accumulated wealth as their natural heirs, but would want to exclude others. Lancaster and Lancaster's biosocial account differs from Engels's in one way pertinent to present considerations. They emphasize scarcity of resources rather than wealth. They argue that with societal evolution and population growth, there is a shift in how family wealth is counted: from family members in foraging societies to scarce material resources in agrarian groups. Unlike Engels, they seem to think that the agrarian revolution did not bring a surplus but that it was a response to overpopulation and scarcity. Families come to restrict claims on their resources rather than attempting to maximize membership. Illegitimacy is only one kind of norm serving to organize and limit claims against the family estate. In one sense, these claims about scarcity do not contradict Engels's notions on wealth accumulation. The Lancasters are speaking about access to resources—land, tools, herd and draft animals—to procure basic necessities. This is a scarcity based on survival needs. Engels, in speaking of the accumulation of wealth and the urge to transmit it to legitimate heirs, talks of a scarcity produced by desire.

There is a second expectation about the link of extended family structure with illegitimacy sanctions. Using Malinowski's notion that the value of offsprings' labor makes for more relaxed controls, the opposite prediction can be made. Since there would tend to be more years of offspring labor in the extended family, there should be less severe sanctions for illegitimacy. This reasoning also needs to be kept in mind as we move along with the analysis, especially since it suggests a relationship opposite in direction to the prediction from other theories.

Measuring Wealth and Scarcity

The new variables in this section are nuclear versus extended family structure, presence or absence of inheritance rules, and presence or absence of food shortage. A cross-cultural code on food storage facilities (Murdock and Morrow 1970) contains information on food *shortage*. This code is a useful measure of scarcity based on survival needs. There seems to be no direct way to measure scarcity produced by desire. Stratification, as the rank structure of desired possessions and statuses, can be conceived as a remote indicator, but it is already in use as a measure of the structuring of power in society. Inheritance rules are the theoretical facet that is readily measurable and closest to scarcity produced by desire (or by necessity) in evolutionary thinking. A cross-cultural code on the presence and type of inheritance rules is available (Murdock 1967) and will be employed in empirical testing. Codes on family structure have also been published (Murdock 1967). From the standpoint of cultural evolutionary theory and biosocial theory, we would expect both the presence of real property inheritance and the presence of extended families to be associated with more severe controls of illegitimacy and to be intervening factors which link illegitimacy to economic, population, and political factors. I will ask whether these family factors and food shortage intervene or interactively impact on illegitimacy sanctions.

FINDINGS ON FAMILY AND INHERITANCE

Empirically, neither extended families nor real property inheritance is significantly associated with illegitimacy sanctions (gamma $= -.02$ for family, and $+.26$ for inheritance). There is little variation among different types of family systems—from nuclear to stem to small and large extended families—in severity of sanctions for illegitimacy. However, there is some cross-cultural variation with different types of inheritance patterns, although it does not fit theoretical expectations. In Table 5.4, the percentage distributions of types of illegitimacy sanctions are very similar for societies having inheritance by males only, regardless of whether the pattern is matrilineal or patrilineal. The percentages for societies without fixed inheritance rules for real property are similar to these. Surprisingly, among societies where both women and men inherit property (but not necessarily equally), the sanctions for illegitimacy tend to be significantly more severe. Repressive sanctions occur in over three-fifths of the sample societies in which both sexes inherit, which is nearly double the proportion found in societies with other inheritance patterns. This pattern of association diverges from the prediction from evolutionary theory in two ways. One is the serendipitous finding on masculine inheritance versus inheritance by

Table 5.4. Severity of Sanctions for Illegitimacy by Rules for Real Property Inheritance

Severity of Sanctions	Type of Rule for Inheritance			
	Absence of Rules	Matrilineal Males Only	Patrilineal Males Only	Both Sexes Inherit
Relaxed	46%	36%	38%	12%
Restitutive	26%	27%	27%	25%
Repressive (Mother and Child)	26%	36%	24%	56%
Repressive (Father also)	3%	0%	11%	6%
Total (N)	35	11	45	16

Note: With inheritance dichotomized as absence of rules vs. presence of any type, gamma = +.26, and is not significant. With inheritance dichotomized as "both sexes inherit vs. other types, gamma = −.40 , pr. < .05.

both sexes, which suggests that repressive illegitimacy sanctions may be linked to a higher status of women, rather than a lower one as the theory holds. The other is the primary finding that the presence of inheritance rules, and patrilineal inheritance in particular, is not a marker for the onset of repressive reproductive controls.

The connections of family and inheritance to illegitimacy are weak links in the causal chains expected from evolutionary theory. The partial gammas in Table 5.5 reaffirm this conclusion regarding family structure. Population and technology do not affect reproductive sanctions solely through family structure, since the partial gammas remain about the same magnitude as the zero-order gammas for all four independent variables. Consequently, there is no way that the extended family can be considered as an intervening factor linking technology, population, and political factors to illegitimacy sanctions.

The question of interactive effects remains. The conditional gammas suggest possible interaction effects, since three of the four gammas for societies with nuclear families are significant, while the corresponding gammas for extended family-based societies are not. However, the test for differences between gammas shows that only sedentism interacts significantly with family patterns.

In the interactive pattern involving the nomadic-sedentary factor, the nomadic societies with nuclear families appear to be different from the rest. Over half of these societies have relaxed mechanisms for handling illegitimacy, and only 9 percent of them have repressive sanctions. Forty-four percent of all other societies in the sample have repressive sanctions, for a 35 percent difference in

Table 5.5. Gammas for Severity of Sanctions by Population and Technology Factors Controlling for Family Structure

Independent Variable	Zero-Order Gamma	Partial Gamma	Conditional Gammas	
			Nuclear Family	Extended Family
Subsistence Economy	+.19	+.16	+.43*	+.01
Fixity of Residence	+.37	+.34	+.63*	+.18
Population Density	+.19	+.16	+.40*	+.03
Community Size	−.09	−.13	+.18	−.29

* The conditional gammas within this category are significant at the .05 level.
i For the relationship of illegitimacy sanctions, dichotomized into less severe vs. repressive) to sedentism, the conditional Q for societies with nuclear families is +.81, while its mate is +.06. $W^2 = 4.76$, pr. < .05.

the proportions having repressive sanctions. The patterns of percentages with repressive sanctions for nonagricultural societies and low-density societies with nuclear families are similar, although not quite so dramatic. Their percentage differences from residual societies are 25 percent and 22 percent, respectively. In all cases, the frequencies of repressive sanctions among low-population, low-technology societies with extended families are very similar to those for the more developed societies. Hence, the nonsignificant findings help to corroborate the significant pattern of interaction.

Evolutionary theory holds that the extended family begins controlling reproduction repressively *in more developed agrarian societies*. The findings indicate instead that this repressive control begins in technologically simple, nomadic societies with sparse population. Among more developed societies, nuclear and extended family systems seem to employ repressive controls of reproduction to about the same extent. These findings call for some revision of evolutionary theory. We need to understand how extended family structures "jump start" the formation of repressive reproductive controls—how they move simple societies ahead of the schedule set by evolutionary theory. I will elaborate on this finding at the end of this chapter.

MALINOWSKI, CULTURAL EVOLUTION, AND THE FAMILY

Malinowski's hypothesis fares no better. I had forecast, from Malinowski's emphasis on the economic value of offspring as a factor in relaxed mechanisms of control of illegitimacy, that extended family systems might be accompanied by less severe sanctions. We see little evidence of this here. We need to take a further look at Malinowski's idea and the evolutionary approach by examining the joint effects of family factors on reproductive controls while holding constant political structure and social stratification. This further analysis indicates that the family neither intervenes nor interacts in the relationships of illegitimacy sanctions with political centralization and stratification.

However, there is a powerful interaction of family structure and police presence on illegitimacy sanctions, as shown in Table 5.6. In societies with police forces, repressive sanctions are associated more with nuclear rather than extended families, but among unpoliced societies those with extended families are more likely to have repressive sanctions. The percentages in the table show that repressive controls are least likely in unpoliced societies with nuclear family systems, with only one-fifth of such societies having repressive sanctions. For the eleven sample societies with nuclear family systems and standing police forces, almost three-fourths utilize repressive measures to control illegitimacy, and none of these have relaxed handling of nonmarital birth. Societies with extended families tend to hover around the intermediate proportion of two-fifths using repressive measures regardless of the presence or absence of police.

Collins's version of evolutionary theory suggests that sanctions are most severe in societies with large fortified households. From the standpoint of this theory, one finding is somewhat anomalous: control through repressive sanctions is most common in societies with police forces and with nuclear family systems. This finding is more in line with Malinowski's idea of the economic value of

Table 5.6. Percent of Societies with Repressive Sanctions for Illegitimacy by Family Structure and Presence of Police, with Conditional Gammas

| Family Type | Percent with Repressive Sanctions | | | | |
| | Police Absent | | Police Present | | |
	%	(N)	%	(N)	Conditional Gammas
Nuclear	20%	(39)	73%	(11)	+.83*
Extended	43%	(44)	40%	(25)	−.07
Conditional Gamma	+.49*		−.60*		

Note: In this and subsequent tables of this format, each percentage is based on the N in parentheses adjacent to it. Thus, 20% of 39 societies with nuclear families and lacking police forces have repressive illegitimacy sanctions.

* Gamma is significant at the .05 level.

Interaction Effect: Using Goodman's test, each pair of gammas differs significantly. With family type controlled, $W^2 = 9.85$, pr. $< .05$. With police presence controlled, $W^2 = 11.97$, pr. $< .05$.

children than with evolutionary theory—assuming that offspring are of greater economic value in extended families.

A multivariate analysis similar to the preceding ones examined the question of whether inheritance rules statistically interact with technological, demographic and political factors to affect illegitimacy sanctions. While no significant interaction occurs, some qualification is in order. Inheritance rules are a much closer concomitant of sociocultural complexity than family structure is. Gammas for the presence of rules for real property inheritance and sociocultural complexity measures are as follows:

—with presence of state +.68
—with presence of police +.75
—with presence of social classes +.76
—with presence of agriculture +.86
—with sedentism +.86
—with population density +.85
—with community size +.65.

When the relationships of these factors to illegitimacy sanctions were examined with inheritance controlled, several subtables had low Ns, skewed marginals, and small cell frequencies. Because of the low frequencies and skewing, there are no significant interaction effects even though there are large differences between Chase for some pairs of subtables. For example, for thirty-four societies without inheritance, only three have an organized police force. Significant associations are unlikely when the marginal frequencies are thirty-one and three. This is the problem of multicollinearity, or correlated independent variables, which makes it difficult to draw valid conclusions from the analysis. I cannot conclude with confidence that property inheritance has any particular role in elaborating the effects of technology, population, political structure, and stratification on illegitimacy sanctions.

The last question of this chapter concerns the interaction of family structure, inheritance rules, and food scarcity on illegitimacy sanctions. Since evolutionary theory presumes the concomitant variation of scarcity, inheritance rules, and family patterns, they ignore possible differences in effects of these variables. The individual effects of these factors might help to ascertain where the theory needs modifying, or where other theories may enter to account for cross-cultural variability in the control of reproduction.

Both inheritance rules and food shortage interact similarly with family structure: each has a significant impact only in societies with nuclear families. This can be seen in Table 5.7. The top portion of the table shows that repressive sanctions are quite uncommon among societies with nuclear families and no inheritance rules for real property. However, repressive sanctions are evident in about two-fifths of societies having inheritance rules, with little variation from this proportion among the categories. In the bottom half of Table 5.7, there is a strong positive association of repressive sanctions with food

Table 5.7. Percent of Societies with Repressive Sanctions for Illegitimacy by Family Structure, Inheritance Rules, and Food Shortage, with Conditional Gammas

Inheritance Rules	Nuclear Family %	Nuclear Family (N)	Extended Family %	Extended Family (N)	Conditional Gamma
	Percent with Repressive Sanctions				
Absent	12%	(16)	42%	(19)	+.67*
Present	45%	(31)	39%	(41)	−.13
Conditional Gamma	+.70*		−.06		
Food Shortage					
Adequate Food Supply	25%	(40)	46%	(52)	+.44*
Some Shortage	67%	(9)	29%	(17)	−.66*
Conditional Gamma	+.71*		−.35		

* Gamma is significant at the .05 level.

Interaction Effect: The differences between the gammas for societies with extended families and societies with nuclear families are both significant, using Goodman's (1966) test. For the association of sanctions with inheritance rules controlling for family structure, $W^2 = 4.63$. For the association of sanctions with food shortage controlling for family structure, $W^2 = 10.41$.

shortage among societies with nuclear families, but a nonsignificant negative association among societies with extended families. Repressive sanctions are most common in societies with nuclear families and periodic food shortages, and least common in nuclear family societies without periodic shortages. Predictions concerning the effects of scarcity and inheritance from evolutionary theory apply only to societies with nuclear family systems. The hypothesis about family structure derived from Malinowski's notion on the economic value of offspring is supported only for societies with periodic food shortages.

RETHINKING THE ROLE OF FAMILY STRUCTURE

Did the evolutionists and Malinowski see opposing principles that are valid only under certain limited circumstances? This may be possible, but it seems more likely that my operational definition of Malinowski's "economic interests in children" is weak. Other factors associated with extended family life may override the effect of economic interests in offspring. The more parsimonious approach in examining the anomalous findings is to view extended family-based societies as different in some important ways from nuclear family-based societies. The common thread in all of the analysis of the role of the family is that predicted relationships occur in societies with nuclear family systems more often than in societies with extended family systems. Based on the findings, we must ask why extended family-based societies may have repressive controls even if there is little development of technology or social hierarchy.

As mentioned at the start of this chapter, there are practical reasons for keeping a tight rein on mating and reproduction in societies with extended families. However, there are cognitive reasons for more intense concerns about reproduction as well. Extended families are relatively permanent units within society in contrast to nuclear families. This permanence may produce a concern about maintaining family lines through orderly reproduction. Nuclear families move through a cycle of formation, growth, shrinkage, and death. While there is a cycle of change for stem families and extended families (Goody 1962; Goody 1972), new units do not by necessity appear and disappear with each passing generation. The family exists for many generations as its members are born, reproduce, and die. Individual extended families thus are stable features of the social landscape, even in nomadic groups. This family is always hierarchical, although the extent and nature of the hierarchy may vary. As women and men live their lives, they experience social mobility within the extended family, moving from lowly positions in infancy and childhood to positions of greater authority and prestige as they achieve new family statuses. While their positions change and their subordination decreases, they never cease to live life outside the intimate authority structure of the extended family.

Surely, lifelong experience in extended families affects people's ideas and values. Todd (1985) uses Freudian theory to argue that the type of family structure in a society or region molds political and religious ideologies. The experience of permanence or impermanence, and of equality or hierarchy in various family relationships shapes people's ideas and values on politics. Todd's theory does not directly link family structure to illegitimacy controls. However, his notion that ideas and attitudes are shaped by family experience suggests a possible *cognitive* and *evaluative* connection between family structure and illegitimacy controls. One can argue that experiencing family as more permanent than individual members leads to more concern with maintaining the family line over the generations through orderly reproduction. With this concern stemming from an authoritarian structure, repressive controls for illegitimacy seem more likely.

A second version of this cognitive and evaluative link of family structure and illegitimacy controls can be derived from Bernard Farber's (1968, 1971, 1973) work. Families and kin groups, according to Farber, develop symbolic estates that include family spirits, renowned deeds of ancestors and living kin, and other meanings attached to membership. Symbolic estates exist in societies even where there is not much in the way of material property. Farber argues that societies have one of two emphases (or paradigms) in kinship. They may emphasize on one hand the differentiation of kin groups from each other, the orderly replacement of group members, and the maintenance of the symbolic estate. On the other hand, a society may emphasize the integration of kin groups, with marriage and alliances being seen as more important. While both emphases are obviously important for any society, groups tend to set more store by one than the other. The emphasis in kinship affects the handling of illegitimacy. Farber (1973) points out that legal corrective actions for illegitimacy take a number of forms: punitive, educational, moralizing, and remedial for any harm done. More stringent actions are indicative of the emphasis on maintenance of the symbolic estate and orderly replacement of members.

While Farber does not make it explicit, we may infer that the permanence of extended families may make the continuity of the symbolic estate more important to a people. For this reason, we can understand that extended family-based societies may see illegitimacy as a greater threat to the preservation and transmission of symbolic family estates.

Biosocial and cultural evolutionary theories tell us that government and class structures in sedentary agrarian societies may give rise to more severe illegitimacy controls because of people's material interests. The research findings, however, show that more severe sanctions occur even in technologically simple, nomadic societies if they have extended family systems. The ideas of Todd and Farber can help to ameliorate the empirical weakness of the theories linking severe sanctions to family resources. Farber's theory helps in understanding how family structure may affect illegitimacy sanctions for cognitive and evaluative reasons, even in the absence of technological development and real property inheritance rules.

NOTES

1. The part played by sexual inequality will be examined in Chapter Seven.

2. Although the gamma of $+.56$ is large, the table on which it is based has a very skewed marginal distribution. There are only four nomadic societies with police in the sample societies for which illegitimacy descriptions are available. It is difficult to draw any reliable statistical conclusion from these data on the joint impact of sedentism and police on illegitimacy.

6

Effects of Descent and Fraternal Interest Groups

Several theories suggest that illegitimacy sanctions are related to descent rules or to marital residence rules. Empirically speaking, it is difficult to separate out the effects of residence and descent because their intercorrelation tends to confound statistical analysis. Patrilineal groups are almost always patrilocal. While matrilineal groups often have matrilocal or avunculocal residence, patrilocal residence is not uncommon. Other types of marital residence pattern occur in matrilineal groups also. Double unilineal and bilateral societies have a great variety of marital residence rules as well. Nonetheless, there is a moderate connection between type of unilineal descent and type of marital residence rule. Because of this recognized interconnection of descent and residence (Murdock 1949; Colson 1950; Driver and Massey 1957; Aberle 1961; Schneider 1961), we must view a hypothesis emphasizing descent rules as competing with a hypothesis emphasizing marital residence. Sociobiology and mid-century functionalism deal with the primary role of descent. FIG group theory emphasizes the primacy of marital residence rules.

FUNCTIONALISM AND SOCIOBIOLOGY

Hypotheses emphasizing the role of descent rules can be derived from functionalism and sociobiology. I criticized the functionalist argument on the role of the father in status placement as not being applicable to matrilineal societies. Clan membership, inheritance, and political succession are taken from one's mother and her brothers in these societies. Fathers usually play a lesser, perhaps negligible, role. This critique can be rephrased as a hypothesis testing the status-placement idea: sanctions for illegitimacy tend to be most relaxed in matrilineal groups, most severe in patrilineal societies, and intermediate in others. A functionalist perspective might see residence rules as a secondary factor in status placement. Since a marital residence rule places a child in a particular geographic and social community, it sets constraints on that child's social locus and available statuses. The father's part in status placement would be most emphasized in patrilocal societies, so more severe sanctions are to be expected there. However, a weaker link would be expected between sanctions and residence than between sanctions and descent.

Some sociobiologists have followed the lead of early evolutionary theory in accounting for matrilineal descent on the basis of uncertainty of biological paternity. If men cannot know with certainty whom their offspring are because of sexual promiscuity, the argument runs, they will maximize inclusive fitness by investing in their sisters' children. At least they are certain to share some genes with their nieces and nephews.

Sociobiologists and others have raised questions about this idea, but it is refusing to die. Since sociobiologists have not explicitly discussed illegitimacy from this line of argument, we can follow up on it to draw out implications for illegitimacy sanctions. If a society were organized around this matrilineal principle of male investment in sister's children, there would not likely be much concern over women having children outside of marriage whether through premarital or extramarital liaisons. The society would not tend to demand restitution or punishment for fathers or mothers of bastard children.

Sociobiology predicts that where paternity is more certain and men invest in their own offspring, patrilineal descent is more likely to occur. Under this condition, nonmarital birth is more likely to stigmatize a woman, bringing shame or reducing her marriageability. The "fatherless" child will not have the same rights as children born in regular unions, nor the advantage of paternal investment. In short, repressive controls are to be expected.

The argument is that promiscuity produces matriliny, which produces relaxed handling of illegitimacy. If this is statistically correct, we expect a strong correlation of matriliny with illegitimacy sanctions. A weaker association of nonmarital promiscuity with sanctions would be expected to disappear when descent is held constant.

Table 6.1 shows the percentage distributions of types of sanctions for illegitimacy within categories of descent. Percentages for matrilineal and patrilineal societies appear in the extreme left and right columns of the table. There is a slight tendency for more severe sanctions in patrilineal groups as posited from the theory, but it is not significant.

Unilineal descent exists when there are kin groups to which people are assigned on the basis of parentage. These groups can be multifunctional and a critical organizing principle of social life, or they can be nearly nominal in importance. A more rigorous test of the functionalist-sociobiological hypothesis would look at closer indicators of status placement and parental investment. Two such indicators are the type of unilineal inheritance rule and succession to the office of local headman. Illegitimacy sanctions are not significantly related to matrilineal or patrilineal succession to the office of local headman, and we saw in the previous chapter that societies with different forms of unilineal inheritance barely differ in their prevalence of repressive sanctions for

Table 6.1. Severity of Sanctions for Illegitimacy by Rule of Descent

Sanction for Illegitimacy	Rule of Descent				
	Matri-lineal	Double	Ambi-lineal	Bilateral	Patri-lineal
Relaxed	47%	33%	0%	39%	33%
Restitutive	29%	33%	33%	22%	23%
Repressive for woman or child	24%	17%	67%	35%	32%
Repressive (father also sanctioned)	0%	17%	0%	4%	8%
Row Total (N)	17	6	3	49	47

Note: When the middle categories of descent rule (double, ambilineal, and bilateral are combined together, gamma = +.12, pr. = .16, which is not significant.

illegitimacy.   These recurrent, nonsignificant findings suggest that functionalism's status-placement function of the father and sociobiology's notion of uncertainty of paternity do not account for severe illegitimacy sanctions.

When the data are examined for a possible impact of extramarital sex on illegitimacy sanctions, only a nonsignificant trend in the predicted direction is found (gamma = −.15), as shown in Table 6.2.   Data codes on both extramarital sex and illegitimacy are in hand for only 45 societies.   Neither of these is a standard ethnographic topic, so descriptions are sparse.   The small number of cases presents difficulties for further analysis, but the findings are suggestive that descent and paternal uncertainty may have very minor separate, additive effects on illegitimacy sanctions, rather than interactive effects.[1]   The sociobiological concern about certainty of paternity then does not seem to account for illegitimacy sanctions.

FRATERNAL INTEREST GROUP THEORY

Paige and Paige (1981) use FIG theory to emphasize the primacy of marital residence over descent in the patterning of legitimacy.   Marital residence rules indicate the strength of FIGs.   As discussed in the Chapter 3, FIGs are local aggregates of kinsmen.   Aggregation is most often accomplished through patrilocal residence.   In matrilineal societies, avunculocal residence helps keep clansmen in spatial contiguity.   Duolocal residence—the pattern wherein husband and wife remain with their natal groups rather than establishing a common residence—also keeps matrilineal kinsmen together.   FIG theory views the

Table 6.2. Severity of Sanctions for Illegitimacy by Frequency of Extramarital Sex for Wives

Sanction for Illegitimacy	Frequency of Extramarital Sex			
	Uncommon	Occasional	Moderate	Near Universal
Relaxed	57%	0%	46%	50%
Restitutive	14%	40%	18%	33%
Repressive for Mother or Child	14%	60%	36%	17%
Repressive (Father Sanctioned Also)	14%	0%	0%	0%
Column Total (N)	7	5	22	6

Note: Gamma = -.15, pr. = .20, not significant.

aggregation or dispersion of kinsmen as a structural feature constraining the ways in which men are able to claim offspring as legitimate. Men are said to crave offspring as political and economic allies. When patrilocal residence unites kinsmen and sorts men into large descent-group-based communities, these men control reproduction through ritual surveillance of women and through contracts with other FIGs. With weak FIGs, men are poorly organized to enforce contracts or to keep guard over women. Instead they ritually involve themselves in childbirth to establish their legitimate claims over their wives' offspring. In Chapter 3, I pointed out that "ritual surveillance" is a more repressive form of control. It also tends to imply more severe sanctions when surveillance breaks down.

What other factors are relevant in this theory? FIG theory views descent as of secondary relevance. First, descent is viewed as an ideology bolstering kinsmen's ability to act on their interests without having any independent effect. This logic implies statistically that a looser association of descent and sanctions will disappear when a closer association of residence and sanctions is controlled. Second, these factors are held to work in these ways only in stateless societies. A centralized government may take over the role of the FIG in enforcing the rules of reproduction. Hence, an interactive effect of FIG structure with state organization is specified by the Paiges. Warfare is another relevant factor. In my earlier critique I argued that the Paiges' theoretical motor—political interests in offspring—may not be constant, but may be induced or enhanced by internal warfare. If my question about internal warfare enhancing political interests is correct, then an interactive effect of warfare and residence on illegitimacy sanctions should appear.

To test these hypotheses, the severity of illegitimacy sanctions is cross-tabulated with marital residence rules, frequency of internal warfare, and measures of state development. There is qualified support for FIG theory. Table 6.3 shows a modest association of illegitimacy sanctions with FIG organization. Repressive sanctions are much more common among societies with kinsmen-aggregating residence rules. Only one-fifth of the matrilocal societies have repressive sanctions for illegitimacy. Repressive sanctions occur in half of the six avunculocal societies in the sample and in over two-fifths of the patrilocal societies. This finding in support of FIG theory is contrary to the prediction from the status-placement hypothesis of functionalism, which holds that descent is a stronger factor than residence. [2]

Parenthetically, the four sample societies with neolocal residence are least likely to have repressive sanctions. None of them do! Several factors may combine to produce this: the absence of FIGs, a low level of hierarchy, and the absence of large extended family groups. In contrast, ambilocal societies, which allow a choice of residence in the communities of the husband's parents or of the wife's parents, are as likely as societies with strong FIGs—that is, patrilocal residence—to have repressive sanctions for illegitimacy.

The FIG theory of ritual reproductive control applies only to stateless societies, and I have suggested that internal warfare stimulates the underlying political intergenerational interest. Neither of these ideas works out in empirical

Table 6.3. Severity of Sanctions for Illegitimacy by Marital Residence Rules

Sanction for Illegitimacy	Marital Residence Rule				
	Matri-local	Ambi-local	Neolocal	Avuncu-local	Patri-local
Relaxed	48%	20%	75%	0%	38%
Restitutive	32%	30%	25%	50%	20%
Repressive for Mother or Child	20%	40%	0%	50%	35%
Repressive (Father Also Sanctioned)	0%	10%	0%	0%	8%
Column Total (N)	25	10	4	6	77

Note: With categories of residence combined and arrayed to show the degree of aggregation of kinsmen as (1) matrilocal, (2) ambilocal and neolocal, and (3) avunculocal and patrilocal, the severity of sanctions is significantly associated with gamma = +.25, pr. < .05.

tests. The frequency of internal warfare is not related to severity of illegitimacy sanctions (gamma = −.05), and when controlled it does not alter the association of illegitimacy sanctions with FIGs. Similarly, the predicted interaction of centralization and FIG structure on illegitimacy sanctions is not found. FIGs and illegitimacy sanctions are as strongly related in state societies and societies with police as in stateless and unpoliced societies.[3]

To sum up, the central hypothesis from FIG theory is supported, and the theory fares somewhat better in testing than do sociobiology and functionalism. However, the key association of sanctions and FIGs is of modest magnitude. The factors of warfare and lack of central control within society, two key elements in the logic underlying the hypothesis, are not confirmed. [4]

THE WEAK LINK OF ILLEGITIMACY TO DESCENT AND RESIDENCE

Other Intergenerational Interests

How is it that our theories of illegitimacy do not apply strongly to descent and marital residence? First, the intergenerational interest in FIG theory may be misconstrued. In reality, perhaps some motives other than political and economic interests in offspring are at work, creating variation in sanctions not accounted for by FIGs. Affective bonding of parent to child and the proper reproduction of group members as a way of justifying the value on one's culture may also be at work in societies with strong FIGs. The impact of parent-child bonds will be considered in a subsequent chapter, but no operational measures of the other motives are available.

Sexual Inequality

FIG theory presumes universal male dominance, although it sees this dominance as being structured differently in strong and weak FIGs. Men are treated as actors and decision makers, while women are reproductive objects men struggle to control. What happens to illegitimacy sanctions when women have more political influence? I will consider this question in the next chapter.

THE DISSOCIATION OF BIOLOGICAL AND SOCIAL PATERNITY?

Another factor in the poor fit of theory to data is variations in the way that societies construe biological fatherhood in relation to social fatherhood. We tend to think that matrilineal groups set less store by biological paternity than patrilocal, patrilineal ones, but this is not necessarily true. Societies have several mechanisms, unrelated to descent or residence, to regulate birth without identifying the genitor as the social father.

Female Initiation

There is a belief, with a limited empirical basis, among some sociocultural anthropologists that matrilineal groups use female puberty rituals instead of marriage to legitimate procreation (Goody 1982). If this were common among matrilineal groups only, it would produce more dissociation of biological and social fatherhood in those groups. However, some patrilineal societies have the same practice, and many matrilineal counter-examples can be cited.

Richards (1956, no. 7) notes that among the matrilineal, matrilocal Bemba, there was no recognition of paternity, and that it was not marriage, but the female initiation rite, or *chisungu*, that was the important factor in legitimating reproduction. However, Richards's description suggests that *chisungu* and marriage are part of the same larger ritual process. Richards describes the process of marrying, not as a brief ceremony, but as a gradual procedure with many exchanges, such as bride service, *and the woman's initiation rite*. Couples usually slept together before the girl reached puberty, and she or her mother started the *chisungu* about the time of the first menses. The elaborate and lengthy ritual was only a part of marriage, but it was the part that legitimated reproduction. This is not strong evidence that puberty rites rather than marriage legitimate procreation, since the two processes interpenetrate. Also, if couples were matched together and often conceived before marriage, there was little dissociation of biological and social fatherhood.

Some other matrilineal (or double descent) groups in Africa have similar practices in which female initiation rites help to legitimate offspring, but marriage is the final step. The Ashanti, a double descent group, went easy on illegitimacy if the woman had passed her puberty rituals and the man acknowledged the child. If a woman had a child before her initiation, she and the genitor were fined heavily and subjected to public obloquy. Reproduction not authorized by initiation was regarded as unclean, and the fine went for purification of ancestral stools. In earlier times, both culprits would have been driven out or killed (Fortes 1950, no. 19).

The matrilineal Mende of Sierra Leone required both women and men to be initiated to have a right to sexual intercourse. The offense of sex with an uninitiated girl was an offense called for compensation and ritual washing. Once a woman passed puberty and initiation, sex was not considered bad, but her parent's permission was required (Little 1951: 144). Perhaps initiation similarly helped legitimate reproduction, but the description is not explicit on this.[5]

These cases show some evidence for the notion that some matrilineal groups use *both* female initiation rites *and* marriage to fully legitimate reproduction. Initiation rites do not replace marriage in this respect and do not always dissociate biological and social fatherhood.

Another problem with the idea that female initiation authorizes reproduction in matrilineal groups is that some patrilineal, patrilocal societies have had similar arrangements. Perhaps the patrilineal groups doing this are fewer in number, but they do exist. The Masai of Kenya are one. Leakey (1930) describes the Masai as having had considerable sexual freedom before initiation, between initiation and marriage, and after marriage. The main restriction was the norm that one should have sex with a person of one's own age-marital status but outside one's subclan. Wives could have sex with married men other than their husbands, but not with a warrior or an uninitiated boy. Uninitiated girls could have sex with uninitiated boys or initiated men, but not with married men. Procreation is a different matter, however.

If an uninitiated girl conceives and her condition becomes known she immediately would be initiated. In the normal way her initiation would take place at her mother's house and the necessary arrangements would be made by her father, but if she is to be initiated because she is with child, the onus of all the arrangements is shifted on to the man who is responsible for the girl's condition, and the ceremony must take place at the man's village. This does not however, mean that the man will have to marry her because of this, but he may do so should both parties desire it. Not only must the man arrange for her initiation and pay all the costs of the ceremony, but he must also give one heifer and a quantity of beer to the girl's father, because he has prevented the father from having the honour of the feast of her initiation. (Leakey 1930, no. 34: 198-199)

Although many details in the initiations differ, the normative necessity of initiation to procreation for the patrilineal Masai is not any less than that of the matrilineal Bemba. They carefully keep track of the biological father also. The Igbo are another African patrilineal group treating illegitimacy less seriously after a woman's initiation (Basden 1921, no. 17).

Similar patterns are found outside of Africa. The Lolo, an Asian patrilineal group, authorize sexual intercourse and procreation by a status-change ritual in which the woman's hair is put into two braids. The ritual ordinarily accompanies marriage, but for "spinsters" of sixteen or seventeen years of age, the ceremony marks the acceptability of their being sexually active without marriage (Lin 1947, no. 67).

Not only do matrilineal groups not use female initiation to legitimate birth, they take nonmarital birth quite seriously. In describing the Trobriand Islanders, it was noted that they do not fit this scenario of casual reproduction by initiated women. Although the Trobriand Islanders did not recognize biological fatherhood, neither did they employ puberty rites to legitimate reproduction outside of marriage. Illegitimacy brought stigma.

Many other matrilineal societies do recognize the biological father and ideally want the biological and social father to be the same. The Palauans deplored bastardy because it meant an economic loss in the exchanges between the father and the mother's brother (Barnett 1949, no. 111). The Goajiro fined the biological father and tried to force a marriage. The lack of marriage brought shame upon the mother of an illegitimate child (Gutierrez de Pineda 1948, no. 159). Bastardy was also deplored and stigmatized among the Nahane. They would try to force the father into marriage, or failing that, to give a gift to the woman's father. Also, the woman could be exiled for a month (Honigmann 1954, no. 129).

Bride Wealth without Marriage

Quite a few societies legitimate children through bride wealth, one of the common transactions accompanying marriage around the world. The institution of bride wealth sometimes dissociates biological and social fatherhood. There is a continuum of dissociation of biological and social fatherhood through bride wealth. Bride wealth payments ordinarily accompany marriage but in the breach may be used to legitimate children without marriage. Children also may go to whomever gives the bride wealth, be it genitor or a social father. In the extreme case, societies practicing bride wealth can ignore biological fatherhood and deal with unwed birth most casually. Since large bride wealth payments tend to be associated with patriliny and patrilocality, we find that some patrilineal groups treat illegitimacy in a relaxed or restitutive way, with little concern that the person identified as the social father also be the biological father. Others try to identify the biological father.

A glance at the case descriptions of bride wealth societies suggests that the greater the dissociation, the more relaxed the handling of illegitimacy. The Massa of Cameroon, a patrilineal, patrilocal group, had a well-described complex arsenal of principles for dealing with illegitimacy. They did not ignore biological fatherhood for legal purposes. The first principle was preventive. Among the Massa, unmarried women had some sexual liberty. Premarital pregnancy was usually followed by quickly negotiating a marriage with bride wealth, which legitimated the child. There was little or no shame involved in this arrangement. It is unclear if there was some degree of shame if there was no marriage, but in the back-up system the main concern seems to have been with the distribution of cattle from the illegitimate child's eventual marriage. If the man was poor and could not pay the bride price, he was still the recognized father and had certain rights in the child. If the child was a son, this child moved to his father's household at maturity. The mother's family raised the child, but the father had to give some cattle for their trouble in raising him. If the child was a girl, she was raised by her mother's family, and the mother's father arranged the marriage of his illegitimate granddaughter and received the bride price. The genitor received one heifer from her bride price when she married. If the mother of the illegitimate daughter married, her husband could not receive the bride price for his stepdaughter, as might happen in some other societies (Garine 1964, no. 27: 159-160). The Massa then did not ignore biological paternity. They preferred to merge biological and social fatherhood in the same relationships, but when the two fatherhoods got separated, the Massa still assigned rights and obligations to the biological father.

Other patrilineal, patrilocal societies do dissociate biological and social paternity. This is commonly done through the mechanism of using the bride price to establish the link between social father and child. Linton (1933, no. 81) mentions that if a Tanala man married a woman with a child, he could at his discretion pay a bit extra on the bride price if he wanted the additional child, or pay at the standard level if he did not want rights in the child. Numerous African societies, such as the Shilluk (Seligman and Seligman 1932, no. 31) and the Nkundo Mongo (Hulstaert 1928, no. 14) legitimate offspring through payment, sometimes with marriage and sometimes without it. Children are simply incorporated as members of the mother's descent group in the absence of bride wealth payment. Although accounts of Igbo reproductive control conflict (Leith-Ross 1939, no. 17; Uchendu 1965, no. 17), Basden (1921, no. 17) relates that after an early betrothal and the start of bride wealth payments, an initiated woman was free to have sex with whomever she wanted before she married at around age sixteen. If she became pregnant before marriage, the offspring was counted as her husband's child.

Other patrilineal, patrilocal societies attempt to keep social and biological paternity identical using more restrictive measures on women or men. These range from enforced marriage to shaming and fines to genital operations and death. Santal village elders would force a man to marry a woman he made pregnant (Mukherjea 1962, no. 62). For the Kazaks, premarital pregnancy brought shame to a woman and her clan. Either a marriage was arranged or abortion was induced to avoid the shame of illegitimacy (Grodekov 1899, no. 65). Herzog (1957, no. 39) reports that a Kenuzi Nubian woman who had premarital sex was killed by her kin. The fate of her partner is not mentioned. This patrilineal, patrilocal group fits the image of sexual control in FIG interest groups well. Capital punishment was probably rare however, for women wore leather garments marking their virginity, and their vaginas were sewn up leaving only a tiny hole making sexual intercourse impossible.

Early Marriage

Early marriage for women, at the onset of the menses or before, effectively prevents premarital sex, pregnancy, and illegitimacy. Our theories have not taken early marriage into account as a means of establishing the social paternity of women's offspring. This strategy is employed in societies with both strong and weak FIGs and in both matrilineal and patrilineal societies. Some societies use early marriage in conjunction with the rule that the groom claims all his bride's offspring. In other groups, there are severe illegitimacy sanctions for any women not marrying early or for those practicing extramarital sex. Early marriage itself is not a sanction. It is neither restitutive nor repressive; it does not seek amends for harm nor punish a woman for her misconduct.[6]

Some matrilineal groups, such as the Bemba (who were mentioned above) the Luguru in Africa (Christensen 1963, no. 10) and the Vedda of India (Seligman and Seligman 1911, no. 80), time marriage with sexual maturity, as do the patrilineal Nyakyusa (Wilson 1977, no. 8). Several other societies, like the

Igbo, who were mentioned before, betroth prepubescent girls with their marriages becoming official after they reach sexual maturity. The Tiwi of North Australia, a double descent group with patrilocal residence (Hart and Pilling 1960, no. 90), and the Shavante, an unusual patrilineal but matrilocal society in South America (Maybury-Lewis 1967, no. 179), marry girls off when they are infants or toddlers. In such cases, if the husband can claim all offspring of his fiance or wife, the problem of illegitimacy is solved.

These varied examples aid in understanding why there is little association between descent or residence on the one hand and the severity of illegitimacy sanctions on the other. Some societies attempt to socially enforce biological relationships, whereas others set less importance on whether the social father is biologically related. In some societies where they occur, bride wealth and early marriage are mechanisms of dissociation of biological and social fatherhood. These factors and the uses of female initiation to partially legitimate reproduction seem to make for less repressive illegitimacy sanctions. Descent and residence do not seem to account for the dissociation of social and biological fatherhood, and hence are less related to severity of illegitimacy sanctions than we have supposed.[7]

CONCLUSION

The role of the father in the child's status placement is more structurally important in patrilineal than in matrilineal societies (Goode 1960; Schneider 1961; Zingo and Early 1994). However, the data suggest that even patrilineal groups can dissociate biological and social fatherhood and still function well. We need to revise the status-placement theory to focus attention on the role of the *social* father, rather than the biological father, in status placement. The question of why some groups attempt to identify the biological father as the social father is quite another question.

NOTES

1. For the 45 cases with data on both extramarital sex and illegitimacy, the zero order gamma for the relationship of sanctions to descent rules (arrayed as matrilineal, other, patrilineal) is +.31, and the partial gamma is +.33. Similarly the association of sanctions with extra-marital sex remains constant when descent is controlled. The zero-order gamma for severity of illegitimacy sanctions and the frequency of extra-marital sex is -.12, increasing to -.17 when descent is controlled. All but one of the five conditional gammas are in the direction of their zero-order counterparts, although the subtable sizes on which they are based drops as low as seven cases. This consistency bolsters the interpretation that descent is not an intervening variable between sexual promiscuity and illegitimacy sanctions.

2. This is evidence against the status-placement idea in that residence is related to illegitimacy sanctions whereas descent rules, the purported primary factor, is not. When the effects of residence and descent on sanctions are examined simultaneously, the results

are inconclusive because of the problem of multicollinearity. The gamma of +. 10 for descent shifts to -.03 when marital residence is held constant. The significant gamma for residence of +.25 drops to +.09 when descent is controlled. The same problem prohibits a sensible examination for interaction effects.

3.   The partial gammas in these three analyses with internal warfare, political centralization, and police organization are virtually identical to the zero-order gammas. Conditional gammas for societies with police and with central polities are just slightly larger than their counterparts.

4.   Homans (1984) criticized the Paiges' work on the basis that the ritual reproductive controls they emphasized for stateless societies also occurred in some states. He believed that the logic underlying the theory and findings was flawed. Homans's critique is a harbinger of the findings here on sanctions for illegitimacy.

5.   Since the description for the Mende is on sex rather than reproduction, and since no sanctions are mentioned for initiated women, this society was not coded on severity of sanctions for illegitimacy. Consequently, it is not included in the quantitative part of this study.

6.   Early marriage fits best here in the relaxed category of mechanisms of control. As a preventive measure, it means that societies do not have to be as concerned with after the fact controls, with pressuring people to legitimate offspring or punishing people for their failure to legitimate. Nonetheless, a few societies practicing early marriage do not take a relaxed approach to sexuality generally, and in this sense the classification of early marriage in the typology of illegitimacy controls may be misleading.

Feminist theorists might argue that women's early marriage indicates greater male control of women's lives. They might feel that early marriage represses women, even if is not a sanction, nor repressive in the Durkheimian sense. In many cases men also are married early, or have limited voice in the selection. Also, mothers may have some input into arranging their daughters' marriages.   If so, then where is the sexual inequality?   If early marriage is to be viewed as an indicator of repression and inequality, it is as closely connected to the power of the elder generation over youth, as of men over women.

7.   Unfortunately, no way was developed to take this factor into account in coding the data for this study. Ethnographic discussions of the ideology of procreation and of the desired fit between biological and social paternity are not common. To hope for comparable data on these factors for a large number of societies would be fruitless.

7

Illegitimacy and Sexual Inequality

In this chapter the association of illegitimacy sanctions to sexual inequality will be examined, first as an individual variable, then with the primary variables of the preceding chapters controlled. Different theories over the past century have explicitly linked the severity of control of illegitimacy to sexual inequality, while others have not emphasized the role of the relative power of women and men. Some examples of these diverse positions can be summarily reiterated here. Beginning with Engels, some theorists have believed that inequality of men and women produces not only greater restrictions, but also a double standard of sexual and reproductive rights. Engels believes that sexual inequality worked in conjunction with greater accumulation of wealth in society to produce repressive controls on sex and reproduction for women. William Goode brings functionalism closer to this position with his emphases on placement in the stratification system and on courtship bargaining power. Guttentag and Secord however feel that greater bargaining power of women (deriving from sex ratio imbalance) leads to more restrictive controls and severe sanctions. Engels's materialist theory, Collins's conflict theory, Lancaster and Lancaster's biosocial theory, and Paige and Paige's fraternal interest group theory all presume a high level of sexual inequality that comes into play only under certain structural conditions. These diverse theories treat sexual inequality as a necessary factor—one that works with other structural factors—to produce repressive controls for illegitimacy. This "working together" translates into a hypothesis of interaction effects.

There is not total agreement on this point. Some theorists, like Malinowski, have not felt that sexual inequality is an important factor. These theories disagree on the relevance and the role of sexual inequality in illegitimacy control systems. Gender theorists emphasize that restrictions on women's behavior, sexuality and reproduction primarily reflect differences in sexual inequality, or are dimensions of sexual inequality (Sacks 1979; Sanday 1981a; Chafetz 1984).

SEXUAL INEQUALITY AS A CONFOUNDING VARIABLE

This situation of theoretical disagreement cries out for an analysis of the relationship of illegitimacy sanctions to sexual inequality. Recent research findings on the extent of variation and the structural correlates of women's power are not always taken into account. Women are not powerless, nor men dominant, to the same degree in all societies. Most cross-cultural scholars today recognize that the observable range of variation in sexual stratification is from sexual equality to extreme male dominance, stopping short of female dominance (Whyte 1978b; Sacks 1979; Sanday 1981a; Chafetz 1984; Hendrix 1994).[1]

Some evolutionary theories presume that sexual inequality is a part of the general process of development of technological complexity and power structures in society. Sexual inequality *is* correlated with technological complexity and hierarchy cross-culturally, but this is by no means a perfect correlation (Friedl 1975; Whyte 1978b; Johnson and Hendrix 1982; Hendrix and Hossain 1988). The effects of technology and hierarchy in societies with more sexual inequality, and in those with less, need to be ascertained separately.

Similarly, the point can be reiterated that the effects of fraternal interest group organization may be confounded with the effects of sexual inequality. Fraternal interest group theory posits that restrictive controls on sex and reproduction stem from the aggregation of kinsmen into competing communities, but empirically these are the very locations where sexual inequality tends to peak (Whyte 1978b; Sanday 1981a). Hence, we need to ask whether sexual inequality makes any difference in the impact of fraternal interest groups on illegitimacy sanctions.

MEASURING SEXUAL INEQUALITY

What kind of measure of sexual inequality should we try to correlate with illegitimacy sanctions? While scholars agree on the cross-cultural range of variability of sexual inequality, they agree less on how to define and measure it.[2] The main point of conceptual agreement is that sexual inequality or women's status must be measured *relative* to men's status. Beyond this, there is much disagreement. For example, Sacks (1979) defines inequality in terms of sex differences in the control of production, leading to differentials in economic autonomy, access to power and authority, a double standard of sexuality, and invidious stereotypes of women; but each of these dimensions must be analyzed for the statuses of *sister* and *wife* separately in kinship structured societies. Whyte (1978b) finds ten loosely intercorrelated dimensions of sexual inequality from a cluster analysis of some fifty items. Emergent dimensions, such as men's and women's relative property control, power in kin contexts, domestic authority, and control of sex, match some dimensions from Sacks's conceptualization. However, other dimensions, like men's fear of women, and value on women's labor, do not match. Sanday (1981a) focuses on the power factor and suggests three major dimensions to sexual inequality. Women's power may be: (1) *ascribed* and justified on the basis of women's creation of life in biological reproduction and chartered in myth; (2) *achieved* by virtue of producing and controlling valued goods for extradomestic consumption leading to political participation and women's organizations; but these two sources of power may be counteracted by (3) *male aggression* when men come to fear women's mythically ascribed power. Sanday combines women's achieved power with male dominance to create a composite variable of *male dominance*. This conceptualization is in some ways more narrow than that of Sacks or Whyte, but broader in adding an ascribed dimension of power. It is different from other measures of sexual inequality in that it is not a measure of relative power of women and men. Chafetz (1984), in an attempt to integrate the comparative literature on sexual inequality, defines sexual inequality as sex difference in access to scarce and valued goods and services. She lists eleven areas where women and men may have differential access—for example, material goods, formal and informal authority and power, prestigious roles, behavioral freedom, and life sustaining requisites. While these dimensions are similar to those of other definitions, Chafetz's conceptualization covers areas that are not explicit in the other definitions, such as discretionary time and opportunities for psychic enrichment and gratification.

The theoretical guidance provided by these diverse definitions would allow the use of a great many different operational definitions of sexual inequality. Two common threads among the definitions, however, are political participation and the control or ownership of material goods as a resource for power. This is also the sort of definition used in those theories of illegitimacy that make sexual inequality an explicit factor.

Three sources of cross-cultural measures of sexual inequality in political participation and economic control are available for use in this research. These are from Whyte's exploratory study of the status of women (1978a, 1978b), Ross's study of women's political participation (1983, 1986), and Sanday's study of male dominance and female power (1981a, 1981b). Each of these presents strengths and problems, but one of Sanday's scales is the most useful. Ross's codes on women's political participation and Whyte's scales on property control and on power in kin contexts are suitable, but share a common problem. Each of these researchers coded alternate societies in the standard sample being used here, reducing sample size by half. Their measures reduce by half the number of cases for statistical analysis. Additionally, Whyte's scale of power in kin contexts is a bit too narrowly delimited. Women may have a voice in community-wide decisions encompassing several kin groups which would not be measured by that scale.

Sanday's measure of women's "economic and political power and authority" is more broadly defined and has data for all adequately described cultures in the standard sample. It contains items on both the control of production and on political organization and participation. Both dimensions are lodged in one

Guttman scale, the type of scale using the most rigorous criteria in its construction. Its shortcoming is that it does not measure women's power relative to men's power. Women's power is measured in terms of absolutes—whether women control the extradomestic distribution of goods they produce *or not*; whether women participate in political decision-making *or not*. It is not a precise indicator of the balance of power of men and women in a society, but cross-culturally compares women's access to resources for power, without reference to men's access.[3]

This shortcoming of Sanday's measure demands a validity check to see whether it is correlated with cross-cultural measures of sex *differences* in power. Both Ross and Whyte measure women's power relative to men's power in the same society. Sanday's female power scale is significantly associated with Ross's female political participation scale (gamma = +.33) and with Whyte's property control scale (gamma = +.34), but not with Whyte's power-in-kin-contexts scale. Since Whyte's two scales are not significantly associated, this last finding is no surprise. The positive correlations of Sanday's scale with the other relative measures suggests that it has considerable validity, in spite of its not being a relative measure of power.[4]

A MISSING LINK BETWEEN ILLEGITIMACY AND FEMALE POWER?

A surprising finding is seen in Table 7.1. Illegitimacy sanctions and female power are not significantly related. The most visible connection between the variables in the table concerns the repressive categories of sanctions, and whether men are sanctioned in addition to the mother or child. All cases where the illegitimate father is penalized along with the mother and child occur in societies where women have some basis in production for power—starting with level four, where women's extradomestic produce is valued, and continuing to the highest levels of female power. While not a statistically significant pattern, this is a substantively interesting one. It suggests that sanctions are more egalitarian when power is more equally shared between the sexes. This may be due to women's voice in calling for more equal punishment in some of these societies. It may stem from women's value as workers and reproducers. Men may want to see that other men who violate workers and reproducers are brought back into line.

ETHNOGRAPHIC EXAMPLES OF SANCTIONS

Examples of repressive sanctions from societies with different levels of female power suggest an interesting pattern. For societies with repressive illegitimacy sanctions, female power seems to make treatment of women and men more balanced. The Tikopia of the Pacific and the Kikyuyu are at extreme ends of the female power scale.

Table 7.1. Severity of Sanctions for Illegitimacy by Female Power

Severity of Sanction	Level of Female Economic and Political Power						
	1	2	3	4	5	6	7
Relaxed	43%	67%	20%	38%	35%	26%	25%
Restitutive	29%	33%	20%	12%	24%	33%	33%
Repressive for Mother or Child	29%	0%	60%	37%	29%	37%	33%
Repressive (Father Also Sanctioned)	0%	0%	0%	12%	12%	4%	8%
Column Total (N)	7	6	5	8	17	27	24

Note: Female power is measured as a Guttman scale: Level 1—absence of any scale traits; level 2—flexible marriage mores; level 3—women produce goods for nondomestic use; level 4—demand for female produce; level 5—women control nondomestic produce; level 6—women participate in political decision making; level 7—women are organized into all-female groups. Gamma = +.14, not significant.

Tikopia's Punishment of Women

The Tikopia, a patrilineal, patrilocal people, are one of the societies with the lowest female power scores—a score of one. Their example shows how women and children become the targets of repressive sanctions in sexually inegalitarian societies. The Tikopia are one of those Pacific island peoples whose attitudes on sex and illegitimacy seem contradictory to Westerners (Firth 1936, no. 100). They were not opposed to premarital sex, and various institutions seem to have encouraged it in the Tikopian youth subculture. Dances were opportunities to initiate intrigues and affairs. Relationships between unmarried lovers were institutionalized and called *tau manoni. Manoni* also referred to aromatic leaves or flowers used as dance ornaments. Sweethearts slept together away from their parental homes and usually had sexual intercourse. These *tau manoni* relationships were the usual route to marriage.

The Tikopia loved children and felt that "children should be born only in a house where they have both parents" (Firth 1936, no. 100). They also believed bastards to be evil. A single woman was ostracized, not for sex, and not for conception, but only if she gave birth without being married. Coitus interruptus was practiced, not always effectively, to avoid conception. The Tikopia believed that conception was caused by semen accumulating and coagulating from repeated frequent intercourse with one person. Infrequent intercourse also was thought to be a contraceptive measure because it prevented the accumulation of semen. The final decision to marry was in the hands of the sweethearts themselves, although others might try to persuade them to marry. Sometimes a person would intentionally prevent withdrawal before ejaculation in hopes of bringing about conception. This might be a bargaining chip against a partner who was reluctant to marry.

Many couples conceived before marriage but few gave birth to bastards. Premarital conception was a crisis, bringing scandal, because of the imminence of unwed birth. Some couples married to avoid ostracism. Firth (1936, no. 100: 535) describes threats and violence sometimes used to bring out the facts about paternity. An informant thought a woman whose sweetheart would not marry might tell him that her kin would slash her throat if he did not marry right away. Failing to move him in this way, suicide might be a remaining option.[5] Sometimes a pregnant woman induced abortion by having someone massage or roll hot stones on her abdomen. Others killed the newborn. Each of these were normative ways, before Christianization, of escaping an untenable situation. Secrecy was observed about the birth of a child to an unmarried women from shame at her unmarried state. No stigma was attached to the act of infanticide itself (Firth 1956-57, no. 100).

Both married and single people practiced abortion and infanticide as backup to coitus interruptus. These practices were less horrible to them than to us today because, the infant had not yet been accepted ceremonially into society and because of their different view of human life.

When the practice of infanticide by the Tikopia is correlated with their ideas of family life on the one hand and their economic situation on the other, it can be seen that they adopt a realistic point of view. To them a human life as such has no sentimental or absolute value. It is to be considered in relation to its position in terms a social structure and economic need; and for them it is preferable to remove unwanted beings immediately from the social scene rather than allow them to endure misery or by their multiplication to be a cause of misery in others. (Firth 1936, no. 100: 530-31)

This realistic point of view does not mean that mothers callously killed unwanted offspring. Firth indicates that other people made these choices and carried them out. Husbands held the right to order their wives' newborns put to death. This was always the husband's decision. First-born children of uncertain paternity, and later-born children for whom there would be no land were sometimes killed, along with illegitimate offspring. In the case of the illegitimate child, the mother's mother might put it to death. Firth quotes an informant on married women's feelings about infanticide: "The woman herself does not call for the death of the child; she has affection for it, but the feelings of the man are not good towards it" (1936, no. 100: 529). An unwed mother's affection also may have been contravened by the actions of others or by her fear of ostracism.

The weight of the system of control of illegitimacy in Tikopia falls on the child and its mother. The immediate threat of scandal, ostracism, and possible abortion or infanticide makes marriage a welcome alternative for her. Illegitimate fathers may have been persuaded or harassed into marriage in some instances, but they were not shamed as the mothers were.

The Kikuyu's More Equal Treatment

The Kikuyu of Kenya are patrilocal and patrilineal like the Tikopia but are at the opposite end of Sanday's female power scale. Their score of seven indicates that women had a voice in decision making and had their own organizations, but the Kikuyu also used repressive sanctions for illegitimacy. Kikuyu institutions allowed many unsupervised opportunities for youth, although their norms discouraged sexual intercourse (Kenyatta 1979, no. 11). Dances were one opportunity, but the institution of *ngweko*, or fondling, was more important. A special hut was used as a place for rendezvous for young men and women. This was a general recreation spot, where youth could eat, drink, and find companionship. *Ngweko* ideally involved what researchers of American dating patterns call "petting," stopping short of full sexual intercourse. The man removed all his clothes, and placed his penis back out of the way between his own thighs. The woman removed only her upper garment, protecting herself from penetration by keeping her leather skirt and apron tucked between her legs.

In this position the lovers lie together facing each other, rubbing their breasts together, whilst at the same time they engage in love-making conversation until they gradually fall asleep. Sometimes the partners experience sexual relief, but this is not an essential feature of the *ngweko*. (Kenyatta 1979, no. 11: 158)

While this looks to be too tempting a situation, these ideals were followed in most instances. Men were expected to show self-control. The peer group itself prosecuted on the complaint of a woman that a man asked her to have sex or tried to remove her garments. It was considered unclean for one partner to contact the other's genitals. Furthermore, brides were expected to be virgins, to have unruptured hymenal membranes when their marriages were consummated. Only occasionally, and after long-standing friendship, did couples break the ban on coitus and conceive a child out of wedlock.

Both the illegitimate father and the illegitimate mother received penalties, with the man's outweighing the woman's. If a man made an unwed woman pregnant, the tribal council fined him "nine sheep or goats." These were given as compensation to the woman's family, but this gave the man no rights to the child. In addition the man was fined "three big, fat sheep" for the council's fee. The women and men of the unwed father's age group would act in concert to caste him out. They made the mother give a feast for the age group and she was subject to ridicule (Kenyatta 1979, no. 11: 160). The feast is not readily characterized as a restitutive sanction nor a repressive one. It is not compensation to a specific injured party but seems to work to reintegrate the mother into the age group. The ridicule and cost of the feast are mild punishments compared to the man's cattle payments.

A turn-of-the-century description generally coincides with this recent one. It pointed out that the illegitimate mother's companions and family made a fuss and disapproved. The man would either have been forced to pay the full bride wealth and marry or to pay ten goats and one sheep (Routledge and Routledge 1910, no. 11).   If a woman would not reveal the name of the man and had a second unwed birth, then her marriage value (in terms of potential bride wealth) would decline.   The fine of nine or ten head of livestock is but a small part of the standard bride wealth.

Table 7.1 shows that women's power has no overall significant effect on the severity of sanctions.   Not surprisingly then we find similarities in the system of control of illegitimacy between the Tikopia and the Kikuyu, patrilineal, patrilocal groups at opposite ends of the female power scale.   However, we see in these case examples that women's power may make a subtle difference in societies with repressive sanctions.   It produces greater comparability of repressive sanctions for illegitimacy in that both partners are punished.   The Tikopia put the shame and stigma almost entirely on the mother and child, although the father sometimes was harassed into marrying the woman.   Among the Kikuyu, women had a share of economic and political power and were involved in enforcing sexual standards and illegitimacy norms.   The unwed father was punished along with the unwed mother.   His sanctions were both restitutive and repressive, while hers were repressive and reintegrative.

ILLEGITIMACY AND OTHER MEASURES OF SEXUAL INEQUALITY

Since the lack of an overall statistical association of reproductive controls and women's power is anomalous, the illegitimacy sanctions variable was cross-tabulated with Sanday's scale items individually and also with other available measures of sexual inequality.   This analysis gives little evidence that repressive illegitimacy sanctions stem from women's powerlessness in itself.   Only two of Sanday's scale items are significantly associated with severity of sanctions—goods produced by women for extradomestic use and demand for these goods—and both of these items are *positively* correlated with severity of sanctions.   Nor are other scales associated with illegitimacy sanctions in the expected direction.   Here are the gammas between severity of sanctions and other scales measuring sexual inequality:

Sanday's other scales:
    Male aggression +.01
    Male dominance −.18

Whyte's scales:
    Property control scale +.05
    Kin power scale +.03
    Value of life scale +.03
    Value of labor scale +.03
    Domestic authority scale +.26, pr. < .05
    Ritualized female solidarity scale +.12
    Control of sex scale −.02

Ritualized fear of women scale (Absence) $+.34$
Joint participation scale $-.28$

Ross's scales:
Female public political participation $-.14$
Female private political participation $-.04$

Among all of the available measures of sexual inequality, only one—women's relative domestic authority—is significantly related to illegitimacy sanctions.[6] It, like Sanday's two items, is related in the opposite direction from the expectation. Two other scales have sizeable, but not significant, associations with illegitimacy sanctions.

The lack of correlation of illegitimacy sanctions to female power needs to be understood in terms of women's and men's intergenerational interests. Possessing power may enable women to voice their interests in the formation of illegitimacy norms and sanctions.   However, both men's and women's intergenerational interests are affected by factors other than sex and gender. Little can be explained by sexual inequality alone. As several theories concur, the effects of sexual inequality need to be examined within the context of other structural factors that trigger intergenerational interests.

FEMALE POWER AND FRATERNAL INTEREST GROUPS

Next we look for answers to the question of how sexual inequality and other factors jointly affect reproductive controls. Paige and Paige (1981) explain repressive reproductive controls over women in patrilocal groups by arguing that men's fraternal interest organization enables them to make contracts for reproductive rights in women: the repressive controls are the *enforcement of this contract*. Their analysis is built upon a presumption of male dominance in all societies, without which the patterns they predict would not be possible. The question of whether sexual inequality may be confounding their analysis needs empirical investigation. A start in that direction is to examine the joint impact of female power and marital residence patterns on severity of illegitimacy sanctions. The Paiges' discussion of two sorts of control of reproduction in strong fraternal interest groups—through ritual surveillance (a more repressive style), or through explicit contracts assigning all a women's children to her husband (a more relaxed style)—led me to hope that women's greater power may account for this relaxation of surveillance and sanctions in one set.

Table 7.2 shows a significant interactive effect in which the empowerment of women affects severity of sanctions in opposite directions in strong and weak fraternal interest groups. Women's power makes for not less, but more repressive sanctions in strong fraternal interest groups however. While neither relationship is significant per se, the difference between them is. Another interpretation is that all of the relationship between severity of sanctions and fraternal interest organization discussed earlier[7] occurs in societies in which

Table 7.2. Percent of Societies with Repressive Illegitimacy Sanctions by Sexual Inequality and Marital Residence

Marital Residence	Female Power		Conditional Gamma
	Low % (N)	High % (N)	
Types not Aggregating Kinsmen	42% (12)	21% (19)	−.46
Patrilocal, Avunculocal	36% (31)	53% (32)	+.34
Conditional Gamma	−.13	+.62*	

* Pr. < .05.
Interaction: W^2 = 4.16, pr. < .05, for the difference between the gammas when FIG strength is controlled.

women wield power. For societies with female power, Table 7.2 shows that repressive illegitimacy sanctions are over two and one-half times as likely to occur in societies with residence rules that aggregate kinsmen as in the residual category of residence rules. In societies where women have little power, there is no association of sanctions and residence. The pattern of interaction is not what was anticipated, but adding women's power to the analysis does sharpen the predictive focus of fraternal interest group theory.

Why does fraternal interest group theory work only for societies with high female power? In the most negative interpretation, the logic of the theory is simply incorrect. It makes correct predictions but for the wrong reasons. In this interpretation, reproductive rituals and restrictions do not really stem from male competition to claim offspring. Reproductive ritual and illegitimacy sanctions are not really extensions of male politics, but some other explanation is needed. From this viewpoint, it is too simplistic and misleading to ground a theory in the idea that all men want to claim children as political and economic allies.

A second interpretation is that the theory is not altogether wrong, but needs to be extended to take into account what might be called "sororal interest groups," or groups of women whether sisters or not, who are organized and engage in regular face-to-face interaction just as fraternal interest groups do. The items in Sanday's female power scale indicate the highest levels of power are women's political participation and *women's groups*. These women's groups are of various sorts: large groups of women may be in frequent contact through food production work, marketing produce in a central marketplace, through groups organized for rituals, or in other ways. This suggests that the theory predicts illegitimacy sanctions primarily for those groups where women have strong associations, and not where they have only weak female social support networks. If this is the case, then reproductive rituals and constraints need to be understood not only in the context of male organization and power but simultaneously in the context of female organization and power. Women may be active agents in the creation of rituals and restrictions along with the men who are the focus of the theory. Men's struggle may not only be with other men as the theory emphasizes, but also with women in some societies.

EFFECTS OF FEMALE POWER AND TECHNOLOGY/POPULATION FACTORS

Most of the effects of the population and technology variables on illegitimacy sanctions noted earlier are not altered when female power is controlled. Female power neither interacts nor intervenes in the relationships of the level of subsistence economy, sedentism, or population density to severity of sanctions. Community size is the one exception to this statement. It has a significant interactive effect with female power as shown in Table 7.3. In societies with smaller communities, women's power is associated with harsher sanctions, but with larger communities, women's power appears to reduce severity of sanctions. Repressive sanctions are found in about half of the societies either with large communities and low female power or with small communities and high female power. Only about one-fourth of other societies have repressive sanctions.

Remember that community size has been the oddball among the technology-population variables. It had no zero-order association with illegitimacy sanction. Also, when the (presumed intervening) stratification and political variables were controlled, it consistently yielded partial associations larger than its zero-order associations. None of the other technology-population variables behaved this way. In interacting with sexual inequality to produce two equal but opposite effects on severity of sanctions, it continues to be intractable. It may be that

Table 7.3. **Percent of Societies with Repressive Illegitimacy Sanctions by Sexual Inequality and Community Size**

Community Size	Female Power		Conditional Gamma
	Low % (N)	High % (N)	
Small	28% (25)	51% (31)	$+.47^*$
Large	50% (18)	25% (20)	$-.50$
Conditional Gamma	$+.44$	$-.52^*$	

* Pr. < .05.

Interaction: For the difference in the gammas for large and small communities, Goodman's test of interaction is significant. $W^2 = 7.71$, pr. < .05

community size is not a mere indicator of technological and demographic development, but that it tells us about the scale of constituent moral and political units in the territorial makeup of some societies.

Modest-sized associations were reported earlier between the three hierarchy variables and illegitimacy controls. Can the predictive power of evolutionary theories be improved by considering the joint effects of stratification or political structure with sexual inequality? Table 7.4, using social stratification and female power as independent variables, suggests that it can. Only one conditional gamma is significant, but there is significant interaction in the table.[8] The impact of social stratification on sanctions is limited to those societies with high sexual inequality. Among societies in which women have more power, regardless of the level of stratification, about two-fifths of these societies employ repressive sanctions for illegitimacy. Among societies where women have little power, the more highly stratified groups are three times as likely, at 78 percent, to have repressive controls as those with less stratification.

Table 7.5 shows a similar significant interactive pattern for the relationship of political centralization and sexual inequality to reproductive controls. The hypothesis of rising severity of sanctions with political development holds only for societies in which women have little political input. When women have little input, societies with central governments are nearly three times as likely as acephalous groups to have repressive sanctions. Among societies where women are more involved in the political process, centralized states are slightly less likely than stateless societies to have repressive controls of illegitimacy. If we look at the table from another angle, we see that women's power significantly contributes to the severity of sanctions in stateless societies, but in centralized states, women's power is a pressure toward more relaxed sanctions.

The same type of significant interaction pattern is seen again, and more strongly, in the relationship of female power and police organization on illegitimacy controls (See Table 7.6). Fully three-quarters of policed societies

Table 7.4. Percent of Societies with Repressive Illegitimacy Sanctions by Sexual Inequality and Level of Social Stratification

Social Stratification	Female Power		Conditional Gamma
	Low % (N)	High % (N)	
Egalitarian or One Division	26% (34)	42% (33)	+.34
More Complex	78% (9)	39% (18)	−.69
Conditional Gamma	+.81*	−.07	

* Pr. < .05.

Interaction: Goodman's W^2 = 7.07, pr. < .05, showing a significant difference between gammas for societies with low female power and with high female power.

Table 7.5. Percent of Societies with Repressive Illegitimacy Sanctions by Sexual Inequality and Political Centralization

Political Centralization	Female Power		Conditional Gamma
	Low % (N)	High % (N)	
Stateless	21% (24)	48% (23)	+.55*
Central Polity	58% (19)	36% (28)	−.42
Conditional Gamma	+.68*	−.25	

* Pr. < .05.
Interaction: $W^2 = 8.38$, pr. < .05, showing a significant difference between gammas for societies with low female power and with high female power.

in which women have little power have repressive controls, nearly double the proportion in societies where women have more power, and over three times greater than societies with low female power and no standing police organization. Three of the four conditional gammas in Table 7.6 are significant. The gammas at the right show that female power actually has significant relationships to severity of sanctions that are in opposite directions from each other, depending on the presence or absence of a standing police force.

EXAMPLES OF THE HIERARCHY-FEMALE POWER INTERACTION

Female power is found to interact with each of the three measures of hierarchy in similar ways. Community size has the same sort of interactive pattern, confirming my suggestion that it is more a measure of the scope of political-moral communities than of demographic development per se. Having firmly established this statistical effect, some elaboration on particular cases can help answer further questions about it. In this interaction, do high and low female power produce the same kinds of relaxed and restitutive control mechanisms, or are there observable differences between them? I will use the interaction of political centralization with female power to answer this question.

Of the nineteen stateless societies with low female power and lacking repressive reproductive controls, thirteen treat illegitimacy in a relaxed rather than a restitutive way. Five of these betroth or marry women off before sexual maturity or have rules specifying that the husband take any offspring existing at the time of marriage. A few of these societies differ in that illegitimate fathers are forced to make restitution by marrying the mother.

The Lolo, an ethnic group in China, provide an example of the first pattern. Young Lolo women and men were free to love and have sexual relations within the limits set by clan exogamy and caste endogamy. Marriage ages for females

Table 7.6. Percent of Societies with Repressive Illegitimacy Sanctions by Sexual Inequality and Presence of Police

Presence of Police	Female Power		Conditional Gamma
	Low % (N)	High % (N)	
Absent	23% (30)	44% (32)	+.44*
Present	75% (12)	35% (17)	−.69*
Conditional Gamma	+.82*	−.18	

* Pr. < .05.
Interaction: $W^2 = 20.46$, pr. < .05.

varied from nine to nineteen, with a preference on odd-numbered years. Ordinarily, a woman changed her hairstyle from a single braid to double rolled braids at the time of marriage to signify her change in status. If she did not marry early, her parents held a public ceremony and braided her hair. This braiding ceremony denoted that she had come of age and could have sexual freedom. Marriage was a complicated process, with parents usually making the selection and a matchmaker doing the negotiating. There was also a preference for marrying cross-cousins. On betrothal bride wealth was agreed upon and was paid in silver, although livestock or other goods might be substituted for the later installments. After the wedding the spouses remained with their families of orientation for the *tao-chi* period (meaning "staying home") for one to five years. During this time the bride was free to have sex with the groom and with other men. Lin gives a vivid description of sex and procreation during the *tao-chi* period.

Day and night she chases and plays around with the young men of the neighborhood or her male cross-cousins. She, too, enjoys sexual freedom. During the same period the groom can also contact the bride and make love. It is only when the bride become pregnant that the groom takes her to his father's house. The first child usually is not the child of the groom, but he has to recognize it as his child. (Lin 1961, no. 67: 81)

Presumably that minority of women who had braiding ceremonies without marrying at the time had the same right of legitimizing offspring when they did eventually marry. If so, the combination of early marriage and the imprecise link of biological and social fatherhood effectively managed the problem of illegitimacy for the Lolo.

An extreme case of early marriage, and one that grates against the American definition of child sexual abuse, is provided by the Shavante of South America. Maybury-Lewis (1967, no. 179) tells us that Shavante teenage males married infant and toddler girls, but without immediate cohabitation. Sometime after the wife reached five years of age, sexual visits began. Girls were usually deflowered by their husbands by the time they reached age eight or ten, without apparent trauma, according to the ethnographer. Later on the husband and wife established a home together.

The eighteen centralized states with high female power that lack repressive controls have a somewhat different pattern. Instead of emphasizing relaxed mechanisms, eleven have primarily restitutive sanctions for illegitimacy. Seven of these—mostly in Africa—require fines, child support, or partial payment of bride wealth. In most of these groups, a hasty marriage is an option, but there is no strong pressure to marry and there is typically little shame attached to illegitimacy. In other societies, the illegitimate child is merely incorporated into the mother's home. In a few societies of this sort, restitution is made by the father through the mechanism of enforced marriage.

The matrilineal Ashanti ideal was that the genitor and pater be the same person, and illegitimate fathers were pressed to acknowledge paternity. No disgrace followed nonmarital birth, so long as the mother had passed her puberty rituals, had not been promiscuous, and the man acknowledged paternity. The acknowledged illegitimate child had full rights in his father's group, but carried a stigma. Fortes (1950, no. 19) points out that *acknowledging* one's bastard included more than mere speech. It meant that the father maintained the mother during her pregnancy, that he gave the customary gifts at delivery that a husband would give to a wife, and that he named the child in a ceremony on the eighth day after its birth, thereby passing on his *ntoro* (spirit, soul, or personality) to the child. Christensen (1954, no. 19) adds that the father had to support the child. In either case, the illegitimate father is under a strain to make recompense. However, if the genitor would not marry the mother nor acknowledge the child, then another man who married the mother would legitimate and claim her bastard child by paying bride wealth.

The Shilluk of Africa used bride wealth to legitimate reproduction in a more relaxed way. Their name for bastard was *okeijo*, meaning "child for whom no bride wealth is paid" (Howell 1953, no. 31: 104). "The position of children born out of wedlock shows the importance of the bride wealth in establishing sociological fatherhood, physiological fatherhood having no legal importance" (Seligman and Seligman 1932, no. 31: 68). If a woman had one illegitimate child, it belonged to the man who gave her father bride wealth. If she had more than one child, they belonged to her own father and became members of his lineage. The father gained two lineage members, but he was not able to get as much bride wealth for his daughter should she eventually marry. Other than this reduction of bride wealth for repeated illegitimacy, the descriptions of the Shilluk system of control do not mention any shame or loss of rights or status for the illegitimate father, mother, or child. There is no mention of the genitor having been forced to make bride wealth payments. Illegitimate fathers apparently had no more obligation and no more claim to their offspring than strangers would have had.

This Shilluk concept of bride wealth as legitimating mechanism was also applied in divorce (Howell 1953, no. 31). The bride wealth was returned in whole or in part on divorce. If a couple divorced after having children, the man could demand return of the cattle only after deducting five head for each girl and two head for each boy.[9] Otherwise, the children became legitimate members of the wife's lineage if the full bride wealth was returned. As noted in Chapter 5, these particular uses of bride wealth dissociate biological and social fatherhood for some proportion of the offspring of a society.

These cases clarify the interaction of female power and societal hierarchy by contrasting the nonrepressive mechanisms in stateless, low female-power societies and in centralized, high female-power situations. The difference is that one set uses predominantly relaxed mechanisms, the other predominantly restitutive. Low female power in stateless societies tends to produce early marriage and other relaxed mechanisms. High female power in centralized societies in contrast tends to occur more in Africa and more often results in men's being coerced to make compensation for illicit reproduction, either through payments or through marriage.

CONCLUSION ON HIERARCHY AND FEMALE POWER

Sexual inequality is a key factor in understanding the conditions under which hierarchical structures promote repressive reproductive controls. Women's power *buffers* the effects of other hierarchical factors, such as centralization, police organization, and stratification. The tendency of hierarchy to produce repressive sanctions occurs almost entirely in those societies with little power for women. Societies in which women have power have an intermediate likelihood of having repressive sanctions. This is a pattern that is predictable from some theories such as Engels, Goode, Collins, and Lancaster and Lancaster. Each of these sees sexual inequality as a necessary condition for the formation of repressive sexual and reproductive controls.

These theories of illegitimacy organized around technological and political development have not adequately grasped the cross-cultural variation in women's power and the way it covaries with other factors. Female power is somewhat correlated with other forms of social hierarchy, but being independent of these other forms to a degree, it interacts powerfully with other measures of hierarchy to relax or restrict reproductive controls. Theories like those of Engels, Goode, Collins, and the Lancasters can easily be revised to take the buffering pattern into account, since they tend to assume that sexual inequality is a necessary factor for repressive sanctions.

A problem for theory is a second part of the buffering effect of women's power. The buffer on the effect of hierarchy works in both directions: among less hierarchical societies, greater female power contributes to more repressive systems of illegitimacy control. These research findings go counter to the direction of relationships posed in the theories. Existing theories may need revision to be able to account for this part of the pattern. Women's power increases their input into norm formation, and thereby affects the mix of intergenerational interests that give rise to illegitimacy sanctions. Theoretical understanding may advance if we attend to the interplay of intergenerational interests in different structural contexts.

NOTES

1. Some suggest that the situation may have been different among indigenous groups before contact with westerners (Sacks 1979) or in prehistoric times (Sanday 1981a). See Hendrix (1994) for a discussion of this as an overly specific false consensus that promotes scholarly solidarity and helps to set a research agenda.

2. The disagreement on definition and measurement suggests a problem about the consensus on the range of variation, namely that it is a false consensus.

3. If one views power as a zero-sum game, then relative and absolute measures of women's power in a society would be identical. When other aspects of inequality are measured however, this is not true. We cannot speak of control of women's sexuality as a sign of inequality unless we also know the extent to which men's sexuality is also controlled. Sanday's scale measures resources for power in terms of control of resources or access to them. It measures women's resources only, without reference to men's resources. Women may control some extradomestic goods, but we do not know how much of a power resource this is until we also know the amount and kinds of extradomestic goods men control. Nonetheless, we should expect some correlation between an absolute measure of women's resources for power and relative measures.

4. The lowest four categories of Sanday's scale are collapsed together for this analysis. It should be mentioned that the magnitude of association of Sanday's female power measure with Ross's scale fluctuates considerably, depending on whether hers is collapsed into a dichotomy (gamma = +.74) or not collapsed at all (gamma = +.32). The Whyte and Ross scales cannot be compared in an exactly comparable way because their data sets have so few cases in common. While each researcher coded every other society in the Standard Cross-Cultural Sample, one did odd numbered cases, the other, even. Ross replaced societies with inadequate description with adjacent cases from the sample, and this procedure produced 22 cases in common between the two data sets. Here are the associations between their scales, based on these few cases. Ross' measure, like Sanday's, is correlated with Whyte's property control scale (gamma = +.60), but less so with his power in kin contexts scale (gamma = +.25, pr. > .05). The three scales with the highest intercorrelation would seem to be the most valid measures of power inequalities between the sexes.

5. One Christianized man wrongly accused of bastardy put out to sea in a canoe in an unsuccessful suicide attempt (Firth 1936 no. 100: 535-536). Firth points out that this man did not want to marry the woman, but the mission teacher overcame his resistance. His kin and the woman's former husband were opposed to the match. His attempted suicide was apparently brought on by these cross-pressures between missionary teachings and indigenous culture and is an atypical response.

6. This scale is not considered as a primary measure of sexual inequality because it is limited in scope to nuclear family relationships. It is made up of three items concerning who has authority over infants, who has authority over children, and whether

husbands have authority over wives. Additionally, it is negatively correlated with other measures of female status (Whyte 1978b).

7. The conditional gamma of = .62 compares with a zero-order gamma of + .32 for severity of sanctions by marital residence with each variable dichotomized and with the cases occurring in Table 7.6 (there is missing data on the female power variable).

8. Another analysis shows that when societies are classified into egalitarian (no classes, castes, slavery, or wealth distinctions) versus those with some stratification, the interaction effect is not statistically significant. The watershed is not with the development of some inequality, but with more complex forms involving at least three levels.

9. A girl was worth 150 percent more cattle than a boy was. One's immediate impression of this is that women must have been highly valued in Shilluk society. Then one's feminist side recalls that men were exchanging cattle for sexual and reproductive rights in women in the bride wealth system. Females were surely being treated as objects. Then again one looks to Sanday's rating of Shilluk women as having the highest score on the female power scale. They participate in politics and are organized into groups, ready for mobilization. This convoluted situation tells us, among other things, that bride wealth systems should not be treated as a mere symptom of men's domination of women. Several of these societies in with high female power and restitutive sanctions *on men* have bride wealth systems. Overall, the presence and type of exchange at marriage are significantly correlated neither with sexual inequality nor with severity of illegitimacy sanctions.

8

Illegitimacy and Parent-Child Ties

This chapter examines the question of how socio-emotional closeness of parents to children combines with other factors to affect illegitimacy sanctions. Malinowski speculated that bonding of parents and children underpins the universal aspect of the principle of legitimacy. Since Malinowski viewed parent-child bonding as a universal constant, he could not conjecture on how it covaries with sanctions in the way he did for economic interests in children. Draper and her associates more recently have substituted the idea of a sensitive learning period in early childhood in which children acquire reproductive strategies. These strategies respond to the variable of the father's closeness or absence. As I argued in Chapter 3, the father-absent strategy should be linked to a more relaxed treatment of illegitimacy.

THEORY AND MEASURES

Malinowski's ideas can be briefly recapitulated: societies require child care and socialization for their survival. While mothers need little social enhancement of their biological urges for child care to guarantee their part in child care and socialization, fathers have a weak biological bond and need an extra push. Either positive inducements or negative sanctions give men this extra push to enact the father role in the family.

Malinowski's insistence on biological constants is problematic, both in the sense of their being "biological" and in the sense of their being invariant. It is not possible with ethnographic data to separate out the biologically induced part of an attachment from the socially induced part.[1] Empirically, we must simply deal with socio-emotional closeness as seen through behavior regardless of its sources.

Malinowski's treatment of the intrinsic bonding of parents to children as a cross-cultural constant also needs to be modified. The closeness of parents and children varies a great deal across cultures. We can examine Malinowski's reasoning by testing whether these closer or more distant bonds between parent and offspring do impact on illegitimacy control systems.

Do close parent-child ties lead to more or less severe sanctions for illegitimacy? Does father-child closeness, the object of Malinowski's and Draper's theories, have the same effect as other intergenerational ties? Does parent-child closeness specify the other factors on illegitimacy control systems? The last question is the most directly relevant to Malinowski's theory. It translates his view of father-infant bonding as a necessary but not sufficient constant factor underlying illegitimacy control systems into a question of interactive association between measurable variables. Since the focus of this chapter is primarily on interactive relationships, no tables will be presented for zero-order and partial gammas, as previous chapters have done. These will be mentioned where appropriate however.

Several published measures of parent-child ties, useful in answering these questions, are available from the Standard Cross-Cultural Sample. Three are used here in dichotomous form. Barry and Paxson's (1971) ratings on the role of the father in infancy and on the role of the father in early childhood are two. Sometimes called "father proximity," each of these ratings combines the physical proximity and presence of the father with his offspring in its early years. The third measure is derived from codes on affection toward children. Barry et al. (1977) published four separate codes for affection toward younger girls, toward older girls, toward younger boys, and toward older boys. These four codes are combined by summation here for the sake of simplicity. This is a measure of affection from adults in general (but most likely from parents and kin) toward children in general.[2] Whereas this code concerns ethnographer statements on affection and emotional closeness to children, the father proximity codes concern statements on whether the father and child are often together in the same social situations. Proximity may be correlated with father-affection, but is not in and of itself a measure of emotional closeness. Thus, the codes differ in terms of dealing with sentiment or behavior; in terms of age status of the child and in reference to the father specifically or to adults in general.

First, the relationships of the parent-child variables to illegitimacy sanctions will be shown. This will be followed by a discussion of the joint effects of parent-child closeness and hierarchy variables.

EFFECTS OF PARENT-CHILD TIES

The impact of parent-child closeness on illegitimacy is more contorted than expected, having both positive and negative effects on the severity of sanctions. General affection toward children makes for more severe sanctions (gamma = +.30), but father-infant proximity is associated with more relaxed handling of illegitimacy (gamma = −.28). The father's relationship with children past infancy is not significantly related to sanctions. Table 8.1 shows joint effects of these variables with sanctions for illegitimacy. There are no significant interaction effects, and the two variables with significant zero-order relationships retain their opposite associations with severity of sanctions when the other is controlled.[3] This suggests that sentiment of adults toward children and the father's involvement with the child affect illegitimacy sanctions independently. Malinowski was not off the mark according to these findings, but the real test is whether there are any statistical interaction effects of father-child relations with social structural factors.

This table shows mixed results for the hypotheses from Draper's theory. The association of illegitimacy sanctions with father-infant proximity is opposite to the prediction that illegitimacy sanctions would be more punitive when fathers are more involved with infants and children. However, father-*child* proximity—which may be equally relevant to Draper's theory—shows a nonsignificant association with illegitimacy sanctions in the predicted direction. Parenthetically, most of the other factors said to precipitate father absence in Draper's theory are not significantly related to illegitimacy sanctions. These include husband-wife sleeping arrangements, male aggression, warfare and nonparental caretakers.

THE INTERACTION OF FATHER-PROXIMITY AND SOCIAL STRUCTURE

In this section, we will take a look at the interaction effects of father-child ties with social structural factors on illegitimacy control systems. Since population and technology factors were found largely to impact on sanctions through the intervening variables of hierarchy and centralization, the former conditions are not examined here. The variables examined for possible interactions with parent-child relationships are the following: social stratification, political centralization, police organization, female power, and marital residence.

First, the variable affection toward children does not appear to interact or intervene in the relationships of these structural factors with illegitimacy sanctions. When affection toward children was held constant, the partial gammas were close in magnitude to the zero-order gammas. Four of the five pairs of conditional gammas were of like direction. Female power was the exception, but even here no significant interaction effect was found.

All of the interaction effects involve the two father-proximity variables. These interaction effects of the two variables have some similarity because the variables are highly correlated. The difference in proximity between the two stages is that in many societies, proximity rises as the infancy stage gives way to childhood. Infant care is usually left to the mother, other women, or siblings of the infant, making father-infant proximity a highly skewed variable. Father-child proximity is somewhat more symmetrically distributed cross-culturally.

Table 8.1. Severity of Sanctions for Illegitimacy by Affection Toward Children, Father-Infant Proximity, and Father-Child Proximity

| | Affection Toward Children | | | | | | Conditional Gamma |
| | Low Affection | | | High Affection | | | |
	Relax.	Rest.	Repr.	Relax.	Rest.	Repr.	
Father-Infant Proximity							
Distant	40%	37%	23%	29%	19%	52%	+.37* (61)
Close	67%	11%	22%	36%	32%	31%	+.41 (31)
Conditional Gamma	-.33 (39)			-.26 (53)			
Father-Child Proximity							
Distant	38%	42%	21%	58%	17%	25%	-.21 (36)
Close	39%	17%	44%	36%	32%	31%	+.06 (56)
Conditional Gamma	+.20 (42)			+.43* (50)			

* Pr. < .05.

Note: Row percentages of subtables total to 100% except for rounding error.

Illegitimacy Controls and Social Hierarchy

Five measures of power structure are police organization, political centralization, level of stratification, marital residence (as an indicator of fraternal interest groups), and female power. All of these variables except police organization showed an interactive effect with one or the other father-proximity variable on illegitimacy sanctions. Part of the reason for a lack of significant interaction between father proximity and police organization may be that each of these variables has a considerable number of cases with no data. Altogether, ten tests yielded seven significant interactions.

Earlier, it was noted that political centralization is associated with more repressive sanctions for illegitimacy. This association occurs only in societies with close father-infant proximity and not in those with more distance between father and infant. Table 8.2 reveals that repressive illegitimacy sanctions are least likely in stateless societies with close father-infant ties and most likely in states with close father-infant ties. There is almost a 50 percent difference in the frequency of occurrence of repressive sanctions between these two categories. Centralized and acephalous societies with less contact between father and infant are intermediate in their propensity to evolve repressive sanctions. Parenthetically, a significant interactive relationship resembling that in Table 8.2 was found when *father-child* proximity was held constant.[4] This finding strengthens the interpretation that father closeness helps to alter the substantive impact of political organization on illegitimacy control systems.

Table 8.3 shows an interactive relationship of the level of stratification and father-infant proximity on repressive sanctions. The pattern of interaction is remarkably like that of the previous table. The level of stratification is significantly related to repressive illegitimacy sanctions only when there is high father-infant proximity. Among societies with father proximity, those with more

Table 8.2. Percent of Societies with Repressive Sanctions for Illegitimacy by Father-Infant Proximity and Political Centralization

Political Centralization	Percent with Repressive Sanctions		Conditional Gamma
	Father-Infant Distant % (N)	Father-Infant Close % (N)	
Stateless	44% (36)	13% (23)	$-.68^*$
Centralized State	37% (38)	60% (10)	$+.44$
Conditional Gamma	$-.16$	$+.81^*$	

* Pr. < .05.

Interaction: The two gammas for the relationships of sanctions to political centralization controlling for father-infant proximity ($-.16$ and $+.81$) are significantly different, with Goodman's $W^2 + 12.61$, pr. < .05.

Table 8.3. Percent of Societies with Repressive Sanctions for Illegitimacy by Father-Infant Proximity and Level of Stratification

Level of Stratification	Percent with Repressive Sanctions		
	Father-Infant Distant % (N)	Father-Infant Close % (N)	Conditional Gamma
Egalitarian or One Division	43% (44)	12% (24)	− .68*
More Complex	37% (30)	67% (9)	+.55
Conditional Gamma	− .14	+.87*	

* Pr. < .05.

Interaction: The two gammas for sanctions by stratification (−.14 and +.87) differ
   significantly, with $W^2 = 14.23$, pr. < .05.

complex stratification systems are 55 percent more likely to have repressive illegitimacy sanctions than those with simple stratification. Undoubtedly the close correlation of these dichotomous measures of stratification and political centralization account for the similarity of Tables 8.2 and 8.3. The proximity of the father to older children shows a similar significant pattern of interaction.[5]

Marital residence, used here as an indicator of fraternal interest group organization, is also more associated with severe sanctions when father and infant are together more, as shown in Table 8.4. About two-thirds of societies with fraternal interest groups have restitutive or repressive sanctions, regardless of father-infant proximity. The same is true for father-distant groups without fraternal interest groups. Societies in which fathers and infants are together more, but without fraternal interest groups, tend to have a different type of illegitimacy control system. Only one-third of these societies have the more severe illegitimacy sanctions. To translate this into causal terms, either distant father-infant ties or fraternal interest groups tend to result in restitutive or repressive illegitimacy sanctions. Close father-infant proximity in societies with weak fraternal interest groups tend to result in relaxed mechanisms for handling illegitimacy. A somewhat similar interaction was found when the proximity of the father to older children was examined.[6]

Female power is found to interact with father-child proximity, but not with father-infant proximity, in its impact on illegitimacy sanctions. Table 8.5 shows how female power makes for milder sanctions when father and child are distant (gamma = −.55), but for more severe sanctions with father-child closeness (gamma = +.56).[7] To compare the impact of sexual inequality on illegitimacy with that of other forms of hierarchy, we need to consider that female power is not a straightforward measure of hierarchy. Rather, female power is likely to

Table 8.4. Percent of Societies with Restitutive or Repressive Sanctions for Illegitimacy by Father-Infant Proximity and Marital Residence

Marital Residence	Percent with Repressive Sanctions		
	Father-Infant Distant % (N)	Father-Infant Close % (N)	Conditional Gamma
Types Dispersing Kinsmen	71% (21)	32% (15)	$-.68^*$
Patrilocal, Avunculocal	66% (53)	67% (18)	$+.01$
Conditional Gamma	$-.12$	$+.60^*$	

* Pr. < .05.

Interaction: The gammas of $-.12$ and $+.60$ for sanctions by father-infant proximity differ significantly, with $W^2 = 3.95$, pr. < .05.

indicate restricted male authority. The range of variation in sexual inequality is commonly taken to be from extreme male dominance to equalitarian relations (Whyte 1978a). If men's authority is tempered to a large extent by female power, then those societies with high female power are more egalitarian. While stratification and political centralization, together with father proximity, make for more severe sanctions, sexual inequality has the opposite effect. It makes for milder sanctions in the presence of father proximity. There may be something about the penetration of sexual inequality into the family that makes its effect on sanctions different. Families and lineages may be the units of stratification systems or the units that are regulated by a central political authority. Sexual inequality exists in this broader, extra-domestic sphere, but is also a part of interaction within families and kin groups.

The findings of this chapter help to extend and specify several theories and hypotheses on illegitimacy. Theories predicting that hierarchy and centralization in society are accompanied by severe illegitimacy sanctions are better supported for those societies wherein fathers are close to their offspring. Societies with distant ties of fathers and offspring tend to show little or no relationship between hierarchy and seriousness of illegitimacy. Sexual inequality is an exception to this, for there the findings do show severe sanctions occurring in more egalitarian societies in which fathers are less involved with infants. The findings of this chapter also specify fraternal interest group theory. FIG theory accounts for illegitimacy sanctions better for societies where fathers are close to their infants and children.

Predictions from Draper's theory on the acquisition of reproductive strategies do not fare well. For the sample as a whole, more punitive treatment of illegitimacy is found with close father-infant ties, not distant ones as predicted.

Table 8.5. Percent of Societies with Repressive Sanctions for Illegitimacy by Father-Child Proximity and Female Power

Female Power	Percent with Repressive Sanctions		Conditional Gamma
	Father-Child Distant % (N)	Father-Child Close % (N)	
Low	47% (21)	22% (18)	−.52
High	21% (19)	50% (28)	+.58*
Conditional Gamma	−.55	+.56*	

* Pr. < .05.
Interaction: The gammas for sanctions by female power differ significantly between societies with high and low father-child closeness. $W^2 = 10.30$, pr. <.05.

Nonetheless, the association between general affection toward children and more severe sanctions may offer support for her recent "stress" interpretation of father-absence (Draper and Belsky 1990; Belsky, Steinberg, and Draper 1991). The interaction effects involving father-offspring ties suggest that a specification is need for the father-absence hypothesis. It works better for societies with central states, with complex stratification, and with high female power. In stateless, in less stratified, and in sexually inegalitarian societies, father-absence seems to promote stronger sanctions rather than weaker ones. The theory may need modification to take these factors into account.

MALINOWSKI'S PUZZLE OF TROBRIAND ILLEGITIMACY SANCTIONS

These findings may help to unravel Malinowski's conundrum of why the Trobriand Island society stigmatizes illegitimacy. Although the Trobriand Islanders saw no biological link between the father and child and fully approved premarital sex, they disapproved of premarital conception and birth. Because of their belief in impregnation by spirit, the Trobrianders did not blame the father for nonmarital pregnancy, but the mother was blameworthy in spite of this theory. While there was pity for the "fatherless" child, the mother lost status and became virtually unmarriageable. By placing the Trobriand Island social structure in the context of the causal relationships tested in this chapter, we may be able to better understand the severity of their control system. First, let's sum up these findings briefly. Malinowski's principle of legitimacy led me to speculate that the bonding patterns of fathers and offspring would interact with features of social structure to impact on illegitimacy norms. The positive relationships of severity of sanctions to fraternal interest groups and hierarchical structures, excepting sexual inequality, are enhanced by father-infant and father-child closeness. Sexual inequality is related to milder sanctions with father-child proximity and harsher ones with father-child distance. The associations are opposite in direction from that of other hierarchical structures.

Trobriand Social Structure

Malinowski described a paramount chief who "owned" all the lands of the Trobriands. He made it clear that ownership is a complex and layered phenomenon with different groups and individuals being able to say they "owned" a given piece of land. Nonetheless, the highly respected chief is unable to collect taxes, compel participation in warfare, and the like. Thus, the Trobriand Islanders are coded in the standard sample as being stateless and without sovereignty being lodged in a political hierarchy. The low degree of political centralization does not contribute to the Trobriands' repressive sanctions for illegitimacy.

The Trobriands have only a moderate level of stratification with only two classes and no slavery. They do not have an aristocratic set of lineages, nor are they socially egalitarian, so social classes are not the factor. It seems that we must look toward men's and women's economic and political organization to solve Malinowski's puzzle.

While Malinowski describes the marital residence rule in the Trobriands as "patrilocal," it is more suitably put into the "avunculocal" category. It is true that wives reside in the husband's village with the husband's kin. However, men, after reaching puberty, are expected to move to their maternal uncle's village. Hence, marital residence is in the village of the husband's maternal uncle. Avunculocal residence aggregates matrilineal kinsmen in the same fashion that patrilocal residence aggregates patrilineal kinsmen: it puts successive generations of male descent group members in the same locale.

Malinowski described the autonomy of Trobriand women. Husbands have little or control over their wives, although women remain under the authority of their matrilineal kinsmen after marriage. Since a man's "sister" usually lives in a different village with her husband and children, male kin are not in constant contact with women members of the clan. On Sanday's female power scale, Trobriand women get the very highest rating, indicating that they have some voice in political decision-making and are organized into female groups. Hence, both men and women have groups through which they can organize for political action, and women have considerable power based on their productive activities.

As mentioned earlier, Trobriand fathers are very much involved in infant and child care and very affectionate toward their offspring. It is the combination of this closeness with female power and organization on the one hand and male organization on the other that can account for the extreme stigma placed on mothers of illegitimate children in the Trobriand Islands. This chapter's findings show that Malinowski was looking in the right direction. The key to his conundrum concerning illegitimacy in the Trobriands is in the linking of family relationships with larger social structures.

NOTES

1. There is of course not a concrete part of any complex behavior that is biological and a concrete part that is social or environmental. There are no purely biological behaviors. People using this sort of language may have in mind the proportions of variance in a type of behavior explained by biological factors and by social factors. Human sociobiologists insist that behavior is always the result of the *interaction* of the individual's biology and environmental factors (van den Berghe 1979) where each constitutes a necessary but not sufficient cause of the behavior. From a longer evolutionary perspective, the individual's biology itself is seen as having coevolved along with prehistoric culture (Parker and Parker 1979), with culture and biology affecting each other. Hence, our biology today may be in part a product of the early social environment to which we adapted. These notions lead us to the interesting view that contemporary behavior is the interactive product of social and biological factors, with the social and biological having previously influenced each other. If we take this view seriously, it becomes an arduous task to separate the social from the biological in contemporary behavior.

2. Codes specifically on parent-child acceptance or rejection are available (Rohner and Rohner 1981). Although these codes could be useful, they have more missing data than the ones selected.

3. The partial gammas for severity of sanctions by affection toward children are $+.38$ and $+.32$ when father-infant proximity and father-child proximity respectively are controlled. With affection held constant, the partial gamma for father-infant proximity remains at $-.28$, and father-child proximity remains unrelated to sanction severity. All three independent variables are dichotomized for calculation of these coefficients.

4. When father-*child* proximity is controlled and severity of sanctions is dichotomized into "relaxed" versus "more severe" categories, the gammas for sanction severity by political organization are $-.04$ for societies with distant father-child relations, and $+.77$ for those with high father-child proximity, with $W^2 = 5.49$, pr. $< .05$.

5. With father-*child* proximity controlled and illegitimacy sanctions collapsed into "relaxed" and "more severe" categories, the difference between the two gammas for sanctions by stratification ($+.02$ for distant father; $+.77$ for close father) is significant at the .05 level, with $W^2 = 4.91$.

6. The gammas for sanctions by marital residence when father-child proximity is distant or close are $-.28$ and $+.49$ respectively, with the latter gamma being significantly different from zero. Additionally there is a significant interaction effect of marital residence with father-*child* proximity on illegitimacy sanctions, collapsed as relaxed versus other: $W^2 = 3.32$, pr. $> .05$. Unlike the pattern in Table 8.4, more severe sanctions are likely either in the absence of both variables or in the presence of both, but less likely when one is present and one is absent.

7. The comparable W^2 coefficient for sanctions by female power with father-*child* proximity controlled is not significant. This is partly due to missing data, bringing the total cases in the computations down to 87. Additionally, the gammas are simply not as strong ($-.18$ for father-distant societies and $+.52$ for father-close societies).

9

Social Structures and Principles of Legitimacy

I have examined theories of illegitimacy from the past century and derived and tested hypotheses from them. My tests are extensive but not exhaustive. They are limited to hypotheses concerning the severity of illegitimacy sanctions and to independent variables published for the Standard Cross-Cultural Sample. The findings do not support one theory over others. Instead they suggest that most every theory has some piece of the total picture. In this chapter I suggest that we need a composite of past theories, and summarize my findings within this framework.

A COMPOSITE FRAMEWORK ON ILLEGITIMACY

The principle of legitimacy is universal, but highly variable. It is universal because birth and death raise too many issues to go unregulated in any society. The principle varies because the issues raised by birth and death vary from one society to another—and from one interest group within society to another—depending on social structure. A society's structure triggers or enables expression of a particular constellation of intergenerational interests, which in turn molds the definition and sanctions for illegitimate birth. The structures of family and kinship and the structures of power and of sentiment within a society are important in triggering intergenerational interests. Structures of power are also important in enabling differential expression of these interests for different groupings.

Figure 9.1 portrays the set of social structures that trigger or enable expression to intergenerational interests within a society, which in turn shape the society's values and norms for illegitimacy. In the theoretical chapters, each theory was seen to be grounded in its own underlying intergenerational interest and stage of the life cycle. Only a few theories these interest or motives in a pluralistic way. The composite model points out that the theories are not so much wrong as that each is a partial view of a complex reality.

MULTIPLE INTERGENERATIONAL INTERESTS

One part of the framework for understanding illegitimacy is the idea of intergenerational interests. These interests of adults in offspring, and of offspring in adults, mold a society's definition and sanctions for illegitimacy. More specifically we may view a society coming to adapt a certain principle of legitimacy because diverse agents create it. Different individuals and groups within a society may have different intergenerational interests, including conflicting ones. Variation in the handling of illegitimacy comes about from the different mixes of motives and life-cycle problems that are activated in different societies and in different subgroups, with some agents having more impact on illegitimacy definitions and sanctions. These intergenerational interests teased out of these theories are:

—a concern among adult men for passing on their wealth to their biological offspring by their wives (Engels 1972).
—a widespread moral concern that the membership of society be replaced in an orderly manner stemming from a value (ethnocentrism) of the culture itself (Davis 1939a, 1939b)
—a concern for all children generalized from one's bonds to one's own children (Malinowski 1930).
—a male concern to claim offspring as economic and political allies (Malinowski 1930; Paige and Paige 1981).
—a male concern to reduce alienation from reproduction (O'Brien 1981).
—a concern in the upper classes of stratified societies that family status be maintained (Goode 1960). Related to this is the idea developed from the research findings that extended families may give rise to similar concerns that a valued group (the permanent family) be perpetuated.
—a concern on the part of the younger generation to acquire the prestige, wealth and possessions, and the offices of elders or the deceased. I mentioned this in Chapter 3 as a neglected basis for theory.

Offsetting these intergenerational interests are other motives that lead men to avoid claims of some offspring upon them. Sociobiologists distinguish between the "cad" and the "dad" reproductive strategies that men may use (Hewlett 1992). Men may employ the cad strategy and invest little or nothing in some offspring, perhaps while claiming and investing in other offspring by other women with the "dad" strategy. These avoidance motives often result in double standards in sexual and reproductive conduct.

FINDINGS ON INTERGENERATIONAL SENTIMENT

Both Engels and Malinowski presumed that illegitimacy norms are grounded in an affectionate bond between father and child. Although the chapter on parent-child ties is more exploratory than others, it shows the importance of explicitly measuring intergenerational interests as variables. I examine two indicators of affective intergenerational interests—general affection toward children, and father-infant proximity—to find whether they are related to illegitimacy sanctions and under what conditions they are related.

On the one hand, societies in which adults hold affection toward children tend to have *more* severe handling of illegitimacy. This indicator of intergenerational affection does not specify the effects of other variables or intervene in any way with the hierarchy variables, sexual inequality, or other variables of this study. Affection for children impacts on illegitimacy sanctions in a way that is completely separate from structural factors.

On the other hand, societies in which fathers are close to their own infants and children tend to have *less* severe sanctions. This finding specifically goes against hypotheses derived from Draper's biosocial theory of father-absence and reproductive strategy. Additionally the father-infant proximity variable, and its twin, father-child proximity, show numerous interactive relations with the hierarchy variables, and this again helps to specify the convergent hypothesis; hierarchy is associated with more severe sanctions when fathers are *more* involved with infants and children. This specific finding could not have been predicted from any given theory of illegitimacy. Malinowski posited that the principle of legitimacy rests on father-child bonding, but did not discuss the direction of covariation. The finding provides a direction and indicates that our theories need to be modified to take parent-child relations into account.[1]

Figure 9.1. A Composite Model for Principles of Legitimacy

Social Structure precipitates $\Longrightarrow$	Inter-Generational Interests mold $\Longrightarrow$	Illegitimacy Definitions and Sanctions
Technology Stratification Centralization Sexual Inequality Form of Family Marital Residence Inheritance Parent-Child Relations	Status Concerns Value on Culture (Ethnocentrism) Emotional Bonds of Parent to Child Men's Alienation from Reproduction Economic and Political Value of Offspring Avoidance of Investment in Offspring Concern with Extended Family Line Adult Offspring's Interest in Claiming Property and Offices of the Deceased	Seriousness Morality Importance of Biology to Social Fatherhood Sanctions Preventions

Father-infant and father-child proximity specifies the effect of structural factors, such as FIGs and sexual inequality, again indicating the importance in distinguishing between bonds to one's own children and affection toward children in general. When father-child ties add a new intergenerational interest into the mix, the principle of legitimacy is sometimes molded into a different shape.

The father-child relationship affects the link between FIG structure and illegitimacy sanctions in that relaxed handling of illegitimacy is likely only when father-infant ties are close and FIGs are weak. This finding may also be helpful in extending FIG theory: parts of the theory may be more valid for societies in which the constellation of intergenerational interests includes close ties of fathers to their own offspring.

One further finding shows the importance of treating the father-child tie as a variable.   Father-infant proximity interacts with female power in affecting sanctions for illegitimacy. Repressive sanctions are more likely either when low female power is combined with distant father-infant ties, or when high female power is combined with close father-infant ties.   To put it differently, the severity of illegitimacy sanctions is positively related to female power in societies with close father-child ties, but inversely related in societies with distant father-child ties. The effect of father-child ties on illegitimacy sanctions depends on women's intergenerational interests which are enabled expression by their power. Theories need to be reshaped around these complex effects.   For example, hypotheses derived from Draper's biosocial theory of father absence predict well for more sexual equalitarian societies, but are incorrect for male dominated societies. Engels's theory predicts severe illegitimacy sanctions with close father-child bonding combined with male dominance, but this set of conditions is one that is empirically less likely to produce severe sanctions.

The evidence garnered in this research does not empirically address intergenerational interests other than sentiment.   Other motives should be translated into measured variables for empirical testing. One society may have strong ethnocentrism and strong father-child bonds that mold the treatment of illegitimacy. In another society, a powerful upper class may have a strong influence in illegitimacy norm formation although there is weak father-child bonding in that strata. With either set of conditions, stringent regulation of illegitimacy can be expected, although its patterning may vary.

The examples of intergenerational sentiment show a need for rethinking the constants in our theories. Conceiving of some factors as constant is a way of simplifying the theorist's task, of focusing attention on one or two factors that are deemed important. Often it is the motive—the intergenerational interest—in the theory that is seen as a constant. A problem with this is that the empirical validity of a theoretical constant is difficult to evaluate. Only by comparing other societies where the so-called constant is empirically absent, or by translating the constant into a variable, can one determine whether the theory is empirically valid.

SOCIAL STRUCTURE AND VARIATION IN ILLEGITIMACY

One key part of the composite framework is the idea that specific social structures trigger, or enable expression of, specific kinds of intergenerational interests between the generations. Figure 9.1 shows a list of often-interacting factors found to be statistically associated with illegitimacy sanctions in this research.

The structural factors in the composite model are of two overlapping types: those that trigger particular interests and those that enable some interest groups to influence norm formation more. Sexual inequality is an example of the first type. It enables men's interests, more than women's, to mold a society's principle of legitimacy. As various theorists have noted, if men are dominant in a society, their views become manifested in norms. Inheritance is an example of the second type of structural factor. Inheritance rules trigger interests of the younger generation in the property of the dead, or reflect the past workings of these interests. Social stratification exemplifies both types of factors. It enables more influence in norm formation for the upper classes but also triggers intergenerational interests among these classes—the maintenance of prestige or social superiority and the greater interests of offspring in the holdings of parents.

The framework contains no typologies of societies. The statistical findings of this study suggest that we need to avoid typologies that presume strong structural clusters or strong correlations among many features of social structure. Engels's typology of evolutionary stages—savagery, barbarism, and civilization—presumes that technology, social hierarchy, and sexual inequality are strongly related.   Cross-cultural research has recognized for decades, however, that while some correlations among aspects of social structure are strong, many are modest. Typologies, by over-simplifying in this way, tend to muddle our vision. This research has shown the utility of keeping variables separate from each other and examining their independent and joint effects.

The main question of my cross-cultural research is how social structure affects the sanctions for illegitimacy. None of the theories attempting to explain why some societies react more strongly to illegitimacy have a monopoly on the truth. In some places there is overlap of the theories, and in others, the factors emphasized in different theories interact to produce repressive treatment of illegitimacy.

A Point of Convergence

Some functionalist, Marxist, and sociobiological theories converge (for different reasons) in the hypothesis that the severity of treatment of illegitimacy increases with increasing sociocultural complexity and social inequality. While Engels's use of evolutionary theory and Marxism was earlier than others to see this connection, functionalists such as Goode, sociobiologists such as Lancaster and Lancaster, and later conflict theorists such as Collins, concur. The findings show some truth to this idea. Repressive illegitimacy sanctions are somewhat more likely with higher levels of technological development. Social hierarchy and centralization is to some degree an intervening link between technological factors and severe sanctions.

The findings suggest that this point of convergence needs to be qualified. While these statistical patterns are generalizable, the correlations are very modest. They are not strong enough to make a case for immutable stages of evolution, punctuated by radical transformations. This point of agreement needs qualification also in that hierarchy interacts with some technological factors, specifically community size and sedentism.

Findings on family structure also help to specify the convergent predictions. While extended family structure in and of itself is unrelated to illegitimacy sanctions, it seems to "jump start" the use of repressive sanctions. These sanctions may occur even in nomadic, decentralized societies if families are extended. This puts repressive sanctions ahead of the schedule from evolutionary theory for those societies with extended families. I argue that more durable extended families may affect illegitimacy sanctions by adding a different interest into a society's constellation of interests. The extended family is a concrete group of everyday experience, existing over many generations of members. Because of this durability, it is a hotbed for a value on the continuity of one's family line and status, or "symbolic estate," as Farber (1968, 1971, 1973) calls it. It is but a short step from this value to a more restrictive and repressive handling of illegitimacy.

Findings on one other family trait, inheritance rules for real property, also suggest a need for reformulating illegitimacy theory. Repressive sanctions do not become more likely with the occurrence of any inheritance rules, or of specifically patrilineal male inheritance rules as Engels suggests. Severe sanctions are more likely with inheritance rules in which both male and female offspring share in the family property. Here again, extended family structure may "jump start" the use of severe sanctions. The findings show an interaction effect in which the extended family is conducive to severe sanctions, even in the absence of any inheritance rules for real property. Other interaction effects—those involving the family structure with food shortage and with police presence—contradict theory and remain anomalous. The anomaly is that under certain conditions, nuclear family societies are most likely to have severe sanctions for illegitimacy.

Another set of issues addressed here concerns the link of illegitimacy to descent and marital residence. The appearance of unilineal descent groups is sometimes seen as a part of the evolution of hierarchy, centralization, and control in society. Sociobiology and FIG theory contain suggestions that matrilineal or matrilocal groups might have more relaxed handling of illegitimacy. Matriliny is unrelated to illegitimacy sanctions, and matrilocality is slightly related. These findings support FIG theory somewhat more than sociobiology.

To deal with these unexpectedly low correlations, I argue through case examples that matrilineal, matrilocal societies do not dissociate biological and social fatherhood as much as has been believed: those in the sample use marriage as the final condition legitimating reproduction. Other case examples show that patrilineal or patrilocal societies dissociate biological and social fatherhood more than has been generally recognized. Bride wealth transactions accompanying marriage sometimes are the mechanism for this. Some societies ask the biological father to pay recompense. Others let any man pay or by default let the child be incorporated into the mother's kin group. These latter societies dissociate biological and social fatherhood more.

A Second Point of Convergence

A second point of theoretical agreement is the view of sexual inequality as a factor conducive to repressive sanctions. Functionalist theories tend to assume that sexual inequality is a constant factor among the world's societies, while evolutionary theories tend to assume a nearly perfect correlation of sexual inequality with other hierarchical factors. I have treated it as a variable that is independent from other inequalities to see if the theories are better supported when there is greater sexual inequality. In other words, I looked for interaction effects that are predictable from the theories if their faulty assumptions on sexual inequality are ignored. The findings suggest that theory needs some revision regarding the role of sexual inequality. Contrary to several theories, sexual inequality by itself is not related to illegitimacy sanctions. However, sexual inequality does specify the first point of theoretical convergence regarding technology and social hierarchy.

The predictions from theory hold only for societies with low female power. Factors such as levels of stratification, political centralization, and police presence make for more severe sanctions only in societies with *low* female power. Societies with high female power tend to have an intermediate chance of having severe sanctions, and social hierarchy and centralization make no difference in the severity of sanctions. Female power, by enabling women's intergenerational interests to have a part in norm formation, appear to buffer the repressive effect of social hierarchy on the control of illegitimacy.

This finding can be incorporated into existing evolutionary and functionalist theories. The interaction effect is fully consistent with what can be predicted from the theories. Both types of theories err in not explicating the place of sexual inequality in sufficient comparative detail. The theories need to be extended to incorporate variation in sexual inequality that is somewhat independent of other forms of inequality.

The findings regarding marital residence and sexual inequality are more problematic for theory. FIG theory is formulated on the assumption that men have power in all societies. The theory presumes that men are the active agents in the formation of reproductive rules and rituals. Women are seen as having little voice in reproductive matters. While the inference is that the theory should predict better when women have little power, the opposite is found, for FIG strength predicts the severity of illegitimacy sanctions better when female power is high! Patrilocal societies have more severe handling of illegitimacy only when women have more economic and political power. I believe the FIG theory needs to include "sororal interest groups" as well, since the theory works primarily for societies in which women are organized into female groups and have some political participation. Men's and women's intergenerational interests may be more polarized and women more ready for mobilization as a bloc in societies having both exclusively male and exclusively female groups.

To sum up, the statistical findings provide an empirical basis for theoretical extensions. Most theories are shown to overstate their cases. While some agreed-upon factors such as the hierarchy and inequality variables are confirmed to be important in the handling of illegitimacy, many specific findings are surprising and may help in extending the theories.

IS THE PRINCIPLE OF LEGITIMACY A CULTURAL UNIVERSAL?

In the late nineteenth century and into the twentieth, a debate was waged on the universality of the family and of the principle of legitimacy. None of the theories from that debate—pro or con—fit this study's data. Engels argued against a universal principle of legitimacy. He believed that early foraging societies made no distinction between legitimate and illegitimate offspring. Among the functionalists, Davis was at the opposite extreme from Engels. He argued that all societies morally condemn illegitimacy. Malinowski's position was intermediate, viewing the principle of legitimacy as a cultural universal that varies somewhat in its application. He believed that the main thrust of the principle is to provide all children with a social father.

How do the three early theories line up with the data? Regarding Engels's cultural evolutionary view, all of the foraging societies studied make some distinction between legitimate and illegitimate offspring, although many handle illegitimacy in a relaxed way. Others punish illegitimacy severely. While some matrilineal groups—presumably an earlier evolved form in Engels's theory—use a girl's puberty rites as part of the legitimation for reproduction, this legitimation is not complete without marriage. In other matrilineal societies, such as the Trobriand Islands, illegitimacy is morally condemned.

Contrary to Davis's theory, the moral condemnation of illegitimacy is not universal. About two-fifths of the sample societies do not morally condemn illegitimacy, but handle it in a relaxed way. The first birth is a common route into marriage in some cultures, or at least does not harm the mother's position in the marriage market. Still other societies rigorously pressure couples into marrying thereby legitimating their offspring, and some societies do this without condemning them for conceiving beforehand. This evidence fits better with Malinowski's speculations that the principle of legitimacy is universal, but flexible. Malinowski correctly saw that some societies use the carrot rather than the stick to enforce the principle of legitimacy. They prefer that children be born to married couples and encourage unwed parents to marry, rather than simply condemning nonmarital conception and birth. Of course, both Davis and Malinowski would agree that repressive punishment may not only have a deterrent effect, but may also prod many other couples toward a hasty wedding.

However, there is even more variation in the handling of illegitimacy than Malinowski realized. He mentioned two variations—positive or negative pressures. There are other preventive ones, such as betrothal or marriage before puberty, and normative abortion or infanticide. Also, there is the alternative use of partial bride wealth payment to legitimate birth without marriage. Malinowski concentrated on how societies try to link the biological mother and father to form a family. Not all societies have this concern. For example, some societies having bride wealth as a transaction accompanying marriage assign the illegitimate child to whomever pays the bride wealth or the relevant part of it. If no one pays the bride wealth, the mother's parents keep the illegitimate child. Some ethnographies indicate no concern that the biological father become the social father of the child. Nonetheless, these added variations do not contradict the spirit of Malinowski's theory in that there is still a social father for the child.

The principle of legitimacy is universal in a very loose sense. No precise rule on nonmarital birth or response to it is universal. The principle of legitimacy is what Needham (1971) calls an "odd-job" term. It takes any meaning from a list of several possibilities (Leach 1955). Two features of a cultural principle of legitimacy appear to be universal, among the sample societies, at least. Minimally, all societies have a social father role, which is multidimensional and varies from society to society. Secondly, all societies have norms regulating reproduction in which the idea of a social father plays some part. Some societies attempt to identify the biological father as the social father. At the other extreme, it is the absence of a social father that defines illegitimacy.

Ordinarily, social scientists believe that it takes a universal to explain a universal. However, this may not be the most fruitful approach to take in explaining the principle of illegitimacy. Since the principle itself is not uniform, the reasons for the principle may not be uniform.

Descriptions for a few sample societies—mostly in the relaxed handling category—make it impossible to say if they make a distinction between legitimate and illegitimate offspring. The problem is that parenthood is multidimensional, and any of several distinctions could be made in the treatment of marital and nonmarital offspring. Some descriptions of relaxed handling are not detailed and rich enough to rigorously ascertain whether the society makes *some* distinction between legitimate and illegitimate birth. They mention the lack of sanctions but do not discuss the actual treatment of nonmarital offspring.

Consider the following examples. The Chukchee were said to rejoice over children so much that they accepted nonmarital birth. They treated illegitimate children lovingly the same as they treated legitimate offspring. Illegitimate children and children of divorce often were housed in the mother's natal home and were difficult to distinguish. This description can be coded as an instance of relaxed handling of illegitimacy. The treatment of illegitimate infants contrasts with the treatment of deformed infants, who were killed (Bogoras 1901, no. 121). This brief description of illegitimacy does not discuss matters of the actual custody, care, support, sponsorship, training and socialization, succession, and inheritance. There is a father role in Chukchee society, but the description does not indicate how it is filled in cases of nonmarital birth.

The Otoro Nuba also have relaxed handling of illegitimacy, but identified the genitor as the social father of the illegitimate child. Children were considered to "belong" to their biological father regardless of whether he was married to the mother (Nadel 1947, no. 30). Nadel states that the Nuba did not define any children as illegitimate. This assessment may be correct in a moral sense, but more information on how children "belong" to genitors is needed to conclude that legitimate and illegitimate offspring were treated the same in all major respects. The Nuba's enforcement of parental rights or obligations of the unwed genitor is consistent with part of Malinowski's principle of legitimacy. Identifying the genitor as the social father is one way of ensuring that all children have social fathers, although it does not make marriage the license for procreation.

In some societies concubinage, marriage, and the principle of legitimacy are institutionalized together. Concubinage is a normative sexual union that exists alongside marriage, but its offspring are not considered legitimate children of the father. Although concubinage contradicts Malinowski's principle of legitimacy, the other family institutions of the same societies are consistent with it. While statistical data from the sample societies are not available, concubinage typically seems to involve a difference in status of the two parties. Some are unions of upper-status men and lower-status women, while others involve men of one society and women of a pariah group or neighboring society considered inferior. Offspring of concubines are not legitimate and do not inherit the father's status or property. While male partners may support concubines and their offspring, they seem to invest less in these offspring than in those by their legal wives. Fathers may have no obligation to invest in them. Offspring of concubines have few, if any, enforceable claims against their biological fathers. Concubinage goes against the central feature of Malinowski's principle of legitimacy in that it is a normative arrangement that does not assign a social father to the child. Within the same societies, children are assigned social fathers when their mothers marry, so the more general practice fits Malinowski's formulation.

This loose, or "odd-job," principle of legitimacy appears to be primordial and universal. It logically underlies other universal or widespread normative features of the family presuming a social father, such as the incest taboo, nuclear family structure, the division of labor by sex, and sexual inequality. Because of its primordial place among cultural rules, the principle of legitimacy needs to be more carefully studied and linked to other basic features of social structure, including the family. As suggested in Chapter 1, research and theorizing on the other universal or widespread features of the family needs to link these features to variation both in illegitimacy norms and in the father role. Research of this kind should help to speed the growth of family theory.

NOTE

1. I have not examined variation in mother-child relations or closeness of the child to other relatives here. Emotional closeness in these relationships may also be linked to illegitimacy sanctions. More work is needed on how the closeness of family and kin ties affects cultural definitions of illegitimacy and its sanctions.

10

American Illegitimacy in Cross-Cultural Perspective

America's principle of legitimacy is shifting within the middle range of the worldwide spectrum. In cross-cultural terms, America is moving from a repressive mode of handling illegitimacy toward a restitutive mode. Today's debates on illegitimacy—or "adolescent pregnancy"—and welfare programs for single parents are taking place at one moment and one location within a broader long-run historical shift in the Western treatment of illegitimacy. Secular changes in law, as well as changes during this century in the community reactions among different subgroups, document this shift. There are elements of repression and restitution in both the law and in community reactions, but the relaxed handling of illegitimacy is less evident.

ACCOUNTING FOR THE TREND IN CROSS-CULTURAL PERSPECTIVE

The cross-cultural research findings show that several combinations of factors are linked to variations in illegitimacy sanctions. Can these findings help us understand the trends in handling illegitimacy in America today? We need to locate America in terms of the important independent variables of this research. In applying the research findings to the American case, several structural features have pushed America toward repressive illegitimacy sanctions. These include:

—a complex multi-tier government with organized standing police and military forces that is grounded in a technologically sophisticated capitalist economy.
—sentimental, affectionate, parent-child ties but only moderate father involvement. Sentimental attitudes toward children have grown over the centuries.
—Increasing father involvement combined with rising sexual equality (if these occur, as some believe) may become a stronger pressure toward more repressive sanctions in the next few decades.

Still other cross-cultural findings suggest pressures toward more restitutive or relaxed handling:

—a neolocal nuclear family-based kinship system lacking fraternal interest groups, lineages, clans, and indeed any kind of larger kinship or family group. Neolocal residence is never found with repressive illegitimacy sanctions in the study sample.
—the shift from unigeniture and equal inheritance to testamentary freedom (Goody et al, 1976). The findings show that inheritance by both sexes—partible inheritance—is linked to repressive sanctions. The testamentary freedom that has come into vogue in Western societies may not have the same effect.
—relatively high female power in combination with complex hierarchy and centralization. In the statistical findings, female power buffers the effect of stratification and centralization. I will argue from the cross-cultural findings that this is an especially important factor in the American trend.

Given these pressures both toward and away from repressive treatment of illegitimacy, from a cross-cultural perspective, it is no surprise that a controversy is raging on nonmarital birth today.

The issues in the debate on controlling illegitimacy come from the middle of the worldwide spectrum. Diverse mechanisms are used to control illegitimacy among the world's societies. In several societies, an early age at marriage reduces opportunities for illegitimacy. America provides an opportunity for illegitimacy by having a growing gap of eight years or more between sexual maturity and marriage (Vinovskis 1988). In other societies, marriage and children are so desirable that couples who conceive then marry eagerly. Similarly, some groups alternately incorporate the child as a member of the mother's family if the father (or a different man) does not give her family a gift to secure rights over the child. Some societies use abortion or infanticide to prevent illegitimate birth without considering these practices to be unfortunate or deviant. In some sample societies abortion is voluntary, and in others, forced. These same practices exist in other sample societies, but the motive behind them is to avoid the stigma of illegitimate birth. Individual women furtively attempt to induce abortions to escape the shame and punishment that comes from illegitimate birth. Some other societies use physical punishment on unwed couples who conceive or, in rare instances, banish or kill the pregnant unwed woman.

Those attending to the debate on the control of illegitimacy know that it is polarized. From a cross-cultural perspective, polarization is not as extreme as it could be. Three different constructions of adolescent pregnancy and birth compete to institutionalize their view: the public health-preventive medicine view; the view of nonmarital sex and reproduction as immoral; and the fiscal view of illegitimacy as costly to society (Nathanson 1991). All three of these constructions agree that illegitimate pregnancy and fertility rates are too high. Civic debate on illegitimacy deals with abstinence and voluntary birth control, voluntary abortion, with child support from unwed fathers, and especially on the role of government. These latter issues include whether government should help reduce illegitimacy rates by providing sex education to encourage chastity, by providing birth control, or by sponsoring voluntary abortions. Also, there is the question of the extent to which government welfare programs should be financially supporting illegitimate mothers and children. Many mechanisms found in the cross-cultural spectrum are *not* being discussed as options in America. These include: having an earlier age at marriage; assigning social fatherhood to the illegitimate child's maternal grandfather; forcing illegitimate parents to marry; forcing abortion; abandoning infants; making illegitimacy a criminal offense subject to fines; imprisonment or corporal punishment; and making illegitimacy a capital offense. The control mechanisms under discussion today come only from the middle of the worldwide spectrum.

ILLEGITIMACY LAW IN AMERICA AND THE WEST

Zingo and Early (1994) note that the U.S. Supreme court has shown no consistent trend in interpreting illegitimacy cases since the landmark decision in *Levy vs. Louisiana* in 1968. However, many of these recent decisions and laws are based on different tenets than in past decades and centuries. If we view the course of the law since ancient Roman times, a consistent trend appears that is not at all visible over a few decades. The importance of parental marriage as the prime determinant of legitimacy has declined, while the genetic tie of parent and offspring has gained in importance. A shift away from repressive sanctions for women and children toward restitutive sanctions for men has accompanied the greater emphasis on biology. Some highlights can demonstrate the general course of change in illegitimacy law.[1]

Illegitimacy Law in Past Centuries

In Roman times, legitimacy was legally defined in terms of a woman's being married at the time of birth. Under Roman law, a child born to an unmarried woman was literally *filius nullius*—son of no one. The illegitimate offspring could not be legitimated by subsequent marriage, could not inherit, and had no right to support or custody from either parent. On the other hand, all children born to a married woman were defined as her husband's legitimate offspring (Jacobs 1932, no. 49; Clarke 1940). There was an escape clause for husbands in the customs of the time. The husband could accept or reject any infant born to his wife at the moment she ritually presented the newborn to him (Belmont 1976). Husbands likely rejected infants they suspected to be offspring of other men. Rejected infants were abandoned to die, but perhaps some of those abandoned were taken into slavery. If a husband accepted the infant when it was presented to him, he could not bastardize it later. It was then his legitimate offspring.

Only gradually have Western societies qualified the presumption that children born in marriage are the legitimate offspring of the husband. Over the centuries husbands have become increasingly able to bastardize their wives' offspring on biological grounds. In England in the late Middle Ages, a husband could bastardize his wife's offspring on the basis of the husband's impotence, a separation by sentence of divorce, or by "the doctrine of the four seas," in which the husband provided evidence that he was outside the country at the time of conception. These grounds put the burden of proof on the husband and restricted the possibilities for bastardizing marital offspring. The doctrine of the four seas provided a basis for bastardization that could be readily documented, but likely left some men with no legal grounds for disclaiming their wives' offspring by other men. Even if a wife ran away with another man and had a child, the child could not be bastardized if the husband were within the king's realm (Clarke 1940). England's doctrine of the four seas lasted into the eighteenth century.

The law today in England, as elsewhere, still presumes the legitimacy of children born into an existing marriage unless the husband takes legal action to bastardize them. Husbands have more leeway to bastardize their wives' offspring than they did in past centuries, as the grounds have more and more come to be based purely on genetic relatedness.

The concept of *filius nullius* continued to influence Western law on nonmarital offspring for centuries. In English common law, as in Rome, an illegitimate offspring could not inherit from father or mother. Neither parent had the right to custody of the child (Clarke 1940; Pollock and Maitland 1968). Before the time of Elizabeth I, bastard children lacking parental care apparently were supported by the local parish, although some of the expense was likely provided by philanthropy (Jordan 1959). The nobility and well-to-do sometimes recognized and cared for their illegitimate offspring, who suffered less social than legal disability (Given-Wilson and Curteis 1984).[2]

Various attempts were made to use the poor law to make unmarried mothers and fathers responsible for their offspring and to end public funding of illegitimacy among the poor. The preamble to an enactment of 1576 foreshadows the moral and economic sides of the debate on welfare and illegitimacy in America today:

Concerning bastards begotten and born out of lawful marriage (an offence against God's law and man's law) the said bastards being now left to be kept at the charge of the parish where they be born, to the great burden of the same parish, and in defrauding of the relief for the impotent and aged true poor of the same parish, and to the evil example and encouragement of lewd life. (quoted in Clarke 1940: 318)

This act placed the responsibility on both parents to provide basic necessities for nonmarital children. The law enabled local officials to collect weekly payments from either parent under penalty of being committed to the workhouse. The government wanted to get rid of "welfare cheats" and to reduce public welfare costs, even if it meant that officials had to track down illegitimate parents and put them into forced labor. Later English enactments backed off from this stance somewhat, but continued to address the issue of illegitimacy.

Illegitimacy Law in the Twentieth Century

By the twentieth century, it became accepted in both England and America that the nonmarital child had rights to custody and inheritance from its mother. The broad current of legal change has been to expand the conditions under which biological fathers and nonmarital offspring have mutual rights and obligations. The law began to allow the mother to bring action against the biological father to secure financial support for the child. In England after 1926, legitimation through subsequent marriage became possible. This was possible in most states of the United States in the first part of this century, although special petition or adoption might be needed in some jurisdictions (Clarke 1940).

Many countries during this century have attempted to equalize the rights of legitimate and illegitimate children. This legislation is often anchored in the value of children's rights and children's welfare. Special committees on children's welfare were established both in the League of Nations (Clarke 1940: 320-321) and in the United Nations. U.N. policy statements on illegitimacy have repeatedly affirmed (in 1948 and 1967) the principle of equal treatment of illegitimate children. According to Tapp (1980) this general principle of equality is now the international norm, with the countries of the old British Commonwealth lagging behind. This type of legislation makes biological fathers responsible for their offspring and guarantees rights of support and inheritance to the offspring, regardless of whether a marriage has occurred. This legal stance, if successfully implemented, would make biology everything and marriage inconsequential, so far as parent-child legal relations are concerned.[3]

Legal enactments of this international norm began early this century. Before the renowned Soviet "experiment," which equalized through weakening family and reproductive ties (Geiger 1968), Norway in 1915 enacted equalization. Norway's law putting the burden on the state to establish paternity of nonmarital children, required child support from the father and added rights of inheritance from the father.

Recent Developments in the United States

In the United States, Arizona and North Dakota soon followed in equalizing some rights of illegitimate children. According to the Arizona law, "Every child is the legitimate child of its natural parents. . . . " (Clarke 1940). Yet, the law would not grant the illegitimate child a right to live with its father if the father were married. Since no other states followed in equalizing the rights of illegitimate offspring, the United States became one of the "laggard" nations noted by Tapp (1980). In California at mid-century for example, the illegitimate child had a right to support from the father and mother, but could receive support from its father only if its mother successfully brought a "paternity suit." The child could be legitimated, and thus inherit, only if the father acknowledged the child and took the child into his home (Kay 1965).

America has moved slowly toward equalization of rights for illegitimate offspring. Some of this movement has been through court precedent. A key 1968 case by the U.S. Supreme Court made some believe that equalization was imminent when it used the equal protection clause of the Fourteenth Amendment to the Constitution for the first time ever in dealing with questions of illegitimacy. The Court declared Louisiana's Wrongful Death Act unconstitutional. This act granted rights of recovery only to legitimate offspring. The Court found a constitutional basis for equal rights of illegitimate offspring vis-à-vis the mother. Writing shortly thereafter, Harry Krause (1971) felt that the reasoning of the court would apply to the paternal side as well, and that the counter-arguments to this application were weak. Krause wrote that the equalization of rights on the paternal side would be only "four dozen cases and a comprehensive new statute away" (1971: 35).

By 1992, the Supreme Court had gotten over halfway to its four dozen cases bearing on the rights and obligations of illegitimate parents and children. However, the Court has not continued to apply and elaborate the reasoning from its 1968 decision as Krause felt it would, although it has removed many of the legal disabilities faced by illegitimate parents and children (Zingo and Early 1994: 41, 94-95; see also Stenger 1981; Dale 1988).

Restitution by Illegitimate Fathers

The Supreme Court is not the only organ of legal change. With federal legislative leadership, state governments have implemented a restitutive approach toward financial support for children of divorced and unwed mothers. Prior to this push, there was little enforcement of child support for children of unwed mothers or divorced custodial mothers. Enforcement had been contingent on mothers bringing suit against fathers to pay child support. Even in successful suits, the courts did not keep records of whether payments were actually made, but merely issued orders to pay. Less than half of absent fathers who owed child support were paying it fully.

The federal legislature passed a bill in 1975 improving child support enforcement, with some amendments in subsequent years. A federal agency— the Office of Child Support Enforcement (OCSE)—was set up to coordinate the work of states. The law was intended to recoup some of the money spent on Aid to Families with Dependent Children (AFDC), which goes primarily to female-headed households. All states now have passed legislation and set up local agencies under the auspices of this federal law (Office of Child Support Enforcement 1986).

Before the 1970s, the major form of restitution for illegitimate fathers was marrying the mother to "set things right." Since that time, fewer illegitimate conceptions are resulting in marriage. Abortion has leveled off, but illegitimate births have continued to rise. The AFDC program enabled mother-child families to survive and enabled many illegitimate fathers to go scot-free with no restitution or penalty. The OCSE works on several fronts to increase the extent to which men make child support payments. The OCSE legislation in most states:

—requires personnel in birth facilities to encourage unwed fathers to register. This creates evidence of paternity.
—makes it mandatory for applicants for AFDC to cooperate in legal action against an absent nonsupporting parent. In certain cases, such as those involving woman-battering, for example, this requirement is waived. This results in more women naming fathers.
—provides for blood testing and genetic testing to provide rebuttable evidence in contested cases. Little genetic testing is actually done, but it apparently is felt to be a good bargaining chip (Cleveland and Williams 1992).
—allows the local agency to garnish income, seize tax returns, revoke drivers and occupational licenses, place liens and seize property of obligors who are behind in child support payments. In the two years following Maine's license revocation law of 1993, obligors paid 25 million dollars (Office of Child Support Enforcement 1995).
—makes interstate nonsupport a federal crime. This law enables federal action to collect support payments from fathers whose children reside in a different state, and who have not provided support for a year or who owe more than $5,000. This legislation helps with the problem of men who move out of state to avoid paying child support (Landstreet, 1994).

The OCSE claims to take in over three dollars for each dollar spent. Collections rose from $500 million dollars in FY 1975 to $2 billion in FY 1983 (Office of Child Support Enforcement 1983). By FY 1990 collections had climbed to just over $6 billion, while expenditures rose less rapidly to $1.5 billion. Collections rose to $8.9 billion by 1993 (Office of Child Support Enforcement 1993). The federal government keeps about one-third of this money, with a larger share going to states and a smaller part going to AFDC families (Office of Child Support Enforcement 1990. The OCSE sees the government shares as repayment for AFDC money going to families. Single mothers can use the services of the child support enforcement agency even if they are not applying for AFDC. If a mother is not going on welfare, any money collected goes to her, except for the expenses of the agency in locating and bringing action against the father.

Some "deadbeat dads" may feel that some of these OCSE measures are repressive. Some OCSE measures, such as license revocation and jail terms, are punitive mechanisms intended to enforce a primarily restitutive treatment of illegitimacy. The restitutive principle is that the illegitimate father is obliged to support his offspring. It is not the father's illegitimacy being punished; it is his failure to fulfill restitutive obligations.

To put this into the categories of the cross-cultural research, American law is moving from one mode of treatment of illegitimacy to another. Illegitimacy law is moving from the repression of mothers and children toward restitution from genetic fathers. Marital status of parents is becoming less relevant, and biology more important. Defining genetic ties as paramount is a practical solution to the problem of the difficult situation into which illegitimate mothers and children are sometimes put. Once identified, genitors are asked to take on some of the obligations toward offspring that social fathers have. Thus, the shift toward equalizing the treatment of illegitimate children has brought gains for illegitimate mothers, as fathers are increasingly pressured to help support illegitimate offspring. America's legal principle of legitimacy then is increasingly one of restitution. The U.S. law lags behind some other nations in this regard but is moving in the same direction as other nations.

SOCIAL REACTIONS TO ILLEGITIMACY AMONG WHITE AMERICANS

Community reactions to illegitimacy have changed parallel to the legal shifts this century. America's premarital sex norms have relaxed somewhat over the course of this century, especially during the 1960s and 1970s. Not only was this a time of sexual revolution but also a time of revolution in courtship and reproduction.[4] America's handling of illegitimacy continues to shift. Before the 1960s, America handled illegitimacy predominantly through informal repressive controls of shaming through rumor and gossip, withdrawal, and personal verbal attack on the unwed pregnant woman (Rains 1971), as do many of the sample societies.

White Shame

Before the sexual revolution of the 1960s and the *Roe vs. Wade* Supreme Court decision legalizing abortion in 1973, the community reaction to illegitimacy was markedly different from today. Extreme shame attached to illegitimate pregnancy and birth for white and black women alike. Becoming an unwed mother was a deviant career (Rains 1971). Illegitimate birth was an absolute disaster because it brought a lifelong stigma for the mother. It could potentially ruin a woman's chances for a good marriage and a middle-class life (Rains 1971; Solinger 1992; Morton 1993). Clinicians have observed that some young unmarried pregnant women attempted suicide, but few did so after the 1960s (Konopka 1966: 127).

This shame extended not just to the unmarried mother, but to her natal family as well, according to anecdotal evidence. Very often the woman and her family tried to keep the pregnancy secret to avoid shame and discrimination from the community. When parents concealed a daughter's pregnancy, this was in part an altruistic act. It was also a selfish act moved by fear of loss of the family's standing in the community (Rains 1971).

Informal community controls were not always effective in preventing pregnancy outside of marriage but were more effective in preventing birth outside of marriage. For the woman who was premaritally pregnant, there were four alternatives: hurriedly marrying the father, illegal abortion, giving the baby up for adoption following a secretive stay in a maternity home, and being a single mom. America has been ambivalent about each of these options.

Avoiding Shame

White women were more likely than black women to hurriedly marry the fathers of their children so that the child was born to a married couple thereby making the birth legitimate. The early birth within marriage aroused talk but was less shameful than an illegitimate child. Some saw marrying the mother as the illegitimate father's duty, and they exerted pressure on the couple to marry even though they knew the marriage might be far from ideal. Many still feel that the young couple gives up major options in life by marrying and having a baby early.

Illegally induced abortion has been used more often by white women than by black women, partly for financial reasons, and partly because of greater opposition among blacks. Even so, whites also regarded illegal abortion as shameful and as a loss for the woman. Abortion's advantage was that it could be done without general public knowledge, and thereby, stigma could be avoided. Even though abortion is legal today, few feel that it is a desirable form of birth control. Rather, it is a last resort.

Adoption in America has been *closed*, but as the stigma of illegitimacy has eased somewhat, adoption is now sometimes *open*. In closed adoption, the birth parents and the adoptive parents are anonymous to each other. While this arrangement may have been devised to make adoption a closer simulation of biological ties, it also offered an opportunity for avoiding the stigma of both abortion and of unwed motherhood. Maternity homes began earlier this century to assist unwed mothers in putting their infants up for adoption. A woman's family could provide a cover story for her being away for six months or more, while she stayed in the maternity home, and then returned home without the baby (Rains 1971; Solinger 1992). Few maternity homes accepted black women.

The maternity home-adoption experience also brought personal losses for the woman. With the practice of closed adoption, there was no possibility of future contact between biological mother and child. Giving a newborn infant up to an unknown family was a major loss. Solinger (1992) calls it a neo-Faustian trade.

In short, for the first two-thirds of this century, the white middle class responded to illegitimacy repressively with informal community stigmatization.

For some women, there was restitution in the form of a hurried wedding, and this helped decrease stigma. For others, there was institutionalized evasion of stigma through closed adoption or illegal abortion. These extraordinary practices of illegal abortion, of giving a child away, never to see it again, and of marrying early and sometimes without love, speak powerfully about the tremendous shame that unmarried pregnant women faced. Illegitimate fathers did not face the same stigma.

Since the 1960s, the degree of shame attached to illegitimacy has declined but has not disappeared altogether.[5] Shame is applied to nonmarital pregnancy and birth less evenly and less severely than in previous generations. Legalized abortion is now a common way for whites to avoid the shame and difficulties of single parenthood, while hurried marriage has declined. The net result is that adolescent childbearing overall has not increased, but *unwed* childbearing among both adolescents and older women has risen (Vinovskis 1988).

REACTIONS TO ILLEGITIMACY WITHIN THE BLACK LOWER CLASS

White and black responses to illegitimacy were more similar before the sexual revolution of the 1960s (Rains 1971; Solinger 1992). For example, Rains (1971) studied adolescents in two maternity homes. She documents that these teenagers of both races felt that illegitimacy is immoral and that most felt ashamed of their pregnancies. The gap between the classes/races has widened recently.

Goode's (1960) status-placement view of illegitimacy predicts that lower classes will have more illegitimacy and react less severely to it. This prediction is correct today, but the research is not of one voice in describing lower-class community reactions to illegitimacy. A few studies describe relaxed handling of illegitimacy while others suggest a mix of responses are occurring. Stack's (1974) ethnography of a mid-western lower-class black community portrays a relaxed handling of illegitimacy. Nonmarital birth brings no objection or shame. The mother's and father's kin networks welcome the child, and assist in its care. The illegitimate father keeps a relationship with the child, even if his bond with the mother lapses. The portrayal of relaxed handling of illegitimacy glosses over differences in views and reactions of members of the community to illegitimacy. Other research finds gender and generational disparities, suggesting a lack of consensus on relaxed handling of illegitimacy.[6] Many lower-class black adults do object to unwed parenthood, but some youth may object less or not at all.

Youth Subcultures

Anderson (1993) holds that a male subculture among inner-city youths is a key factor in illegitimacy. The male subculture awards prestige points to members who have casual sex with women and for deceiving and manipulating women for sex. Female teens and adults do not value uncommitted sex. Teenage women dream of having a stable marriage, a nice home, and then children. Women try to avoid having children while single, but some engage in sex to keep a boyfriend, especially if the woman believes the man is interested in marriage. Unintended pregnancy often results from this manipulative interaction, with consequences for both partners. The man loses face among his peers if he admits paternity and marries. However, the woman and her family will want to name the father. Many men accept paternity without marrying and are recognized as fathers within the community. A man may at first take some interest in his child, but he tends to drop his romantic relationship with the mother, then has little contact with his child. The woman and her kin, perhaps with the aid of the father's kin, are left to raise the child with occasional help from the father.

Anderson shows for one community that lower-class black illegitimacy is not normative but stems from gender and generational conflicts. Other research confirms Anderson's view. Barnes (1987) finds a black male youth subculture within a different community, which also values casual sex and devalues marriage. She also agrees that men often terminate their relationships as lovers to single women whom they impregnate, although some continue. Sullivan (1993: 71) reports that these relationships often continue, but are "volatile."

Unmarried Motherhood as a Status Transition

One interpretation of adolescent illegitimacy in lower-class black communities is that having a child is a mark of adulthood, a valued status transition to adulthood. The transition-to-adulthood interpretation suggests that single women choose to have children, that unwed motherhood is seen as a positive good, and that there is no community negative reaction. Research has not detected these patterns. Anderson (1993) is quite clear on unwed pregnancies being mostly unintentional. Barnes (1987) finds that six-tenths of a small sample of unwed pregnancies were unintentional. In another sample Barnes (1987) studied, half of the unwed mothers became pregnant intentionally apparently out of spite: they wanted get to even with their own mothers. Williams (1992) suggests that most of the illegitimate pregnancies in her study are unintentional, but the intentional pregnancies are telling. One person said she used pregnancy to draw her mother's attention away from partying and a lover. Another blamed two pregnancies on her rebelliousness, which she blamed on her bad relationship with her mother. These pregnancies that are based on ulterior motives or are unintended suggest that unmarried motherhood is deviant and not a normative step toward adulthood.

Evidence on community reactions to illegitimate pregnancy also shows that the response is not positive, but ambivalent and diverse (Barnes 1987; Williams 1992). These reactions include informal repressive sanctions such as shunning by siblings and fellow students, negative expressions from parents, and rumor and gossip in the community and school. Some pregnant women come to feel ashamed in this situation. On the other hand, many parents are happy to have grandchildren. Sometimes peers lend their support, and some unwed mothers feel satisfied (Barnes 1987).

The Age Gap in Illegitimacy

The narrow focus on adolescent pregnancy pushes one to assume that the illegitimate fathers involved in "adolescent pregnancy" are teenagers. In a majority of cases this may be true, but adult men also exploit adolescent girls, both black and white. In some cases the "boyfriends" are not in the ideal age bracket as potential marriage partners but are in their twenties, and sometimes older. Barnes (1987) finds several pregnancies resulting from sexual abuse by men in the home, and one in which a woman allowed her 13-year-old daughter to date a 35-year-old man. This age gap is consistent with the interpretation that young men who exploit teenage girls sexually are not conforming to adult norms.

In summary, the black lower class attaches less shame to illegitimacy than whites do. This community has not shifted to a fully relaxed handling of illegitimacy. There is a sexual and reproductive double standard, with many community members viewing illegitimate pregnancy as deviant. Some sanctions for this deviance are repressive and some are restitutive. Informal repressive sanctions against the mother include social withdrawal, rumor, and gossip. Restitution is asked of biological fathers in the form of visiting the child, giving gifts, and offering some financial support. Children are incorporated into the kin networks of mothers often with important links to the father's kin.

REPRODUCTIVE TECHNOLOGY

Over two decades ago, Toffler (1970) warned that new developments in reproductive technology would shatter existing definitions of parenthood. Court cases now are reported in the mass media on artificial insemination, in vitro fertilization, frozen embryos, and surrogate motherhood. Legal scholars write on the challenge reproductive technology offers to the definitions of parent and motherhood (Wadlington 1983; Barnett 1985; Stumpf 1986). Some argue that reproductive technology enables adults to claim unrelated children as their legitimate offspring in a new way. If true, this technology would imply a transformed principle of legitimacy—one in which reproduction is linked neither to biology nor marriage, and one which creates new forms of parenthood.

Is technology really changing our legal definitions and community reactions to illegitimacy? For the most part the courts are interpreting reproductive technology issues within the existing legal framework on parenthood, legitimacy, and adoption (Edwards 1991). A brief review will show that if there are to be new definitions of parenthood and the family, they lie in the future.

Artificial Insemination by Anonymous Donor

Artificial insemination by anonymous donor (AID) has been in use for some time. A decade ago over 250,000 American children had been born through AID (Blank 1984). The medical community has attempted to establish AID as a fertility aid only for married couples in which the husband is sterile and to restrict its use by unmarried women. Donor anonymity and husband's consent to the wife's insemination are stressed in anticipation of legal questions about the obligations for the donor—the biological father—to the child. Legal questions concerning the legal rights and obligations of the biological father have in fact been raised in instances where women asked friends or acquaintances to donate semen without anonymity. Some cases involving child custody and inheritance have raised the question of the legitimacy of the child produced through AID. The mother's husband typically adopts her AID child, since the genetic father is unknown. Several states have passed legislation regulating AID, generally making the husband the legitimate father if he has given prior consent and if a physician has performed the insemination.

These laws may appear to legitimate nonmarital reproduction in a new way. However, when married couples use AID, the legal situation parallels the long standing law that children born to the wife are presumptively the husband's children. Only he can bastardize them (Krause 1983). If the husband and wife consent to the procedure, there are some grounds for considering AID children legitimate under prior law.

Feminists are concerned with medical and legal controls on reproductive technology (Arditti et al. 1984; Corea 1985). While the medical establishment has attempted to maintain hegemony over AID, the procedure is easily carried out by individuals without physician intervention. Lesbian feminist communities practice "self-insemination" as an alternate path to motherhood. A few friends contribute semen, which is mixed together to conceal the identity of the genetic father. The mix is then injected into the woman's vagina with a turkey baster (Hornstein 1984).

Klein (1984) reports on a London-based lesbian community practicing and encouraging self-insemination since 1978. She notes, "Women who decide on self-insemination question the patriarchal concept of biological parenthood" (Klein 1984: 388). The courts may eventually find that single women have the same right as married women to AID. Alternately, courts or legislatures may decide that children have a right to two parents, or that the preservation of the family takes priority over reproductive rights.

The courts have been hard on lesbian mothers, disallowing adoption by same-sex couples and denying custody rights over biological offspring from previous marriages. No state currently permits marriage by same-sex couples. A letter in the feminist newsjournal, *Off Our Backs* ("Lesbian Custody Battle" 1989), suggests that the movement for gay and lesbian rights is as strong a force for change as is reproductive technology. Lynn and Lisa describe their end run by means of adoption around the legal fatherhood question. They asked the court in Washington state to permit Lynn to adopt Lisa's biological daughter. They feared that if Lisa died, Lynn might loose guardianship of the child, and they also wanted to secure rights for social security and insurance benefits for the child through Lynn (who works as a family therapist). The court allowed Lynn to adopt the child.

The accumulation of legal adoptions by same-sex couples will signal a drastic change in America's principle of legitimacy. Is Lynn the legal father, a second mother, or are both generic co-parents? It will depart from Malinowski's principle that "one man" is the social father, and that marriage is a license for parenthood. Lynn becomes a female father, or perhaps a generic parent, in this case. Several societies within the ethnographic spectrum allow same-sex marriage and parenthood. These cases are ones in which an exceptional person of one sex *acts* in the opposite gender role.

In the case of Lynn and Lisa, reproductive technology as such is not challenging family law. The case is about adoption and social parenthood, but is stimulated by the lesbian and gay rights movement. Members of this movement challenge the legal principle of legitimacy both by using reproductive technology and also by attacking presumptions of the law about parenthood.

Surrogate Motherhood

The misnamed practice of "surrogate motherhood"[7] can dissociate social and biological motherhood—and fatherhood. Surrogacy can also be combined with in vitro fertilization and embryo transfer. If genetic material other than that of the contracting couple and the surrogate is used, this combination can produce up to five different kinds of parents: a genetic father, a social father, a genetic mother, a gestational mother, and a social mother (Edwards 1991). The more typical procedure involves a couple contracting with a woman to be artificially inseminated with the husband's sperm, to carry the fetus, to give up all rights to the child, and to allow the wife of the couple to adopt it, often in exchange for some amount of money and insurance coverage.

Several court cases have determined that the payment of money violates adoption laws, and that the rights to privacy and to reproduce do not override the prohibition on baby selling and buying (Blank 1984; Shannon 1988). The case of *Baby M* in New Jersey is the most famous, but in the end it set no precedents. In *Baby M*, Bill Sterns contracted a surrogacy arrangement with Mary Beth Whitehead and her husband. Whitehead decided to keep the baby and refused the $10,000 payment specified in the contract. The case raised many difficult questions regarding surrogacy: breach of contract by refusing to surrender the baby; a custody dispute between two biological parents who are unmarried; legality of payment for surrogacy; and issues on the status of surrogacy centers (Shannon 1988; Andrews 1989).

After a bitter struggle, the case was decided by the New Jersey Supreme Court in 1988. In the final decision, *Baby M* was decided on the same tenets as custody disputes in divorces—the best interest of the child and the biological parent's rights (Chessler 1988; Shannon 1988). The Court voided both the surrogacy contract and the adoption, thus restoring Whitehead's parental interest. Stern's permanent custody of the child was judged to be in the best interest of the child, and Whitehead received visitation rights as a biological parent.

A less-notorious California case involved both a surrogacy and embryo transfer, but also was interpreted in terms of the rights of biological parents. A white couple, Mark and Crispina Calvert, contracted with Anna Johnson, a black woman, to bear a child. Crispina Calvert had had a hysterectomy so the couple had the wife's ovum fertilized in vitro, then implanted in Anna Johnson. During the pregnancy, Johnson decided that she did not want to give up the baby. The court considered the possibility of the child having two mothers, Calvert and Johnson, but decided that it might be confusing and not in the best interest of the child. The court ruled against Johnson on the ground that she was not genetically related to the child she had carried. The California Supreme Court upheld this decision but held that both Crispina Calvert and Anna Johnson had acceptable proof of maternity. It then based its decision on the intentions of Johnson and the Calverts, which had been for Crispina Calvert to become the mother of the child (Cordes 1993a; 1993b).

In both surrogacy cases the courts used existing law on biological parentage as a basic tenet for decisions. The California lower court specified that the meaning of biological mother is *genetic mother*, not *gestational mother*, although the higher court sidestepped this question.[8] These decisions are *refining* family law more than challenging it. Legal experts recognize that additional regulation of reproductive technology is needed (Krause 1983; Garrison 1988), and that many ethical and legal questions remain to be worked out regarding human reproductive technology.

While reproductive technology may yet bring about changes in America's legal principle of legitimacy, they are not likely to be radical changes for most people. First, reproductive technology is used by a small minority of those couples who have fertility problems. Most Americans will continue reproducing through sexual intercourse. Second, while litigation involving reproductive technology is dramatic, most people using reproductive technology never go to court. Surrogacy is the most controversial practice, but it is not becoming common and does not produce much litigation[9] (Garrison 1988). Whether reproductive technology will change the American principle of legitimacy depends on whether small interest groups can mobilize sentiment to change the basic understanding of the family as people experience it. This seems unlikely within the next few generations, especially in light of the structural factors and intergenerational interests affecting America's principle of legitimacy.

WOMEN'S ROLE IN SHAPING THE AMERICAN PRINCIPLE OF LEGITIMACY

What human agents and intergenerational interests have reshaped America's principle of legitimacy into a more restitutive form that makes little distinction between biological and social fatherhood? The cross-cultural composite framework presented in Chapter 9 can be applied in a limited way. I want to argue that women's intergenerational interests, along with men's, have been formative over the past century in American views of illegitimacy. In the cross-cultural findings, female power *buffers* the effect of hierarchy on the severity of illegitimacy sanctions. American women's efforts have been consistent with this since the last century. Middle-class and upper-class women have worked to make the treatment of illegitimacy less repressive for women and children. These women:

—have worked to design and implement welfare programs for all mothers.
—have been fundamental in the organization and staffing of maternity homes, which have attempted to re-integrate illegitimate mothers into society and recently to reduce stigma.
—have pressed legal cases on behalf of offspring that have expanded the conditions for postpartum legitimation, and thereby inheritance.

Three cultural themes gaining strength in the late 1800s and early 1900s form a backdrop to women's efforts in norm creation and implementation—the ideas of women's separate sphere, of the family wage, and of the priceless child. These themes began to alter the kinds of intergenerational interests in play and offered women a power base. It is important to understand the intergenerational interests pushed into action by these cultural themes.

Interests in One's Own Children

The value of children as economic assets to parents has declined in Western societies, partly as a consequence of industrialization and partly as a result of laws restricting child labor. Children were employed in the early factories, offices, department stores, and even in mines, so industrialization was not the prime factor reducing their economic utility. The passage of child labor laws—grounded in a new definition of the child as emotionally priceless—further restricted opportunities for children's employment outside the home (Zelizer 1985). These laws were intended to advance children's safety and well being, but they also had the effect of making children even more of an economic liability to parents than before.[10]

Until the 1970s family law in the United States assumed that the husband more than the wife has the duty of supporting the family (Weitzman 1985). A similar idea—the family wage—was a slogan used by the labor movement to help secure higher wages for men. Wrapped in this slogan was the familistic ideal that the husband should be solely responsible for providing for the whole family, while the wife maintained the home and nurtured the children. Women's groups did not protest this idea but supported laws placing work restrictions on women (Skocpol 1992). The family wage and restrictions on child labor meant that men fiscally invested more in children.

The upshot of the male-provider pattern is that it yields a different intergenerational interest for men than for women. Men may want to minimize financial obligations by restricting the conditions for legitimate claims for support from unmarried mothers and offspring. Men may also want to reduce the extent to which the costs of illegitimacy come from their own pockets.

Intrinsic Interests in One's Own Children

American fathers, like fathers in most of the sample societies, typically do not develop the depth of emotional tie to offspring that mothers do. Father-child involvement is typically moderate. American middle-class fathers would be scored in the middle of the cross-cultural father-infant proximity scale (Barry 1995), and not in the high end of the scale. Studies of household labor show that fathers typically do little infant and child care (DeStefano and Colasanto 1990). Following infancy, fathers may come to have somewhat more contact, but the major responsibility for children typically remains with the mother.

Studies of the division of labor in the home usually consider only two-parent homes. Father-absence further reduces men's involvement with infants and children. Many infants and children experience extended periods in mother-only households, resulting from illegitimacy or divorce. Despite the fact that many states have omitted the presumption of the mother being the more fit parent from divorce and child custody law, the great majority of couples still elect to have the mother be the physical custodian of the children (Weitzman 1985). The percentage of children in mother-headed homes tripled over the past thirty years, and stood at 23 percent overall, with over half of black children in mother-headed homes in 1992 (DaVanzo and Rahman 1993).

Intrinsic Interests in All the Group's Children

Today Americans value children in general as objects of affection. A separate issue from parents' bonds to their own children is the cultural definition of children as special, and adult affection toward children in general. The West has evolved a social definition of children as precious, innocent, and in special need of guidance and protection. Aries (1962) traces the definition of childhood back several centuries among the elite classes of Europe and suggests that the definition of children as special and in need of protection gradually trickled down the class ladder.[11] Zelizer (1985) documents that the early twentieth century brought the widespread American acceptance of the definition of the child as economically worthless, but emotionally priceless. This new definition of childhood de-emphasized the labor power of children and contributed to the enactment of restrictive child labor laws earlier this century.

The new definition of childhood brought about a different kind of interest in children's well-being. Children had been evaluated by the courts previously as a means—in terms of their financial earning power. By the 1930s they became evaluated as emotionally priceless. During the 1940s middle-class parents brought child-rearing practices into congruence with the new definition of the child. This decreased the use of physical punishment, and parents began to consider the child's needs and self-fulfillment more (Bronfenbrenner 1963). This powerful new definition, and the intergenerational interests it created, stimulated "child saver" movements that view children as innocent victims. Recent "child saver" movements include the movement against child abuse, and the children's rights movement (Best 1990).

The definition of children as priceless makes arguments in favor of children's well-being more compelling. By the same token the new definition can make women and men more sympathetic to programs intended to improve the unfortunate conditions of illegitimate children, so long as these programs did not work against other values. A major issue in the current welfare debate is the extent to which the AFDC program works against other values—whether it encourages more illegitimacy, unemployment, and welfare dependency rather than the well-being of children.

Women's Work in Norm Formation

The new definition of childhood was linked to the earlier doctrine of men's and women's separate spheres, which saw motherhood as sacred, and elevated the moral status of married women of the "better" classes. Women were to be experts in domestic matters and in morality, and in caring for priceless children. While women did not have the vote, the idea of woman's domesticity gave women more power on issues within their sphere. Women activists used the idea of women's domesticity to expand their influence into the community and eventually into federal government. They presented welfare and morality issues as falling within women's special sphere and mobilized enough women to make their interests known.

During the 1910s and 1920s the federal government enacted welfare programs for women and children. Mother's pensions and maternal-infant health programs were put into place largely through the efforts of nationwide women's organizations. While these programs were short-lived, they show clear examples of women's work in norm creation. Skocpol (1992) calls these welfare programs created by women in the interest of women and children *maternalistic* rather than *paternalistic* welfare policies.

In America women organized and gained power on certain issues. They formed two nationwide groups—the National Congress of Mothers and the General Federation of Women's Clubs. These organizations pushed for federal and state legislation on behalf of all mothers in need—whether they be married, widowed, or unmarried mothers. Their effectiveness can be seen in the fact that three-quarters of the states passed mother's pension laws during the 1910s and 1920s.

Women reformers from the middle and upper classes saw welfare benefits for poor women as a way of honoring all mothers and helping children. "The originators of the mother's pension laws intended to include needy mothers in the same moral universe as themselves, providing them with regular and nondemeaning material assistance to make it possible for them to realize a version of the same basic ideals of homemaking and motherhood to which the ladies themselves aspired" (Skocpol 1992: 479). These ideals can be seen in the requirements for receiving a pension. A pension brought with it the requirement to be a morally "fit" mother and to keep a "suitable home." This was a policy against drunkenness and sexual permissiveness.

In practice there was a negative side to these welfare programs. The matter of keeping a suitable home introduced an element of control into the pension plan. The pension was not sufficient income in itself, so mothers had to take part-time jobs or take work into their homes. While the original intent was to help all needy mothers, unwed mothers were among those less likely to receive assistance. The pensions were based on matching state and federal funds, so they were usually underfunded. Pennsylvania had as many people on the waiting list as it was funding. Minorities and unmarried mothers were sometimes excluded, contrary to the original intent. By 1931, only three states explicitly allowed unmarried mothers to receive pensions (Skocpol 1992: 466).

Women's groups pushed through a federal bill for women's and children's health in 1921. Under its auspices, almost three thousand prenatal centers were set up around the country, health conferences were held, literature distributed, and visits made to millions of homes by health workers in the following seven years. Like the intention of the mother's pension plan, this bill provided health assistance to all women, regardless of whether they were wed or unwed, rich or poor. Women administered and worked in this program. It emphasized midwives rather than physicians as birth professionals. The program needed its funding renewed after its first five years. It continued to struggle along until it expired in 1929. This demise was partly due to the efforts of the American Medical Association, whose members wanted to move into the territory occupied by midwives. Partly, there was an unsympathetic Congress and President.

The main thrust of women's intergenerational interests is visible in the maternalist welfare programs. They had an intrinsic interest in emotionally priceless children. Their concern for morality reflected middle-class and upper-class women's expanded domestic sphere. Programs were conceived universalistically in the interests of all mothers and children. This universalism made little distinction in the treatment of married and unmarried mothers, although they would have judged the unmarried mother to be immoral or unfortunate and encouraged her return to the moral community. Putting this universalistic ideal into practice proved more difficult.

These maternalist programs of the 1910s and 1920s are the precursors of America's welfare programs today. Later programs drew heavily on them. There are many parallels with current programs such as AFDC and WIC. It is likely that some of women's intergenerational interests underlying the programs of the 1910s and 1920s carried over into more recent welfare programs.

Women's Interests in Illegitimacy Control

Women's work in implementing illegitimacy norms and sanctions can also be seen in their work in founding, administering and staffing homes for unmarried mothers (Kunzel 1993). In the 1800s evangelical religion offered a rationale for these homes—salvation and re-entry into the moral community for women in trouble.

The maternity home movement had roots in the separate spheres doctrine. The first home and the largest organization was initiated by a wealthy man, Charles Nelson Crittenton (Kunzel 1993: 14). Evangelical women were important in setting up and operating homes for unwed mothers across the country—more than 200 homes by the 1920s. Women worked with the Salvation Army, the National Florence Crittenton Mission (named after Charles Crittenton's daughter) and other groups. The homes opened their doors free of charge initially for any pregnant unmarried women who wanted to re-enter the moral community, although few homes catered to black women. Evangelical women's moral authority in this effort came both from religion and from the separate spheres doctrine which equated femininity and morality. Because of their natural abilities, it was argued, women needed little or no training to be competent maternity-home workers. After all, a maternity home was a home, and women knew more about care of children and keeping the institution homelike.

After 1920, the maternalist movement began to lose some moral authority in the maternity home movement. Social work, with its clinical scientific emphasis, began to replace the maternalist bent in the maternity homes. This was not a casual or smooth shift in orientation, but a protracted struggle between two factions of women to define illegitimacy. Nonetheless, the homes still attempted to bring women back into the moral community. The work still involved some degree of resocialization of wayward girls and women, but the model changed from one of immorality to one of delinquency (Kunzel 1993). Like some other forms of deviance in America, illegitimacy was medicalized (Nathanson 1991). After social workers became more dominant, the maternity homes began to help mothers place their children for adoption, thereby helping them conceal pregnancies from their local communities and avoid being outcast and stigmatized as unwed mothers.

There is an irony in the history of maternity homes. While the staff of the maternity homes felt they were being benevolent, the illegitimate mothers often saw the homes as places of punishment. They felt they were incarcerated because of the close moral supervision, and the requirement to stay for a specified time. In fact, some were sentenced to maternity homes by the courts. Other women during this time turned to maternity homes only after failing to find abortionists (Kunzel 1993). Once in the maternity home women were interrogated on the details of their sex lives and pregnancies. They were required to work. Their mail was opened. Not surprisingly, there were complaints, acts of resistance, and occasional attempts to run away from maternity homes (Kunzel 1993).

Why did women of the reputable classes elect to work with unwed mothers and not with unwed fathers? Maternity home staff often looked for, and often heard, accounts of male culpability—of seduction, for example—in women's stories of how they became pregnant. Yet the thought of working to change men seems scarcely to have been expressed in the maternalist movement. Part of the answer to this question too lies in the doctrine of separate spheres. Perhaps activists saw illegitimate mothers, more than illegitimate fathers, as capable of being resocialized into the moral community. They likely perceived illegitimate mothers as being more culpable because it was "woman's sphere" to uphold morality. The end result of the path chosen was a continued double standard in illegitimacy, but one that gave some respite from the more repressive treatment of women and children from previous times.

Interests of Offspring

One other cluster of interests and life-cycle stages is important in the shift in the American handling of illegitimacy. Offspring may have intergenerational interests in the property, or in other benefits, from the deceased. Death triggers this set of intergenerational interests. The idea of an interest triggered by death is grounded in evidence rather than in theory. A glance at court cases concerning illegitimate parents and offspring in the United States reveals that many cases are brought by adult offspring, or by their mothers on their behalf, following the death of a parent (Kay 1965; Zingo and Early 1994). For example, Kay analyzes 27 cases concerning the question of what it means for the illegitimate child to be "received into the family" in the California law.

Most of the 27 cases involve unmarried mothers and were brought to court after the death of the father. They represent an attempt by the child or his mother to establish that the child had been legitimated by the father during his lifetime in order to qualify the child as heir of its father. (Kay 1965: 62)

All 27 cases concern inheritance. In these cases, mothers acting on behalf of immature offspring, or the offspring themselves, have advanced their economic interests following the death of the father. In bringing legal actions, they helped to elaborate case law on illegitimacy. The intergenerational interests of these women were not moralist, but interests in the economic welfare of themselves and of their own offspring.

CONCLUSION

These examples of women's involvement in national welfare programs, maternity homes, and case law are not the whole story of how America's principle of legitimacy came to be more restitutive. They provide insights into how women were both important agents in molding illegitimacy norms and key players in the control of illegitimacy. The historical examples of women's agency in molding the principle of legitimacy are consistent with the buffering effect of female power in the cross-cultural findings—specifically, that hierarchy and centralization are more likely to produce repressive sanctions when women have little power and are unorganized. After American women organized and gained input into policy and the institutions dealing with illegitimacy, there was more movement toward restitution. Early practices continued to shame women and to allow illegitimate fathers to slip away without punishment. In recent decades, policies have de-emphasized stigma and turned toward restitution by the biological father. While women's efforts alone by no means account for this transition, it cannot be understood without taking their interests as women and as mothers into account.

Despite being a centralized, hierarchically organized society, America is moving toward restitutive social and legal treatments of illegitimacy. Historical studies document that women's efforts have been important in the formation of a more restitutive treatment of illegitimacy in America. This is predictable from the cross-cultural finding that female power buffers the effect of hierarchy to produce less repressive sanctions for nonmarital conception and birth. Had there been cross-cultural testing during the heyday of explicit theorizing on illegitimacy, we would have more readily understood that the shift toward restitution is grounded in basic secular trends in Western social structure.

NOTES

1. There have been backflows and eddies in certain times and locations. For example, after some social revolutions, illegitimacy law has been tossed out by the new regimes only to be reinstated later (Coser and Coser 1974).

2. It seems to be the nonmarital offspring of noble *men* who chose to maintain a relationship with them. They could still bask in family honor, although to a lesser degree, and display a modified version of the family herald, or crest (Boutell 1970). The historical record is startlingly quiet on the fate of illegitimate offspring of noble *women*, and on the fate of offspring of men who were not socially recognized.

3. Equalizing the rights of illegitimate children cannot be a complete success so long as legal marriage is recognized and children born in marriage can be in custody of both parents in a common residence. Nonmarital offspring cannot have the same level of interaction and care from both parents that marital offspring have. Further, testamentary freedom for parents prevents equality for illegitimate children, since they can be legally disinherited. If illegitimate children's right to inherit has precedence over the parental testamentary freedom, then testamentary freedom is lost and illegitimate children are guaranteed more than legitimate children are. Finally, since fathers cannot be

discovered, tracked down, or made to pay recompense in all cases, equality of legitimate and illegitimate offspring can be only a general principle or goal of law, rather than a concrete reality. Davis (1939b) has clear reasoning on this problem of the difficulty of ending the disabilities of illegitimate children.

4. Female premarital sex activity increased just after the turn of the century, then again during the sixties and seventies. The practice of dating coincided with the first, and living together with the second. There have been two sexual revolutions this century, and a third around the end of the colonial period of American history (Vinovskis 1988).

5. Most of the recent research on adolescent pregnancy in general samples or in the middle class is of an abstract psychological nature. This massive body of research tends not to describe concrete social interaction patterns, parental reactions, shame, and the like, but rather with questions such as locus of control, self-esteem, and a host of similar issues. Concrete descriptions of personal and community reactions to illegitimacy in the lower class black community are more plentiful.

6. Alternately, there may be regional variation, or variation according to neighborhood composition. Stack's (1974) study finding relaxed treatment of illegitimacy was done in a midwest neighborhood where most residents were poor. Some of the other studies finding some repressive reactions were conducted in states along the east coast.

7. The so-called surrogate usually is the biological parent and always is the one who goes through labor and childbirth. This labeling seems to be a bit of clinical flim-flam, designed to make infertile couples feel that they can have their "own" child, and to disallow any claims of the biological mother on her child.

8. The California Supreme Court's principle that parenthood is an intentional act might seem to challenge family law. However, the court used the principle in very restricted circumstances, so that there are very few applications. The court used intention to become a parent as a way of testing which of two legal mothers to grant rights over the child. The court probably did not mean to imply, for example, that parents have no rights or obligations when they conceive unintentionally.

9. Andrews (1989) suggests that surrogacy centers' attempts to minimize contact between surrogate parents and adoptive parents creates more hard feelings and a greater sense of loss for the surrogate. Her suggestion is that is surrogacy should be redefined as a gift-exchange relationship rather than a contractual one, with the surrogate mother having more opportunity to maintain a relationship with the child as it matures.

10. Some believe that children still can be good economic investments among the poor. In public debate today, the charge is made that mothers receiving payments from AFDC are having children for economic gain. However, the level of pay from AFDC and related programs is rarely enough for illegitimate mothers to rise above the poverty line and probably never as much as minimum wage would pay for their hours in child care. The hidden motive behind these charges likely is resentment at having to help bear the cost of raising other people's children, especially illegitimate children.

11. Other family historians (Mount 1982; Pollock 1983) suggest that parent-child relations and family interaction generally have not changed radically. In part this disagreement stems from a focus on social definitions by one group and social interaction by the other. Family interaction probably has changed less radically than cultural definitions and ideals.

Appendix A: Variables Used in the Study

Previously published variables are presented in alphabetical order. The sources cited are listed in the references.

Achieved Female Economic and Political Power and Authority (Sanday 1981b); called "female power" here.

Affection Toward Children. The average score from Barry et al. (1977) on four variables: affection toward boys and toward girls in early childhood and in later childhood. These are part of their codes on child training.

Community Size (Murdock and WIlson 1972).

Density of Population (Murdock and Provost 1973).

Descent (Murdock and Wilson 1972).

Fixity of Residence (Murdock and Provost 1973).

Frequency of Extramarital Sex for Wives (Broude and Greene 1976).

Frequency of Internal Warfare (Wheeler 1987).

Inheritance of Real Property (Murdock 1967).

Marital Residence (Murdock and Wilson 1972).

Political Sovereignty (Tuden and Marshall 1972); called "political complexity" here.

Presence of Police (Tuden and Marshall 1972).

Preservation and Storage of Food (Murdock and Morrow 1970).

Prevailing Form of Family Organization (Murdock 1967).

Role of Father During Early Childhood (Barry and Paxson 1971); called father-child proximity or involvement here.

Role of Father During Infancy (Barry and Paxson 1971); called father-infant proximity or involvement here.

Severity of Sanctions for Illegitimacy. This is an original code for this study.

Social Stratification (Murdock and Provost 1973).

Subsistence Economy (Murdock 1967).

Descriptions of the severity of illegitimacy sanctions were coded from sources in the Human Relations Area Files, and from other published ethnographies. Graduate assistants helped in the initial research using the cumbersome sixty-item coding schemes mentioned in Chapter Four, and at various points in extracting material from the Human Relations Area Files and ethnographies. I have classified societies into the set of four categories used here, sometimes using the descriptions extracted by assistants, but often returning to HRAF or the ethnographies to check on uncertainties.

Coding reliability for this typology is substantial, as indicated by agreement between two coders on a subsample of ethnographic descriptions. To ascertain coding reliability, a convenience subsample of sixteen societies was selected and coded independently by a graduate assistant. Intercoder reliability was adequate, with identical codes on 88 percent or fourteen of the sixteen cases.

The validity of the measure of illegitimacy sanctions is apparent in its correlations with other conceptually similar variables. The gammas for the association of severity of illegitimacy sanctions with three somewhat similar variables is as follows:

Consequences for adolescent premarital pregnancy (Anderson et al. 1994)—
Gamma = +.40, pr. < .05, N = 38.

Norms for female premarital sex (Murdock 1967)—
Gamma = +.31, pr. < .05, N = 97.

Attitude toward premarital sex for females (Broude and Greene 1976)—
Gamma = +.38, pr. < .05, N = 105.

Sexual freedom for adolescent boys (Barry and Schlegel 1984)—
Gamma = −.33, pr. < .05, N = 103.

Sexual freedom for adolescent girls (Barry and Schlegel 1984)—
Gamma = −.31, pr. < .05, N = 107.

All five correlations of illegitimacy sanctions with other similar variables are in the expected direction. The levels of association are moderate, which is to be expected. None of these other measures of sex and illegitimacy reactions are built upon the distinction between repressive and restitutive sanctions, and several focus on sexuality rather than pregnancy, and on adolescence rather than the sometimes broader premarital period.

Appendix B: Bibliography on Ethnographic Sources on Illegitimacy

This bibliography gives the sources used for the illegitimacy codes for each society in the study. When possible, I used the copy, or translation of the work available in the Human Relations Area Files. Sources are organized by culture and listed by the number assigned for the Standard Cross-Cultural Sample (Murdock and White 1969). Sources for a given culture are then listed in alphabetical order. The number before each work refers to its relative utility in coding for the severity of sanctions for illegitimacy. References in the chapters to these works contain the SCCR society number in addition to the author's name and date of publication.

1. NAMA HOTTENTOT

2. Dapper, O. 1933. "Kaffraria or Land of the Kafirs, also Named Hottentots." In I. Schapera and B. Farrington (Eds.), *The Early Cape Hottentots*. Cape Town: Van Riebeeck Society, 1-77, 301-309.
1. Schapera, I. 1930. *The Khoisan Peoples of South Africa*. London: Routledge and Sons.

2. KUNG BUSHMEN

4. Fourie, L. 1928. "The Bushmen of South West Africa." In *The Native Tribes of South West Africa*. Cape Town: Cape Times, 89-105.
2. Marshall, Lorna. 1957. "N!ow." *Africa*. 27:232-240.
3. Marshall, Lorna. 1965. "!Kung Bushmen of the Malahara Desert." In J. Gibbs Jr. (Ed.), *Peoples of Africa*. N.J.: Holt, Rinehart and Winston, 241-278.
1. Schapera, I. 1930. *The Khoisan Peoples of South Africa*. London: Routlege and Sons.

3. THONGA

1. Junod, H. A. 1927. *The Life of a South African Tribe.* vol. II, 2d ed. London: Macmillan.

4. LOZI

1. Gluckman, M. 1951. "The Lozi of Barotseland in Northwestern Rhodesia." In E. Colson and M. Gluckman (Eds.), *Seven Tribes of British Central Africa.* Manchester: Manchester University Press, 1-93.

5. MBUNDU

1. Childs, G. M. 1949. *Umbundu Kinship and Character.* London: International African Institute.
2. Hambly, W. D. 1934. "The Ovimbundu of Angola. Field Museum of Natural History." *American Anthropologist* 36: 157-167.

6. SUKU. No information.

7. BEMBA

1. Richards, A. I. 1956. *Chisungu: A Girls' Initiation Ceremony Among the Bemba of Northern Rhodesia.* London: Faber and Faber.

8. NYAKYUSA

1. Wilson, M. 1977. *For Men and Elders.* New York: Africana Publishing for the African International Institute.

9. HADZA. No information.

10. LUGURU

1. Christensen, J. B. 1963. "Utani: Joking, Sexual License, and Social Obligations Among the Luguru." *American Anthropologist* 65: 1314-1327.

11. KIKUYU

1. Kenyatta, J. 1954. *Facing Mount Kenya: The Tribal Life of the Kikuyu.* London: Secker and Warburg.
2. Routledge, W. S., and Katherine Routledge. 1910. *With a Prehistoric People.* London: Edward Arnold.

12. GANDA

1. Mair, L. P. 1934. *An African People in the Twentieth Century*. London: Routlege and Sons.
2. Mair, L, P. 1940. *Native Marriage in Baganda*. London: Oxford University Press for the International Institute for African Languages and Cultures.
3. Roscoe, J. 1911. *The Baganda: An Account of Their Native Customs and Beliefs*. London: Macmillan.

13. MBUTI

1. Turnbull, C. M. 1962. *The Forest People*. 3d ed. New York: Simon and Schuster.

14. NKUNDO MONGO

1. Hulstaert, G. E. 1928. *Le Mariage des Nkundo*. Bruxelles: G. van Campenhout.

15. BANEN. No information.

16. TIV

1. Akiga. 1939. *Akiga's Story*. Rupert East (trans. & ed.). International Institute of African Languages and Cultures 15.
2. Bohannon, P. 1957. *Tiv Farm and Settlement*. London: Her Majesty's Stationery Office.
4. Bohannon, P., and L. Bohannon. 1958. *Three Source Notebooks in Tiv Ethnography*. New Haven: HRAF Press.
3. Downes, R. M. 1933. *The Tiv Tribe*. Kaduna: Government Printer.

17. IGBO

1. Basden, G. T. 1921. *Among the Ibos of Nigeria*. London: Seeley, Service and Company.
4. Green, M. M. 1947. *Ibo Village Affairs*. London: Sidgwick and Jackson.
3. Leith-Ross, S. 1939. *African Women*. London: Routledge and Kegan Paul.
2. Uchendu, V. C. 1965. *The Igbo of Southeast Nigeria*. New York: Holt, Rhinehart and Winston.

18. FON

2. Bohannon, L. 1949. "Dahomean Marriage: A Reanalysis." *Africa* 19: 273-278.

1. Herskovits, M. J. 1938. *Dahomey*. New York: J. J. Augustin.

19. ASHANTI

2. Christensen, J. B. 1954. *Double Descent Among the Fanti*. New Haven: Human Relations Area Files, 14.
1. Fortes, M. 1950. "Kinship and Marriage Among the Ashanti." In A. R. Radcliffe-Brown and D. Forde (Eds.), *African Systems of Kinship and Marriage*. London: Oxford University Press for the African International Institute, 252-284.
3. Rattray, R. S. 1929. *Ashanti Law and Constitution*. Oxford: Clarendon Press.

20. MENDE. No information.

21. WOLOF

3. Ames, D. W. 1953. "Plural Marriage Among the Wolof in the Gambia." Ph.D. dissertation, Northwestern University.
1. Fayet, M. J. L. 1939. *Coutume des Ouolof Musulsmans (Cercle du Baol)*. Comite d'Etudes Historiques et Scientifiques de l'Afrique Occidentale Francaise, Publications, Serie A, 8:147-193.
4. Gorer, G. 1935. "Book One: Senegalese." In *Africa Dances*. London: Faber and Faber, 25-79.
2. Irvine, J. T. 1974. "Caste and Communication in a Wolof Village." Ph.D. dissertation, University of Pennsylvania.

22. BAMBARA

3. Dieterlen, G. 1951. *Essai sur la religion Bambara*. Paris: Presses Univeritaires de France.
1. Henry, J. 1910. *L'ame d'un Peuple Africain: Les Bambara, Leur Vie Psychique, Ethiques, Sociale, Religieuse*. Munster: W. Aschendorff.
2. Monteil, C. 1924. *Les Bambara du Segou et du Kaarta*. Paris: LaRose.

23. TALLENSI

1. Fortes, M. 1949. *The Web of Kinship Among the Tallensi*. London: Oxford University Press.

24. SONGHAI

1. Miner, H. 1953. *The Primitive City of Timbuctoo*. Princeton: Princeton University Press.

25. WODAABE FULANI

2. Dupire, M. 1963. "The Position of Women in a Pastoral Society. In D. Paulme (Ed.), *Women of Tropical Africa*. Berkeley: University of California Press, 47-92.
1. Wilson-Haffenden, J. R. 1927. "Ethnological Notes on the Shuwalbe Group of Borroro Fulani." *Journal of the Royal Anthropological Institut* 57: 275-294.

26. HAUSA

2. Greenberg, J. H. 1947a. *The Influence of Islam on a Sudanese Religion.* New York: J. J. Augustin.
3. Greenberg, J. H. 1947b. "Islam and Clan Organization among the Hausa." *Southwestern Journal of Anthropology* 3: 193-211.
1. Smith, M. 1955. *The Economy of Hausa Communities of Zaria.* London: Her Majesty's Stationery Office.

27. MASSA

1. Garine, Igor de. 1964. *Les Massa du Cameroun.* Paris: Presses Universitaires de France.

28. AZANDE

2. Evans-Pritchard, E. E. 1937. *Witchcraft, Oracles, and Magic among the Azande.* Oxford: Clarendon.
1. Lagae, C. R. 1926. *Les Azande ou Niam-Niam.* Bruxelles: Vromant.
4. Larken, P. M. 1930. "Impressions of the Azande." *Sudan Notes and Records* 13: 99-115.
3. Reynolds, H. 1904. "Notes on the Azande Tribe of the Congo." *African Society Journal* 3: 238-246.

29. FUR. No information.

30. OTORO NUBA

1. Nadel, S. F. 1947. *The Nuba.* London: Oxford University Press.

31. SHILLUK

1. Butt, A. 1952. "The Shilluk." In *The Nilotes of the Anglo-Egyptian Sudan and Uganda.* London: International African Institute, 45-67.

3. Howell, P. P. 1953. "Observations on the Shilluk of the Upper Nile. Customary Law: Marriage and the Violation of Rights in Women." *Africa* 23: 94-109.
2. Seligman, C. G., and B. Z. Seligman. 1932. "The Shilluk." In *Pagan Tribes of the Nilotic Sudan*. London: Routlege and Sons, 37-105.

32. MAO

1. Grottanelli, V. L. 1940. *I Mao*. Rome: Missione Etnografica nel Uollega Occidentale 1: 1-387.

33. KAFA. No information.

34. MASAI

2. Hollis, A. C. 1905. *The Masai: The Language and Folklore*. Oxford: Clarendon.
1. Leakey, L. 1930. "Some Notes on the Masai of Kenya Colony." *Journal of the Royal Anthropological Institute* 60: 185-209.
3. Maguire, R. A. J. 1928. "The Masai Penal Code." *Africa Society Journal* 28: 12-18.

35. KONSO

1. Hallpike, C. R. 1972. *The Konso of Ethiopia*. Oxford: Clarendon Press.
2. Jensen, A. E. 1936. *Im Lande des Gada*. Stuttgart: Strecker und Schroder.

36. SOMALI. No information.

37. AMHARA

1. Messing, S. D. 1957. *The Highland-Plateau Amhara of Ethiopia*. Ph.D. dissertation, University of Pennsylvania.

38. BOGO. No information.

39. KENUZI NUBIANS

1. Herzog, R. 1957. *Die Nubier*. Berlin: Akademie-Verlag.

40. TEDA. No information.

41. TUAREG

1. Lhote, H. 1944. *Les Touaregs du Hoggar*. Paris: Payot.

42. RIFFIANS

1. Coon, C. S. 1931. *Tribes of the Rif*. Cambridge: Peabody Museum of American Archaelogy and Ethnology.

43. EGYPTIANS. No information.

44. HEBREWS

2. Mace, D. R. 1953. *Hebrew Marriage*. New York: Philosophical Library.
1. Patai, R. 1961. *Sex and Family in the Bible and the Middle East*. Garden City: Doubleday.

45. BABYLONIANS

1. Delaporte, L. J. 1970. *Mesopotamia*. New York: Barnes and Noble.

46. RWALA BEDOUIN

1. Musil, A. 1928. *The Manners and Customs of the Rwala Bedouins*. New York: American Geographical Society.

47. TURKS. No information.

48. GHEG ALBANIANS. No information.

49. ROMANS

2. Jacobs, A. C. 1932. "Illegitimacy, Legal Aspects." Pp. 582-6. in E. Seligman and A. Johnson (Eds.), *Encyclopedia of the Social Sciences*. New York: Macmillan.
1. Pomeroy, Sarah B. 1975. *Goddesses, Whores, Wives and Slaves: Women in Classical Antiquity*. New York: Schocken.
3. Queen, S., and R. Habenstein. 1967. *The Family in Various Cultures*. Philadelphia: Lippincott.

50. BASQUES

1. Douglass, W. A. 1969. *Death in Murelaga*. Seattle: University of Washington Press.

2. Douglass, W. A. 1989. Personal communication.

51. RURAL IRISH

1. Arensberg, Conrad and Solon T. Kimball. 1940. *Family and Community in Ireland*. Cambridge: Harvard University Press.

52. NORTHERN LAPPS

1. Pehrson, Robert N. 1957. *The Bilateral Network of Social Relations in Konkama Lapp District*. Bloomington: University of Indiana Press.

53. YURAK SAMOYED. No information.

54. RUSSIANS. No information.

55. ABKHAZ. No information.

56. ARMENIANS. No information.

57. KURD. No information.

58. BASSERI. No information.

59. PUNJABI. No information.

60. MARIA GOND

2. Elwin, V. 1947. *The Muria and Their Ghotul*. Bombay: Oxford University Press.
1. Grigson, W. V. 1949. *The Maria Gonds of Bastar*. London: Oxford University Press.

61. TODA

2. Peter, Prince. 1955. "The Todas." *Man* 55: 89-93.
1. Rivers, W. H. R. 1906. *The Todas*. London: Macmillan.

62. SANTAL

1. Mukherjea, C. 1962. *The Santals* rev. 2d ed. Calcutta: A. Mukerhee.

63. UTTAR PRADESH. No information.

64. BURUSHO. No information.

65. KAZAK

2. Grodekov, N. I. 1899. *Kirgizy i Karakirgizy Syr-Dar'inskoi Oblasti*. Vol. 1. Tashkent: Lekhtin.
1. Hudson, A. E. 1938. *Kazak Social Structure*. Yale University Press.

66. KHALKA (OUTER MONGOLIA)

1. Vreeland, H. H. 1954. *Mongol Community and Kinship Structure*. New Haven: Yale University Press.

67. LOLO

1. Lin, Y. 1947. *The Lolo of Liang Shan*. New Haven: HRAF Press.

68. LEPCHA

1. Gorer, G. 1938. *Himalayan Village: An Account of the Lepchas of Sikkim*. London: J. H. Hutton.
2. Morris, J. 1938. *Living with Lepchas*. London: W. Heinemann.

69. GARO

3. Buring, R. 1963. *Rengsanggri: Family and Kinship in a Garo Village*. Philadelphia: University of Pennsylvania Press.
2. Choudhury, B. 1958. *Some Cultural and Linguistic Aspects of the Garos*. Guahati: Assam, B.N., Dutti Borooah, B. L., Lawyer's Book Stall.
1. Costa, G. 1954. "The Gara Code of Law." *Anthropos* 49: 1041-1066.

70. LAKHER

1. Parry, N. E. 1932. *The Lakhers*. New York: Macmillan.

71. BURMESE

1. Spiro, M. E. 1977. *Kinship and Marriage in Burma*. Berkeley: University of California Press.

72. LAMET. No information.

73. VIETNAMESE

3. Brodrick, Alan. 1942. *Little China: The Annamese Lands*. London: Oxford University Press.
1. De, Tran Dinh. 1951. "Notes on Birth and Reproduction in Vietnam." Results presented by Margaret Coughlin. Unpublished Manuscript. New Haven: HRAF.
2. Tran-Van Trai. 1942. *La Famille Patriachale Annamite*. Paris: P. Lapagesse.

74. RHADE (EWE)

1. Donoghue, J. D., D. D. Whitney, and I. Ishino. 1962. *People in the Middle*. East Lansing: Michigan State University Press.

75. KHMER. No information.

76. SIAMESE (THAI)

1. Hanks, J. R. 1963. *Maternity and Its Rituals in Bang Chan*. Ithaca: Cornell University, Department of Asian Studies.

77. SEMANG. No information.

78. NICOBARESE

1. Whitehead, G. 1924. *In the Nicobar Islands*. London: Seeley, Service and Company.

79. ANDAMANESE

1. Radcliffe-Brown, A. R. 1922. *The Andaman Islanders*. Cambridge: Cambridge University Press.

80. FOREST VEDDA

1. Seligmann, C. G., and B. Z. Seligmann. 1911. *The Veddas*. Cambridge: Cambridge University Press.

81. TANALA

1. Linton, R. 1933. *The Tanala*. Field Museum of Natural History Anthropological Series, 21: 1-334.

82. NEGRI SEMBILAN. No information.

83. JAVANESE

1. Geertz, H. 1961. *The Javanese Family*. New York: Free Press.
2. Jay, R. R. 1969. *Javanese Villagers*. Cambridge: MIT Press.

84. BALINESE

2. Belo, Jane. 1949. *Bali: Rangda and Barong*. New York: J. J. Augustin.
3. Covarrubias, M. 1937. *Island of Bali*. New York: Knopf.
4. Geertz, H., and C. Geertz. 1975. *Kinship in Bali*. Chicago: University of Chicago Press.
1. Haar, B. ter. 1948. *Adat Law in Indonesia*. New York: Institute of Pacific Relations.

85. IBAN

2. Gomes, E. H. 1911. *Seventeen Years Among the Sea Dyaks of Borneo: A Record of Intimate Association with the Natives of the Borneon Jungles*. London: Seeley.
3. Roth, H. L. 1892. "The Natives of Borneo." *Journal of the Royal Anthropological Institute* 21: 11-137.
4. Roth, H. L. 1893. "The Natives of Borneo." *Journal of the Royal Anthropological Institute* 22:22-64.
1. Sutlive, V. H., Jr. 1972. *From Longhouse to Pasar: Urbanization in Sarawak, East Malaysia*. Ph.D. dissertation, University of Pittsburgh.

86. BADJAU

1. Nimmo, H. A. 1970. "Badjau Sex and Reproduction." *Ethnology* 9: 251-262.
3. Nimmo, H. A. 1972. *The Sea People of Sulu*. San Francisco: Chandler.
2. Nimmo, H. A. 1988. Personal Communication.

87. TORADJA

1. Adriani, N. and A. C. Kruijt. 1912. *De Bare'e Sprekende Toradjas van Midden-Celebes* 2d Vol., 2d ed. Amsterdam: N. V. Noord-Hollandsche Uitgevers Maatschappij.

88. TOBELORESE. No information.

89. ALORESE. No information.

90. TIWI

2. Goodale, J. C. 1971. *Tiwi Wives*. Seattle: University of Washington Press.
1. Hart, C. W. M., and A. R. Pilling. 1960. *The Tiwi of North Australia*. New York: Holt.

91. ARANDA. No information.

92. ORAKIVA. No information.

93. KIMAM

1. Serpenti, L. M. 1965. *Cultivators in the Swamps*. Assen: Van Gorcum.

94. KAPAUKU

1. Pospisal, Leopold J. 1958. *Kapauku Papuans and their Law*. New Haven: Yale University Press.

95. KWOMA

1. Whiting, J. W. M. 1941. *Becoming a Kwoma*. New Haven: Yale University Press.

96. MANUS. No information.

97. NEW IRELAND

1. Powdermaker, H. 1933. *Life in Lesu*. New York: Norton.

98. TROBRIANDERS

1. Malinowski, B. 1926. *Crime and Custom in Savage Society*. New York: Harcourt, Brace.
2. Malinowski, B. 1927a. *Sex and Repression in Savage Society*. New York: Harcourt, Brace.
4. Malinowski, B. 1927b. *The Father in Primitive Psychology*. New York: Norton.
3. Malinowski, B. 1929. *The Sexual Life of Savages in Northwestern Melanesia*. New York: Horace Liveright.

99. SIUAI

1. Oliver, D. L. 1955. *A Solomon Island Society*. Cambridge: Harvard University Press.

100. TIKOPIA

1. Firth, R. 1936. *We, the Tikopia*. London: Allen and Unwin.
2. Firth, R. 1956/57. "Ceremonies for Children and Social Frequency in Tikopia." *Oceania* 27: 12-55.
3. Rivers, W. H. R. 1914. "Tikopia." In *The History of Melanesian Society* Vol. I. Cambridge: Cambridge University Press, 298-362.

101. PENECOST. No information.

102. FIJIANS. No information.

103. AJIE. No information.

104. MAORI. No information.

105. MARQUESANS

1. Handy, E. S. C. 1923. *Native Culture of the Marquesas*. Honolulu: Bernice P. Bishop Museum.

106. SAMOANS

1. Mead, Margaret. 1928. *Coming of Age in Samoa*. New York: William Morrow.

107. GILBERTESE

1. Lundsgaarde, Henry. *Cultural Adaptation in the Southern Gilbert Islands*. Eugene: Department of Anthropology, University of Oregon.

108. MARSHALLESE

1. Chave, M. E. 1947. *The Changing Positions of the Mixed-Bloods in the Marshall Islands*. No Publisher.
5. Erdland, A. 1914. *Die Marshall-Insulaner*. Munster: W. Aschendorff.
4. Finsch, O. 1893. "Marshall-Archipel" *Ethnologische Erfahrungen und Belegstucke aus der Sudsee*. 3: 119-383.

3. Mason, L.   1954.   "Relocation of the Bikini Marshallese."   Ph.D. dissertation, Yale University.
2. Spoehr, A.   1949.   *Majuro: A Village in the Marshall Island.*   Chicago: Field Museum of Natural History.

109. TRUKESE

2. Bollig, Laurentius.   1927.   *Die Bewohner der Truk-Inseln.   Religion,Leben und Kurze Grammatikeines Mikronesiervolkes.*   Munster in Westphalia: Aschendorffsche Verlags-buchhandlung.
1. Fischer, A. M.   1963.   "Reproduction in Turk."   *Ethnology* 2: 526-40.

110. YAPESE

2. Hunt, E. E., Jr., D. M. Schneider, N. R. Kidder, and W. D. Stevens. 1949.   *The Micronesians of Yap and Their Depopulation.*   Washington: Pacific Science Board, National Research Council.
1. Muller, W.   1917.   *Yap.*   In G. Thilenius (ed), *Ergbnisse der Sudsee-Expedition 1908-1910* Part 2, B, iii.   Hamburg: Friederichsen, 1-380.

111. PALAUANS

1. Barnett, H. G.   1949.   *Palauan Society.*   Eugene: University of Oregon Press.

112. IFUAGO

1. Barton, R. F.   1919.   *Ifugao Law.*   Berkeley: University of California Press.

113. ATYAL. No information.

114. CHINESE. No information.

115. MANCHU

1. Shirokogoroff, S. M.   1924.   *Social Organization of the Manchus.*   Royal Asiatic Society, North China Branch, Extra Vol. 3: 1-194.

116. KOREANS

3. Bishop, I. L.   1898.   *Korea and Her Neighbors.*   New York: F. H. Rouell.
4. Hamel, H.   1918.   "The Description of the Kingdom of Corea."   *Royal Branch Transactions* 9: 92-148.

2. Knez, E. I. 1960. *Sam Jong Dong: A South Korean Village*. Dissertation. Syracuse University.
1. Osgood, C. B. 1951. *The Koreans and Their Culture*. New York: Ronald Press.

117. JAPANESE

1. Beardsley, R. K., J. W. Hall, and R. E. Ward. 1959. *Village Japan*. Chicago: University of Chicago Press.
3. Embree, J. F. 1944. *Suye Mura, A Japanese Village*. Chicago: University of Chicago Press.
2. Norbeck, E. 1954. *Takashima*. Salt Lake City: University of Utah Press.

118. AINU. No information.

119. GILYAK

1. Schrenck, L. von. 1881. *Die-Volker des Amur-Landes: Reisen und Forschungen in Amur-Lande in den Jahren 1854-1856*. St. Petersburg: Kaiserliche Akademie der Wissenschaften.
2. Shternberg, L. 1933. *Giliaki, Orochi, Gol'dy, Negidol'tsy, Ainy; Stat'i I Materialy*. Koshkin: Khaboravsk Daligiz.

120. YUKAGHIR. No information.

121. CHUKCHEE

1. Bogoras, W. 1901. *The Chukchee*. Memoirs of the American Museum of Natural History 11: 1-703.

122. INGALIK

1. Osgood, C. 1958. *Ingalik Social Culture*. Yale University Publications in Anthropology 55: 1-289.

123. ALEUT. No information.

124. COPPER ESKIMO. No information.

125. MONTAGNAIS

1. Lips, D. E. 1947. *Naskapi Law*. Pp. 397-492 in American Philosophical Society. Phildelphia, 397-492.

2. McGee, J. T. 1961. *Cultural Stability and Change Among the Montagnais Indians of the Lake Melville Regions of Labrador*. Washington, D.C.: Catholic University of American Press.

126. MICMAC

1. Denys, N. 1908. "The Description and Natural History of the Coasts of North America." In W. F. Ganong (ed.), *Publications of the Champlain Society* 2: 399-452, 572-606.

127. SAULTEAUX (OJIBWA)

1. Landes, R. 1937. *Ojibwa Sociology*. New York: Columbia University Press.

128. SLAVE

1. Helm, J. 1961. *The Lynx Point People*. Bulletin of the National Museum of Canada 176: 1-193.

129. KASKA (NAHANE)

1. Honigmann, J. J. 1954. *The Kaska Indians*. New Haven: Yale University Publications in Anthropology 51: 1-163.

130. EYAK. No information.

131. HAIDA

1. Murdock, G. P. 1934. "Kinship and Social Behavior among the Haida." *American Anthropologist* 36: 355-385.

132. BELLACOOLA

1. McIlwraith, T. F. 1948. *The Bella Coola Indians*. Toronto: University of Toronto Press.

133. TWANA. No information.

134. YUROK

5. Erikson, E. H. 1943. *Observations on the Yurok*. Berkeley: University of California Press.

3. Kroeber, A. L. 1925. "Yurok." *Handbook of the Indians of California* 78: 1-97.
4. Thompson, L. 1916. *To the American Indian.* Eureka, CA: Cummins Print Shop.
2. Waterman, T. T. 1920. *Yurok Geography.* Berkeley: University of California Press.
1. Waterman, T. T., and A. L. Kroeber. 1934. *Yurok Marriages.* Berkeley: University of California Press.

135. EASTERN POMO

1. Gifford, E. W. 1937. *Culture Element Distributions: IV, Pomo.* Berkeley: University of California Press.
2. Loeb, E. M. 1926. *Pomo Folkways.* Berkeley: University of California Press.

136. YOKUTS. No information.

137. WADADIKA. No information.

138. KLAMATH

2. Clifton, J. A., and D. Levine. 1963. *Klamath Personalty.* Lawrence, KS: University of Kansas Dept. of Sociology and Anthropology.
1. Spier, L. 1930. *Klamath Ethnography.* University of California Publications in American Archeology and Ethnology 30: 1-338.
3. Vogelin, E. W. 1942. *Culture Element Distribution: XX, Northeast California.* Anthropological Records 7: 47-251.

139. KUTENAI

1. Turney-High, H. H. 1941. *Ethnography of the Kutenai.* Memoirs of the American Anthropological Association 56: 1-202.

140. GROS VENTRE. No information.

141. HIDATSA. No information.

142. PAWNEE

2. Dorsey, G. A., and J. R. Murie. 1940. *Notes on Skidi Pawnee Society.* Field Museum of Natural History Anthropological Series 27: 67-119.
1. Weltfish, G. 1965. *The Lost Universe.* New York: Basic.

143. OMAHA

2. Fortune, R. F. 1932. *Omaha Secret Societies*. Columbia University Contributions to Anthropology 14: 1-193.
1. Mead, M. 1930. *The Changing Culture of an Indian Tribe*. Columbia University Contributions to Anthropology 15: 1-313.

144. HURON

1. Trigger, B. G. *The Huron Farmers of the North*. New York: Holt, Rhinehart and Winston.

145. CREEK. No information

146. NATCHEZ

1. Swanton, J. R. 1911. *Indian Tribes of the Lower Mississippi Valley*. Bulletin of the Bureau of American Ethnology 43: 1-387.

147. COMANCHE

1. Hoebel, E. A. 1940. *The Political Organization and Law-Ways of the Comanche Indians*. Memoirs of the American Anthropological Association 54:1-149.

148. CHIRICAHUA APACHE

1. Opler, M. E. 1941. *An Apache Life-Way*. Chicago: University of Chicago Press.

149. ZUNI

1. Smith, W., and J. M. Roberts. 1954. *Zuni Law*. Papers of the Peabody Museum, Harvard University 43: 1-185.

150. HAVASUPAI (PLATEAU YUMANS)

2. Smithson, C. L. 1959. *The Havasupai Woman*. Department of Anthropology.University of Utah Anthropological Papers 38: 1-170.
1. Spier, L. 1928. *Havasupai Ethnography*. Anthropological Papers of the American Museum of Natural History 29: 81-408.

151. PAPAGO

2. Joseph, A., R. B. Spicer, and J. Chesky. 1948. *The Desert People*. Chicago: University of Chicago Press.

1. Underhill, R. M.   1939.   *Social Organization of the Papago Indians*. Columbia Unviversity Contributions in Anthropology 30: 1-280.

152. HUICHOL

1. Zingg, R. M.   1938.   *The Huichols*.   University of Denver Contributions to Anthropology 6: 1-826.

153. AZTEC.   No information.

154. PAPOLUCA

1. Foster, G. M.   1942.   *A Primitive Mexican Economy*.   Monographs of the American Ethnological Society 5: 1-115.

155. QUICHE.   No information.

156. MISKITO.   No information.

157. BRIBRI.   No information.

158. CUNA

2. Bell, E. Y.   1908-9.   "The Republic of Panama and its People."   *Annual Report of the Board of Regents, Smithsonian Institution*; 607-637.
1. Marshall, D. S.   1950.   "Cuna Folk."   Unpublished manuscript in partial fulfillment for the A. B. degree, Harvard University.

159. GOAJIRO

1. Gutierrez de Pineda, V.   1948.   *Organizacion social en la Guajira*.   Revista des Instituto Etnologica Nacional 3: ii, 1-255.

160. HAITIANS

1. Herskovits, M. J.   1937.   *Life in a Haitian Valley*.   New York: Knopf.

161. CALLINAGO

1. Taylor, Douglas M.   1938.   *The Caribs of Dominica*.   Washington, D.C.: Government Printing Office.

162. WARAU

3. Kirchoff, P. 1948. *The Warrau.* Bulletin of the Bureau of American Ethnology 143: 869-881.
1. Wilbert, J. 1972. "The Warao of the Orinoco Delta." In J. Wilbert (Ed.), *Survivors of Eldorado: Four Indian Cultures of South America.* New York: Praeger.
2. Wilbert J. and M. Layrisse. 1980. *Demographic and Biological Studies of the Warao Indians.* Los Angeles: UCLA Latin American Center Publications.

163. YANOMAMO

1. Chagnon, Napolean A. 1968. *The Fierce People.* New York: Holt, Rhinehart and Winston.

164. CARIB. No information.

165. SARAMANCA. No information.

166. MUNDURUCU. No information.

167. CUBEO

1. Goldman, I. 1963. *The Cubeo Indians.* Illinois Studies in Anthropology 2: 763-798.

168. CAYAPA

1. Altschuler, M. 1965. "The Cayapa." Ph. D. dissertation, University of Minnesota.

169. JIVARO

1. Harner, M. J. 1972. *The Jivaro.* New York: Doubleday, for the American Museum of Natural History.

170. AMAHUACA

1. Huxley, M., and C. Capa. 1964. *Farewell to Eden.* New York: Harper and Row.

171. INCA. No information.

172. AYMARA. No information.

173. SIRIONO. No information.

174. NAMBICUARA

1. Levi-Strauss, C.   1948.   "La vie familiale et sociale des Indiens Nambikwara." *Journal de la Societe des Americanistes* 37: 1-131. Paris.
2. Levi-Strauss, C. 1961. *A World on the Wane*. London: Hutchinson.
3. Oberg, K.   1953.   *Indian Tribes of Northern Mato Grosso, Brazil*. Washington, D.C.: Government Printing Office.

175. TRUMAI

1. Murphy, R. F., and B. Quain. 1955. *The Trumai Indians of Central Brazil*. Monographs of the American Ethnological Society 24: 1-108.

176. TIMBIRA. No information.

177. TUPINAMBA. No information.

178. BOTOCUDO. No information.

179. SHAVANTE

1. Maybury-Lewis, D. 1967. *Akwe-Shavante Society*. Oxford: Clarendon Press.

180. AWIEKOMA (CAINGANG)

Henry, J. 1941. *Jungle People*. Richmond: Wm. Byrd Press.

181. CAYAPA. No information.

182. LENGUA. No information.

183. ABIPON. No information.

184. ARAUCANIANS
3. Faron, Louis C. 1961. *Mapuche Social Structure*. Urbana: University of Illinois Press.

2. Hilger, M. I. 1957. *Araucanian Child Life and Its Cultural Background*. Smithsonian Miscellaneous Collection 133: 1-495.
1. Titiev, M.   1951.   *Araucanian Culture in Transition*.   Occasional Contributions from the Museum of Anthropology, University of Michigan 15: 1-164.

185. TEHUELCHE. No information.

186. YAHGAN

2. Cooper, John M. "The Yahgan." In Julian H. Steward (ed.), *Handbook of South American Indians* 1. Washington, D.C.: Government Printing Office, 81-106.
1. Guisinde, Martin. 1937. *Die Yamana*. Modling bei Wien: Anthropos-Bibliothek.

References

Aberle, David F. 1961. "Matrilineal Descent in Cross-Cultural Perspective.
In David M. Schneider and Kathleen Gough (Eds.), *Matrilineal Kinship*.
Berkeley: University of California Press, 655-730.

Adams, David B. 1983. "Why There Are So Few Women Warriors."
Behavior Science Research 18: 196-212.

Anderson, Elijah. 1993. "Sex Codes and Family Life among Poor Inner-City
Youth." In William J. Wilson (Ed.), *The Ghetto Underclass*. Newbury
Park, California: Sage, 76-95.

Anderson, Judith, Charles Crawford, Joanne Nadeau, and Tracy Lindberg.
1994. "Female Beauty and Adolescent Sexuality: SCCS Codes." *World
Cultures* 1994: 19-23.

Andrews, Lori. 1989. *Between Strangers: Surrogate Mothers, Expectant
Fathers, and Brave New Babies*. New York: Harper and Row.

Arditti, Rita, Renate Duelli Klein and Shelley Minden. 1984. *Test Tube
Women*. London: Verso.

Aries, Philippe. 1962. *Centuries of Childhood*. New York: Knopf.

Aronoff, Joel, and William Crano. 1975. "A Re-Examination of the Cross-
Cultural Principles of Task Segregation and Sex Role Differentiation in the
Family." *American Sociological Review* 40: 12-20.

Bachofen, J. J. 1861. *Das Mutterrecht*. Stuttgart: Krais and Hoffman.

Barnes, Annie S. 1987. *Single Parents in Black America*. Bristol, Indiana:
Wyndham Hall.

Barnett, Daniel L. 1985. "In Vitro Fertilization: Third party Motherhood and
the Changing Definition of Legal Parent." *Pacific Law Journal* 17: 231-259.

Barry, Herbert III. 1995. Personal Communication.

Barry, Herbert III, Lili Josephson, Edith Lauer, and Catherine Marshall. 1977.
"Agents and Techniques for Child Training: Cross-Cultural Codes 6."
Ethnology 16: 191-225.

Barry, Herbert III, and L. Paxson. 1971. "Infancy and Childhood: Cross-Cultural Codes 2." *Ethnology* 10: 446-508.

Barry, Herbert III, and Alice Schlegel. 1984. "Measurements of Adolescent Sexual Behavior in the Standard Sample Societies." *Ethnology* 23: 315-329.

Belmont, Nicole. 1976. "Levana; or How to Raise up Children." In Robert Forster and Orest Ranum (Eds.), *Family and Society: Selections from the Annals*. Baltimore: Johns Hopkins University Press, 1-15.

Belsky, Jay, Laurence Steinberg, and Patricia Draper. 1991. "Childhood Experience, Interpersonal Development, and Reproductive Strategy: An Evolutionary Theory of Socialization." *Child Development* 62: 647-670.

Berkner, Lutz. 1972. "The Stem Family and the Developmental Cycle of the Peasant Household: An Eighteenth Century Austrian Example." *American Historical Review* 77: 398-418.

Best, Joel. 1990. *Threatened Children*. Chicago: University of Chicago Press.

Blake, Judith. 1961. *Family Structure in Jamaica*. New York: Free Press.

Blake, Judith. 1979. "Structural Differentiation and the Family: A Quiet Revolution." In Amos Hawley (Ed.), *Societal Growth*. New York: Free Press, 179-201.

Blank, Robert H. 1984. *Redefining Human Life*. Boulder, Colo.: Westview.

Blumberg, Rae L. 1978. *Stratification: Socioeconomic and Sexual Inequality*. Dubuque, Iowa: William C. Brown.

Blumberg, Rae L. 1984. "A General Theory of Gender Stratification." In Randall Collins (Ed.), *Sociological Theory, 1984*. San Francisco: Jossey-Bass, 23-99.

Booth, Alan, David R. Johnson, Lynn White, and John N. Edwards. 1984. "Women, Outside Employment, and Marital Instability." *American Journal of Sociology* 90: 567-583.

Boutell, Charles. 1970. *Boutell's Heraldry*. Revised by J. P. Brooks-Little. London: Fredrick Warne.

Briffault, Robert. 1931. *The Mothers*. New York: Macmillan.

Briffault, Robert, and Bronislaw Malinowski. 1956. *Marriage Past and Present*. Boston: Porter Sargent.

Bronfenbrenner, Urie. 1963. "The Changing American Child—A Speculative Analysis." In Neil J. Smelser and W. J. Smelser (Eds.), *Personality and Social Systems*. New York: John Wiley, 347-356.

Broude, Gwyn J. 1980. "Extramarital Sex Norms in Cross-Cultural Perspective. *Behavioral Science Research* 15: 181-218.

Broude, Gwyn J., and Sarah Greene. 1976. "Cross-Cultural Codes on Twenty Sexual Attitudes and Practices." *Ethnology* 15: 409-429.

Chafetz, Janet S. 1984. *Sex and Advantage*. Totowa, N.J.: Rowman and Allenheld.

Cherlin, Andrew. 1978. "Remarriage as an Incomplete Institution." *American Journal of Sociology* 84: 634-650.

Cherlin, Andrew. 1981. *Marriage, Divorce, Remarriage*. Cambridge: Harvard University Press.

Chessler, Phyllis. 1988. *Sacred Bond: The Legacy of Baby M*. New York: Times Books.

Clarke, Helen I. 1940. *Social Legislation*. New York: Appleton-Century.

Cleveland, Barbara C., and Andrew M. Williams. 1992. *Paternity Establishment: State Innovations*. METS Periodic Report No. 1. Office of Child Support Enforcement, USDHHS.

Coale, Ansley J. 1965. "Appendix: Estimates of Average Household Size." In A. J. Coale, et al. *Aspects of the Analysis of Family Structure*. Princeton: Princeton University Press, 64-69.

Collins, Randall. 1971. "A Conflict Theory of Sexual Stratification." *Social Problems* 19: 3-21.

Collins, Randall. 1975. *Conflict Sociology*. New York: Academic Press.

Collins, Randall. 1988. *Sociology of Marriage and the Family*. Chicago: Nelson-Hall.

Colson, Elizabeth. 1950. "Some Types of Family Structure amongst the Central Bantu." In A. R. Radcliffe-Brown and Daryll Forde (Eds.), *African Systems of Kinship and Marriage*. London: Oxford University Press, 207-251.

Coontz, Stephanie, and Peta Henderson. 1986. *Women's Work, Men's Property*. London: Verso.

Cordes, Renee. 1993a. "California Court Upholds Surrogacy Agreement: Appeal Planned." *Trial* 29 (May): 91.

Cordes, Renee. 1993b. "Parentage Disputed in Surrogacy Case." *Trial* 29, July: 91-93.

Corea, Gena. 1985. *The Mother Machine*. New York: Harper and Row.

Coser, Rose Laub, and Lewis A. Coser. 1974. "The Principle of Legitimacy and Its Patterned Infringement in Social Revolutions." In Rose Laub Coser (Ed.), *The Family: Its Structures and Functions*. New York: St. Martin's, 94-106.

Coulson, Margaret, Brank Magas, and Hilary Wainwright. 1975. "'The Housewife and her Labour under Capitalism:' A Critique." *New Left Review* 89: 59-71.

Dale, Michael J. 1988. "The Burger Court and Issues of Illegitimacy." *Children's Rights Legal Journal* 9: 9-15.

Daly, Martin, Margo Wilson, and Suzanne J. Weghorst. 1982. "Male Sexual Jealousy." *Ethology and Sociobiology* 3:11-27.

D'Andrade, Roy G. 1966. "Sex Differences and Cultural Institutions." In Eleanor E. Maccoby (Ed.), *Development of Sex Differences*. Stanford: Stanford University Press, 174-202.

DaVanzo, Julie, and M. Omar Rahman. 1993. *American Families: Trends and Policy Issues*. Santa Monica, Calif.: RAND.

Davis, Kingsley. 1939a. "The Forms of Illegitimacy." *Social Forces* 18: 77-89.

Davis, Kingsley. 1939b. "Illegitimacy and the Social Structure. *American Journal of Sociology* 4: 215-233.

Davis, Kingsley. 1941. "Intermarriage in Caste Societies." *American Anthropologist* 43: 376-395.

Davis, Kingsley. 1949. *Human Society*. New York: Macmillan.

Davis, Kingsley. 1985. "Introduction: The Meaning and Significance of Marriage in Contemporary Society." In Kingsley Davis and Amyra Grossbard-Schechtman (Eds.), *Contemporary Marriage*. New York: Russell Sage.

Delaney, Carol. 1986. "The Meaning of Paternity and the Virgin Birth Debate." *Man* (New Series) 21: 494-513.

DeStephano, Linda, and Diane Colasanto. 1990. "Unlike 1975, Today Most Americans Think Men Have It Better." *Gallop Poll Monthly* 293: 25-36.

Devereaux, George. 1955. *A Study of Abortion in Primitive Societies*. New York: Julian.

Divale, William T., and Marvin B. Harris. 1976. "Population, Warfare, and the Male Supremacy Complex." *American Anthropologist* 78: 521-538.

Draper, Patricia. 1989. "African Marriage Systems: Perspectives from Evolutionary Ecology." *Ethology and Sociobiology* 10: 145-169.

Draper, Patricia, and Jay Belsky. 1990. "Personality Development in Evolutionary Perspective." *Journal of Personality* 58: 141-161.

Draper, Patricia, and Henry Harpending. 1982. "Father Absence and Reproductive Strategy: An Evolutionary Perspective." *Journal of Anthropological Research* 38: 255-273.

Draper, Patricia, and Henry Harpending. 1987. "A Sociobiological Perspective on the Development of Human Reproductive Strategies." In Kevin M. MacDonald (Ed.), *Sociobiological Perspectives on Human Development*. New York: Springer-Verlag, 340-372.

Driver, Harold B., and W. Massey. 1957. "Comparative Studies of North American Indians." *Transactions of the American Philosophical Society* 47: 165-456.

Durkheim, Emile. 1964. *The Division of Labor in Society*. Glencoe, Free Press. Translated by George Simpson.

Edwards, John N. 1991. "New Conceptions: Biosocial Innovations and the Family." *Journal of Marriage and the Family* 53: 349-360.

Eekelaar, John M., and Sanford N. Katz. 1980. *Marriage and Cohabitation in Contemporary Societies*. Toronto: Butterworths.

Elbow, Margaret, and Judy Mayfield. 1991. "Mothers of Incest Victims: Villains, Victims, or Protectors?" *Families in Society* 72: 78-85.

Ember, Carol R. 1978. "Men's Fear of Sex With Women." *Sex Roles* 4: 657-78.

Ember, Carol R. 1981. "A Cross-Cultural Perspective on Sex Differences."
In R. H. Munroe, R. L. Munroe, and B. B. Whiting (Eds.), *Handbook of
Cross-Cultural Human Development*. New York: Garland, 531-580.

Ember, Melvin. 1974. "Warfare, Sex Ratio, and Polygyny." *Ethnology* 13:
197-206.

Ember, Melvin. 1975. "On the Origin and Extension of the Incest Taboo."
Behavioral Science Research 10: 249-281.

Ember, Melvin. 1985. ""Alternative Predictors of Polygyny." *Behavioral
Science Research* 19: 1-23.

Ember, Melvin, and Carol R. Ember. 1971. "The Conditions Favoring
Matrilocal Versus Patrilocal Residence." *American Anthropologist* 73: 571-
595.

Engels, Frederick. 1972. *The Origin of the Family, Private Property, and the
State*. (Originally published in 1884.) New York: Pathfinder.

Erickson, Kai T. 1964. "Notes on the Sociology of Deviance." In Howard S.
Becker (Ed.), *The Other Side*. New York: Free Press, 9-21.

Fairchilds, Cissie. 1984. *Domestic Enemies: Servants and their Masters in Old
Regime France*. Baltimore: Johns Hopkins University Press.

Farber, Bernard. 1968. *Comparative Kinship Systems*. New York: Wiley.

Farber, Bernard. 1971. *Kinship and Class*. New York: Basic Books.

Farber, Bernard. 1973. *Family and Kinship in Modern Society*. Glenview,
Ill.: Scott, Foresman.

Firestone, Shulamith. 1970. *The Dialectic of Sex*. New York: William
Morrow.

Fjellman, Stephen M. 1979. "Hey, You Can't Do That: A Response to Divale
and Harris's 'Population, Warfare and the male Supremacist Complex'."
Behavior Science Research 14: 189-200.

Flandrin, Jean-Louis. 1979. *Families in Former Times*. London: Cambridge
University Press.

Flinn, Michael. 1981. *The European Demographic System*. Baltimore: Johns
Hopkins University Press.

Fox, Robin. 1967. *Kinship and Marriage*. Baltimore: Penguin.

Freidl, Ernestine. 1975. *Women and Men: An Anthropologist's View*. New
York: Holt, Rhinehart and Winston.

Gardiner, Jean. 1975. "Women's Domestic Labour." *New Left Review* 89: 47-
58.

Garrison, Marsha. 1988. "Surrogate Parenting: What Should Legislatures Do?
Family Law Quarterly 22: 149-172.

Gaulin, Steven J. C., and Alice Schlegel. 1980. "Paternal Confidence and
Paternal Investment: A Cross Cultural Test of a Sociobiological Hypothesis."
Ethology and Sociobiology 1: 301-309.

Geiger, H. Kent. 1968. "The Fate of the Family in 1944." In N. W. Bell and
E. F. Vogel (Eds.), *A Modern Introduction to the Family*. New York: Free
Press, 48-67.

Gill, Derek. 1977. *Sexuality, Illegitimacy, and the Status of Women*. Oxford: Basil Blackwell.

Given-Wilson, Chris, and Alice Curteis. 1984. *The Royal Bastards of Medieval England*. London: Routledge and Kegan Paul.

Glendon, Mary Ann. 1987. *Abortion and Divorce in Western Law*. Cambridge: Harvard University Press.

Gluckman, Max. 1967. *Custom and Conflict in Africa*. New York: Barnes and Noble.

Goodale, Jane C. 1971. *Tiwi Wives*. Seattle: University of Washington Press.

Goode, William J. 1960. "Illegitimacy in the Caribbean Social Structure." *American Sociological Review* 25: 21-30.

Goode, William J. 1964. *The Family*. Englewood Cliffs, N.J.: Prentice-Hall.

Goode, William J. 1982. *The Family* 2nd ed. Englewood Cliffs, N. J.: Prentice-Hall.

Goodman, Leo A. 1966. "On the Multivariate Analysis of Three Dichotomous Variables." *American Journal of Sociology* 71: 290-301.

Goody, Esther. 1982. *Parenthood and Social Reproduction*. Cambridge: Cambridge University Press.

Goody, Jack. 1962. *Developmental Cycle in Domestic Groups*. Cambridge: Cambridge University Press.

Goody, Jack. 1976. *Production and Reproduction*. Cambridge: University of Cambridge Press.

Goody, Jack, Joan Thirsk, and E. P. Thompson. 1976. *Family and Inheritance*. Cambridge: Cambridge University Press.

Gordon, Michael, and Susan S. Creighton. 1988. "Fathers as Sexual Abusers in the United Kingdom." *Journal of Marriage and the Family* 50: 99-105.

Gough, Kathleen. 1968. "Is the Family Universal?—The Nayar Case." In N.W. Bell and E. F. Vogel (Eds.), *A Modern Introduction to the Family*. New York: Free Press, 80-96.

Greene, Penelope J. 1978. "Promiscuity, Paternity, and Culture." *American Ethnologist* 5: 151-9.

Guttentag, Marcia, and Paul F. Secord. 1983. *Too Many Women? The Sex Ratio Question*. Beverly Hills: Sage.

Hajnal, John. 1965. "European Marriage Patterns in Perspective." In David Glass and D. E. C. Eversley (Eds.), *Population in History*. London: Edward Arnold, 101-146.

Hannan, Michael T., Nancy B. Tuma, and Lyle P. Groeneveld. 1977. "Income and Marital Events." *American Journal of Sociology* 86: 1186-1211.

Harris, Marvin. 1977. *Cannibals and Kings*. New York: Random House.

Hartley, Shirley Foster. 1975. *Illegitimacy*. Berkeley: University of California Press.

Hartung, John. 1982. "Polygyny and the Inheritance of Wealth." *Current Anthropology* 23: 1-12.

Hartung, John. 1985. "Matrilineal Inheritance: New Theory and Analysis." *The Behavioral and Brain Sciences* 8: 661-686.

Hendrix, Lewellyn. 1975. "Nuclear Family Universals: Fact and Faith in the Acceptance of an Idea." *Journal of Comparative Family Studies* 6: 125-138.

Hendrix, Lewellyn. 1993. "Illegitimacy and other Purported Family Universals." *Cross-Cultural Research* 27: 212-231.

Hendrix, Lewellyn. 1994. "What Is Sexual Inequality? On the Definition and Range of Variation." *Cross-Cultural Research* 28: 287-307.

Hendrix, Lewellyn, and Zakir Hossain. 1988. "The Mode of Production and the Status of Women." *Signs* 13: 437-453.

Hendrix, Lewellyn, and Willie Pearson, Jr. 1995. "Spousal Interdependence, Female Power, and Divorce: A Cross-Cultural Examination." *Journal of Comparative Family Studies* 26: 217-232.

Hewlett, Barry S. 1992. *Father-Child Relations: Cultural and Biosocial Contexts*. New York: Aldine de Gruyter.

Homans, George C. 1984. "Sex and Power in Simple Societies." *American Journal of Sociology* 89: 941-944.

Homans, George C. 1987. *Certainties and Doubts*. New Brunswick, N.J.: Transaction Books.

Homans, George C., and David M. Schneider. 1955. *Marriage, Authority, and Final Causes*. Glencoe: Free Press.

Hopkins, Keith. 1980. "Brother-Sister Marriage in Roman Egypt." *Comparative Studies in Society and History* 22: 303-354.

Hornstein, Francie. 1984. "Children by Donor Insemination: A New Choice for Lesbians." In R. Arditti, et al. (Eds.), *Test Tube Women*. London: Verso, 373-381.

Hughes, Austin L. 1988. *Evolution and Human Kinship*. New York: Oxford University Press.

Hupka, Ralph B., and James M. Ryan. 1990. "The Cultural Contribution to Jealousy: Cross-Cultural Aggression in Sexual Jealousy Situations." *Behavior Science Research* 24: 51-72.

Hynes, Eugene. 1985. "The Decline and Fall of the Irish Stem Family." Paper presented at the Annual Meeting of the Midwest Sociological Society.

Isaacs, Stephen L., and Renee J. Holt. 1987. "Redefining Procreation: Facing the Issues." *Population Bulletin* 42 (3).

Jacobs, A. C. 1932. "Illegitimacy, Legal Aspects." In *Encyclopedia of the Social Sciences*. 1st. ed. Pp. 582-586.

Johnson, G. David, and Lewellyn Hendrix. 1982. "A Cross-Cultural Test of Collins's Theory of Sexual Stratification." *Journal of Marriage and the Family* 44: 675-687.

Jordan, W. K. 1959. *Philanthropy in England 1480-1660*. London: George Allen and Unwin.

Kang, Gay E. 1979. "The Nature of Exogamy in Relation to Cross-Allegiance/ Alliance of Social Units." *Behavioral Science Research* 14: 255-276.

Kang, Gay E., Susan Horan, and Janet Reis. 1979. "Comments on Divale and Harris's 'Population, Warfare and the Male Supremacist Complex'." *Behavioral Science Research* 14: 201-210.

Kaufman, Irving, Alice L. Peck, and Consuelo K. Tagiuri. 1954. "The Family Constellation and Overt Incestuous Relations between Father and Daughter." *American Journal of Orthopsychiatry* 24: 266-277.

Kay, Herma Hill. 1965. "The Family and Kinship System of Illegitimate Children in California Law." In Laura Nader (Ed.), *The Ethnography of Law*, Special Publication of *American Anthropologist* Vol. 67, Part 2, 57-81.

Keesing, Roger M. 1975. *Kin Groups and Social Structure.* New York: Holt, Rhinehart and Winston.

Klaus, Marshall H., and John H. Kennell. 1976. *Maternal-Infant Bonding.* St. Louis: Mosby.

Klein, Renate Duelli. 1984. "Doing It Ourselves: Self Insemination." In R. Arditti, et al. (Eds.), *Test Tube Women*. London: Verso, 383-390.

Konopka, Gisela. 1966. *The Adolescent Girl in Conflict.* Englewood Cliffs, N.J.: Prentice-Hall.

Krause, Harry. 1971. *Illegitimacy: Legal and Social Policy.* New York: Bobbs-Merrill.

Krause, Harry. 1983. "Artificial Conception: Legislative Approaches." *Family Law Quarterly* 19: 185-206.

Kriege, E. J., and J. D. Kriege. 1943. *The Realm of a Rain Queen.* London: Oxford University Press.

Kunzel, Regina G. 1993. *Fallen Women, Problem Girls.* New Haven: Yale University Press.

Lamb, M. E., and C. P. Hwang. 1982. "Maternal Attachment and Mother-Neonate Bonding: A Critical Review." In M. E. Lamb and A. L. Brown (Eds.), *Advances in Developmental Psychology*. Volume 2. Hillsdale, New Jersey: Lawrence Erlbaum, 1-38.

Lamb, Michael E., Joseph H. Pleck, Eric L. Charnov, and James A. Levine. 1987. "A Biosocial Perspective on Paternal Behavior and Involvement." In Jane B. Lancaster, et al. (Eds.), *Parenting across the Life Span*. New York: Aldine de Gruyter, 111-142.

Lancaster, Chet, and Jane B. Lancaster. 1987. "The Watershed: Change in Parental-Investment and Family-Formation strategies in the Course of Human Evolution." In Jane B. Lancaster et al. (Eds.), *Parenting Across the Life Span: Biosocial Dimensions*. New York: Aldine De Gruyter for the Social Science Research Council, 187-206.

Landstreet, Eleanor H. 1994. "Prosecuting Criminal Nonsupport." *Child Support Report* 16, 1: 6.

Laslett, Peter. 1980. "The Bastardy Prone Sub-Society." In Peter Laslett et al. (Eds.), *Bastardy and its Comparative History*. Cambridge: Harvard University Press, 217-240.

Laslett, Peter, Karla Osterveen and Richard M. Smith. 1980. *Bastardy and its Comparative History*. Cambridge: Harvard University Press.

Leach Edmund R. 1955. "Polyandry, Inheritance, and the Definition of Marriage." *Man* 54: 182-186.

Leavitt, Gregory C. 1990. "Sociobiological Explanations of Incest Avoidance: A Review of Evidential Claims." *American Anthropologist* 92: 971-993.

Lee, Gary R. 1982. *Family Structure and Interaction*. Minneapolis: University of Minnesota Press.

"Lesbian Custody Battle." 1989. *Off Our Backs* 19 (8): 27.

Levi-Strauss, Claude. 1969. *The Elementary Structures of Kinship*. New York: Beacon.

Levy, Marion J., Jr. 1965. "Aspects of the Analysis of Family Structure." In A.J. Coale, L. A. Fallers, M. J. Levy, Jr., D. M. Schneider and S. S. Tompkins, *Aspects of the Analysis of Family Structure*. Princeton: Princeton University Press, 1-63.

Levy, Marion J., Jr. 1966. *Modernization and the Structure of Societies*. Princeton: Princeton University Press.

Levy, Marion J., Jr. 1989. *Our Mother-Tempers*. Berkeley: University of California Press.

Levy, Marion J., Jr., and Lloyd A. Fallers. 1959. "The Family: Some Comparative Considerations." *American Anthropologist* 61: 647-651.

Little, Kenneth. 1951. *The Mende of Sierra Leone*. London: Routledge and Kegan Paul.

Mackey, Wade C. 1985. *Fathering Behaviors: The Dynamics of the Man-Child Bond*. New York: Plenum.

Malinowski, Bronislaw. 1926. *Crime and Custom in Savage Society*. London: Routledge and Kegan Paul.

Malinowski, Bronislaw. 1927. *Sex and Repression in Savage Society*. London: Routledge and Kegan Paul.

Malinowski, Bronislaw. 1929. *The Sexual Life of Savages*. London: Routledge and Kegan Paul.

Malinowski, Bronislaw. 1930. "Parenthood: The Basis of Social Structure." In V. F. Calverton and Samuel D. Schmalhausen (Eds.), *The New Generation*. New York: Macula, 113-168.

Malinowski, Bronislaw. 1956. "Personal Problems." In Robert Briffault and Bronislaw Malinowski, *Marriage Past and Present*. Boston: Porter Sargent, 74-83.

Malinowski Bronislaw. 1963. *The Family Among the Australian Aborigines*. London: University of London Press.

Mead, Margaret. 1935. *Sex and Temperament in Three Primitive Societies*. New York: William Morrow.

Middleton, Russell. 1962. "Brother-Sister and Father-Daughter Marriage in Ancient Egypt." *American Sociological Review* 27: 603-611.

Miller, Brent C. and Kristin A. Moore. 1990. "Adolescent Sexual Behavior, Pregnancy, and Parenting: Research through the 1980s." *Journal of Marriage and the Family* 52: 1025-1044.

Minturn, Leigh. 1985. "A New Look at the Universal Incest Taboo." Paper presented at the Annual Meeting of the Society for Cross-Cultural Research.

Montagu, M. F. Ashley. 1956. "Introduction." In Robert Briffault and Bronislaw Malinowski, *Marriage Past and Present*. Boston: Porter Sargent, 2-18.

Morgan, Lewis Henry. 1963. *Ancient Society*. (First published in 1877). Cleveland: World.

Morton, Marian J. 1993. *And Sin No More: Social Policy and Unwed Mothers in Cleveland, 1855-1990*. Columbus, Ohio: Ohio State University Press.

Mount, Ferdinand. 1982. *The Subversive Family*. London: Unwin Paperbacks.

Munroe, Robert L., and Ruth H. Munroe. 1992. "Fathers in Children's Environments: A Four Culture Study." In Barry S. Hewlett (Ed.), *Father-Child Relations: Cultural and Biological Contexts*. New York: Aldine de Gruyter, 213-230.

Murdock, George P. 1937. "Comparative Data on the Division of Labor by Sex." *Social Forces* 15: 551-553.

Murdock, George P. 1949. *Social Structure*. Glencoe, Ill.: Free Press.

Murdock, George P. 1967. *Ethnographic Atlas*. Pittsburgh: University of Pittsburgh Press.

Murdock, George Peter, and Diana O. Morrow. 1970. "Subsistence Economy and Supportive Practices: Cross-Cultural Codes 1." *Ethnology* 9: 302-330.

Murdock, George Peter, and Katerina Provost. 1973. "Factors in the Division of Labor By Sex: A Cross-Cultural Analysis." *Ethnology* 12: 203-225.

Murdock, George Peter, and Douglas R. White. 1969. "Standard Cross-Cultural Sample." *Ethnology* 8: 329-369.

Murdock, George Peter, and Suzanne F. Wilson. 1972. "Settlement Patterns and Community Organization." *Ethnology* 11: 254-295.

Nathanson, Constance A. 1991. *Dangerous Passage*. Philadelphia: Temple University Press.

Needham, Rodney. 1962. *Structure and Sentiment*. Chicago: University of Chicago Press.

Needham, Rodney. 1971. "Remarks on the Analysis of Kinship and Marriage." In Rodney Needham (Ed.), *Rethinking Kinship and Marriage*. London: Tavistock, 1-34.

O'Brien, Mary. 1983. *The Politics of Reproduction*. Boston: Routledge and Kegan Paul.

Office of Child Support Enforcement. 1983. *Kids, They're Worth Every Penny*. Child Support: An Agenda for Action. Office of Child Support Enforcement, USDHHS.

Office of Child Support Enforcement. 1986. *History and Fundamentals of Child Support Enforcement*. 2nd. ed. Prepared by National Institute for Child Support Enforcement for the Office of Child Support Enforcement, USDHHS.

Office of Child Support Enforcement. 1990. *Child Support Enforcement: Fifteenth Annual Report to Congress for the Period Ending September 30, 1990*. DHHS Publication No. (ACF) 92-33001.

Office of Child Support Enforcement. 1993. *18th Annual Report to Congress*. Listed on the World-Wide Web of the Internet.

Office of Child Support Enforcement. 1995. "License Revocation the Maine Way." *Child Support Report* 17, 4: 1-2.

Ogburn, William F., and Clark Tibbits. 1934. "The Family and its Functions." In Report of the President's Committee on Social Trends, *Recent Social Trends in the United States*. New York: McGraw-Hill, 661-708.

O'Neill, Brian Juan. 1978. *Social Inequality in a Portuguese Hamlet*. London: Cambridge University Press.

Otterbein, Keith F. 1968. "Internal War: A Cross-Cultural Study. *American Anthropologist* 70: 277-89.

Otterbein, Keith F. 1970. *The Evolution of War*. New Haven: HRAF Press.

Otterbein, Keith F., and Charlotte S. Otterbein. 1965. "An Eye for an Eye, a Tooth for a Tooth: A Cross-Cultural Study of Feuding." *American Anthropologist* 67: 1470-1482.

Paige, Jeffery M. 1974. "Kinship and Polity in Stateless Societies." *American Journal of Sociology* 80: 310-20.

Paige, Karen Ericksen, and Jeffery M. Paige. 1981. *The Politics of Reproductive Ritual*. Berkeley: University of California Press.

Parker, Hilda, and Seymour Parker. 1979. "The Myth of Male Superiority: Rise and Demise." *American Anthropologist* 81: 289-309.

Parker, Hilda, and Seymour Parker. 1986. "Father-Daughter Sexual Abuse." *American Journal of Orthopsychiatry* 56: 531-49.

Parker, Seymour. 1976. "The Precultural Basis of the Incest Taboo." *American Anthropologist* 78: 285-305.

Parsons, Talcott, and Robert F. Bales. 1955. *Family, Socialization, and Interaction Process*. Glencoe, Ill.: Free Press.

Pearson, Willie Jr., and Lewellyn Hendrix. 1981. "Divorce and the Status of Women." *Journal of Marriage and the Family* 41: 375-385.

Pollock, Linda A. 1983. *Forgotten Children: Parent-Child Relations from 1500 to 1900*. Cambridge: Cambridge University Press.

Pollock, Sir Frederick, and Frederic William Maitland. 1968. *The History of English Law Before the Time of Edward I*. (First published in 1895). Cambridge: Cambridge University Press.

Poster, Mark. 1978. *Critical Theory of the Family*. New York: Seabury.

Radcliffe-Brown, A. R. 1950. "Introduction." In A. R. Radcliffe-Brown and Daryll Forde. *African Systems of Kinship and Marriage*. London: Oxford University Press, 1-85.

Radcliffe-Brown, A. R. 1965. *Structure and Function in Primitive Society*. New York: Free Press.

Rains, Prudence Mors. 1971. *Becoming an Unwed Mother*. Chicago: Aldine-Atherton.

Reiss. Ira L., and Gary R. Lee. 1988. *American Family Systems*. New York: Holt, Rhinehart and Winston.

Rodman, Hyman. 1966. "Illegitimacy in the Caribbean Social Structure: A Reconsideration." *American Sociological Review* 31: 673-83.

Rohner, Ronald P. 1975. *The Love Me, They Love Me Not*. New Haven: HRAF Press.

Rohner, Ronald P. 1980. "Worldwide tests of Parental Acceptance-Rejection Theory: An Overview." *Behavioral Science Research* 15: 1-22.

Rohner, Ronald P., and Evelyn C. Rohner. 1981. "Parental Acceptance-Rejection and Parental Control: Cross-Cultural Codes." *Ethnology* 20: 245-60.

Ross, Heather, and Isabel Sawhill. 1975. *Time of Transition*. Washington, D.C.: Urban Institute.

Ross, Marc H. 1983. "Political Decision Making and Conflict." *Ethnology* 22: 169-92.

Ross, Marc H. 1986. "Female Political Participation: A Cross-Cultural Explanation." *American Anthropologist* 88: 843-858.

Rossi, Alice S. 1984. "Gender and Parenthood." *American Sociological Review* 49: 1-19.

Rothman, Barbara Katz. 1989. *Recreating Motherhood*. New York: Norton.

Ruse, Michael. 1985. *Sociobiology: Sense or Nonsense? Episteme, Vol. 8*. Dordrecht: D. Reidel.

Russell, Diana E. H. 1984. "The Prevalence and Seriousness of Incestuous Abuse." *Child Abuse and Neglect* 8: 15-22.

Sacks, Karen. 1979. *Sisters and Wives*. Westport, Conn.: Greenwood.

Sanday, Peggy R. 1981a. *Female Power and Male Dominance: ON the Origins of Sexual Inequality*. Cambridge: Cambridge University Press.

Sanday, Peggy R. 1981b. "Female Power and Male Dominance: Cross-Cultural Codes." *World Cultures* 4, 1.

Scanzoni, Letha D., and John Scanzoni. 1988. *Men, Women, and Change*. 3rd. ed. New York: McGraw-Hill.

Schlegel, Alice. 1977. *Sexual Stratification: A Cross-Cultural View*. New York: Columbia University Press.

Schlegel, Alice. 1989. "Gender Issues and Cross-Cultural Research." *Behavior Science Research* 23: 265-280.

Schlegel, Alice, and Rohn Eloul. 1988. "Marriage Transactions: Labor, Property, Status." *American Anthropologist* 90: 291-309.

Schneider, David M. 1961. "The Distinctive Features of Matrilineal Descent Groups." In David M. Schneider and Kathleen Gough (Eds.), *Matrilineal Kinship*. Berkeley: University of California Press, 1-35.

Seccombe, Karen and Gary R. Lee. 1986. "Female Status, Wives' Autonomy, and Divorce: A Cross-Cultural Study." *Family Perspective* 20: 241-9.

Seccombe, Wally. 1973. "The Housewife and her Labour under Capitalism." *New Left Review* 83: 3-24.

Seccombe, Wally. 1975. "Domestic Labour: Reply to Critics." *New Left Review* 89: 85-96.

Seemanova, Eva. 1971. "A Study of Children of Incestuous Matings." *Human Heredity* 21: 108-128.

Shannon, Thomas A. 1988. *Surrogate Motherhood*. New York: Crossroad.

Shepher, Joseph. 1971. "Mate Selection among Second Generation Kibbutz Adolescents and Adults." *Archives of Sexual Behavior* 1: 108-128.

Shepher, Joseph. 1983. *Incest: A Biosocial View*. New York: Academic.

Shorter, Edward. 1971. "Illegitimacy, Sexual Revolution, and Social Change in Modern Europe." *Journal of Interdisciplinary History* 2: 237-272.

Shorter, Edward. 1975. *The Making of the Modern Family*. New York: Basic Books.

Siskind, Janet. 1978. "Kinship and the Mode of Production." *American Anthropologist* 80: 860-72.

Skocpol, Theda. 1992. *Protecting Soldiers and Mothers*. Cambridge, Massachusetts: Belknap Press.

Skolnick, Arlene S. and Jerome. H. Skolnick. 1989. *Family in Transition*. 6th ed. Boston: Little, Brown.

Solinger, Rickie. 1992. *Wake Up Little Suzie*. New York: Routledge.

South, Scott J. 1988. "Sex Ratios, Economic Power and Women's Roles." *Journal of Marriage and the Family* 50: 19-31.

Spiro, Melford E. 1965. *Children of the Kibbutz*. New York: Schocken.

Stack, Carol B. 1974. *All Our Kin*. New York: Harper and Row.

Stenger, Robert L. 1981. "Expanding Rights of Illegitimate Children, 1968-1981." *Journal of Family Law* 19: 407-444.

Stephens, William N. 1963. *The Family in Cross-Cultural Perspective*. New York: Holt, Rhinehart, and Winston.

Stinchcombe, Arthur. 1968. *Constructing Social Theories*. New York: Harcourt, Brace and World.

Strong, Bryan, and Christine DeVault. 1986. *The Marriage and Family Experience*. St. Paul: West.

Stumpf, Andrea E. 1986. "Redefining Mother: A Legal Matrix for New Reproductive Technologies." *Yale Law Journal* 96: 187-208.

Sullivan, Mercer. 1993. "Absent Fathers in the Inner City." In William J. Wilson (Ed.), *The Ghetto Underclass*. Newbury Park, California: Sage, 65-75.

Swanson, Guy E. 1968. "To Live in Concord with Society." In Albert J. Reiss (Ed.), *Cooley and Sociological Analysis*. Ann Arbor: University of Michigan Press, 87-124.

Swanson, Guy E. 1969. *Rules of Descent*. Anthropological Paper No. 39, Museum of Anthropology, University of Michigan, Ann Arbor.

Swanson, Guy E. 1974. "Descent and Polity: The meaning of Paige's Findings." *American Journal of Sociology* 80: 321-28.

Talmon, Yonina. 1964. "Mate selection in Collective Settlements." *American Sociological Review* 29: 491-508.

Tapp, Pauline. 1980. "The Social and Legal Position of children of Unmarried Cohabitation." In John M. Eekelaar and Sanford N. Katz (Eds.), *Marriage and Cohabitation in Contemporary Societies*. Toronto: Butterworths, 437-449.

Todd, Emmanuel. 1985. *The Explanation of Ideology*. Oxford: Basil Blackwell.

Toffler, Alvin. 1970. *Future Shock*. New York: Random House.

Trivers, Robert L. 1972. "Parental Investment and Sexual Selection." In Bernard Campbell (Ed.), *Sexual Selection and the Descent of Man*. Chicago: Aldine, 136-179.

van den Berghe, Pierre L. 1979. *Human Family Systems*. New York: Elsevier.

Vinovskis, Maris A. 1988. *An "Epidemic" of Adolescent Pregnancy?* New York: Oxford.

Wadlington, Walter. 1983. "Artificial Conception: The Challenge for Family Law." *Virginia Law Review* 69: 465-514.

Weitzman, Lenore J. 1985. *The Divorce Revolution*. New York: Free Press.

Westermarck, Edward. 1894. *The History of Human Marriage*. London: Clay and Sons.

Wheeler, Valerie. 1987. "A Cross-Cultural Study on the Nature of War." *World Cultures* 3 (1).

Whiting, John W. M., and Beatrice Whiting. 1975. "Aloofness and Intimacy of Husband and Wife." *Ethos* 3: 183-207.

Whyte, Martin King. 1978a. "Cross-Cultural Codes Dealing with the Relative Status of Women." *Ethnology* 17: 211-237.

Whyte, Martin King. 1978b. *The Status of Women in Preindustrial Societies*. Princeton: Princeton University Press.

Williams, Constance W. 1992. *Black Teenage Mothers*. Lexington Mass.: Lexington Books.

Wilson, Peter. J. 1983. *Man, the Promising Primate*. 2nd. ed. New Haven: Yale University Press.

Winch, Robert F. and Rae Lesser BLumberg. 1968. "Societal Complexity and Familial Organization." In Robert F. Winch and Louis W. Goodaman (Eds.), *Selected Studies in Marriage and the Family*. 3rd. ed. New York: Holt, Rhinehart and Winston, 70-92.

Wolf, Arthur. 1966. "Childhood Association, Sexual Attraction, and the Incest Taboo." *American Anthropologist* 70: 883-898.

Wolf, Arthur. 1968. "Adopt a Daughter-in Law, Marry a Sister." *American Anthropologist* 70: 864-874.

Wolf, Arthur, and Chieh-shan Huang. 1980. *Marriage and Adoption in China, 1845-1945*. Stanford: Stanford University Press.

Zaretsky, Eli. 1976. *Capitalism, the Family, and Personal Life*. New York: Harper Colophon.

Zelizer, Viviana. 1985. *Pricing the Priceless Child*. New York: Basic Books.

Zingo, Martha T. and Kevin E. Early. 1994. *Nameless Persons*. Westport, Conn.: Praeger.

Index

73, 77-92, 106, 107, 137, 138-40

Davis, Kingsley, 6, 7, 9, 10, 11, 27-31, 33, 50, 52, 69, 72, 73, 134, 140, 141
Delaney, Carol, 49, 50
Descent: empirical findings, 93-103; in theories, 30-31, 41-42, 45, 46-7, 51, 64; in Trobriand Islands, 23-24. *See also* Matriliny
Deviant career, illegitimacy as, 32, 152
Division of labor by sex, 8, 9
Doctrine of the four seas, 148
Draper, Patricia, 5, 45, 47-48, 123-25, 130, 135, 136
Durkheim, Emile, 60

Early marriage, 64, 69, 70, 71, 72, 102-3, 118, 120, 141
Engels, Frederick, 7-8, 13, 18-21, 30, 34, 35, 40, 42, 46, 50, 53, 62, 73, 84, 105, 120, 134, 136, 137, 138, 140
Ethnocentrism, 31, 134
Extended family. *See* Family structure
Extramarital sex: empirical findings, 94-96; in theories, 20-21, 28-28, 31, 46-7, 48, 63-64, 69, 70

Family structure, 6, 27, 78, 84-92, 138, 146
Family universality, 6-7
Father, biological. *See* Genitor
Father, social: as linchpin of family universals, 3-11; differentiated from biological father, 63-68, 98-103, 118, 120, 139, 147; in America, 145, 150-52, 155; in Davis, 27-31; in the later

functionalists, 31-35, 158; in Malinowski, 3-4, 22-27, 140
Father-absence, 5, 45, 47-48, 123-30
Father-child proximity, 124-30
Fatherhood, culturally defined, 39, 41, 46-50, 52, 64, 69, 73
Father-infant proximity, 124-30
Father-involvement. *See* Father-child proximity; Father-infant proximity
Female power: findings 105-22, 127-31, 136-37, 139: in America, 145, 146, 160-65; measurement, 106-8. *See also* Sexual inequality
Filius nullius 147, 148
Food quest. *See* Subsistence economy
Food shortage, 85, 89-90
Fraternal interest group theory, 40-43, 93-103
Functionalism, 6-7, 8, 22-39, 51-57, 73, 77, 83, 93-95, 97, 105, 137-39, 140

Generic children, 2
Genitor, 11, 14, 25, 30, 31, 35, 60, 62, 63-64, 66, 69, 70, 98-103, 119, 139, 141, 142, 149, 152, 157, 158, 166; identity with social father, 19-21, 28-30, 98-103
Genitrix, 62-63, 158
Goode, William, 11, 31-35, 52-53, 69-70, 73, 77, 83, 103, 105, 120,, 135, 154
Guttentag, Marcia, 43-44, 53, 105

Home for unwed mothers. *See* maternity home

Illegitimacy: cross-class, 34-35, 67-68 (*see also* Concubinage);

About the Author

LEWELLYN HENDRIX is Associate Professor of Sociology at Southern Illinois University in Carbondale. His articles have appeared in publications such as *The Sociological Quarterly*, *Journal of Comparative Family Studies*, and the *American Journal of Sociology.*

ISBN 0-89789-467-7

9 780897 894678

90000>

EAN

HARDCOVER BAR CODE